16/31.

£3-
g

EARTH AND ALTAR

D0587953

The Alcuin Club exists to promote the study of Christian liturgy in general, and in particular the liturgies of the Anglican Communion. Since its foundation in 1897 it has published over 120 books and pamphlets. Members of the Club receive publications of the current year *gratis*.

Information concerning the annual subscription, applications for membership, and lists of publications is obtainable from the Treasurer, 5 St Andrews Street, London EC4A 3AB (Telephone 01-583 7394).

EARTH AND ALTAR

The Evolution of the Parish Communion
in the Church of England to 1945

DONALD GRAY

ALCUIN CLUB COLLECTIONS No. 68

Cover design by Timothy Gray

Copyright © Donald Gray 1986

ISBN 0 907547 55 9
First published 1986
for the Alcuin Club
by Canterbury Press Norwich
St Mary's Works, St Mary's Plain,
Norwich NR3 3BH

Canterbury Press Norwich is a publishing imprint of Hymns Ancient & Modern Ltd

Filmset by Eta Services (Typesetters) Ltd., Beccles, Suffolk
Printed in Great Britain by Anchor Brendon, Ltd.

To
Joyce

Contents

Part Three

THE EMERGENCE OF THE PARISH COMMUNION

Part Four

CONCLUSION   217

Part Five

Bibliography

Foreword

I count it an honour to be invited to contribute a foreword to this book, *Earth and Altar*, written by my friend, Donald Gray, to celebrate the fiftieth anniversary of the publication of that seminal work, *The Parish Communion*, edited by Fr Gabriel Hebert, SSM. To one who as an undergraduate was a pupil of Austin Farrer, and has throughout his ministry expounded the relevance of the eucharist to man's life in society, the theme of *Earth and Altar* met with deep appreciation, and its exposition with increasing delight. It records a period of exciting development in theological understanding and in the practice of worship which will surely retain a place of importance in the history of the Church of England.

The social gospel has, of course, its roots in much Old Testament teaching, which our Lord emphasised in his own teaching and practice—for example, in his parable of the sheep and the goats, and in the feet-washing at the Supper. But the pride of natural man did not find it easy to accept, witness the disorders at the Lord's Supper in the Corinthian Church, or the seating arrangements in our own churches in the eighteenth and early nineteenth centuries, with their benches for the poor, and well-cushioned pews (sometimes with a fireplace) for the wealthy. St Paul had to remind us of our calling, 'how that not many wise men after the flesh, not many mighty, not many noble, are called; but God hath chosen the weak things of the world to confound the things that are mighty.'

Yet, to those who could see, it was all there at the Christian eucharist, when 'high and low, rich and poor, one with another' received from the impartial hand of God the bread of heaven and the cup of salvation. It is this sense of the unity of mankind under the fatherhood of God and the saving work of Christ and in the fellowship of the Spirit, which the parish communion proclaims wherever its reality is truly understood. The eucharistic gathering is a blue-print of the divine kingdom come on earth to those who have eyes to see. It is the Christian calling to reproduce in the society of mankind what we know and experience at the altar.

The great merit of *Earth and Altar* is that in it the author so clearly and cogently traces the theology which ultimately gave rise to the parish communion and to the liturgical movement in the Church of England from the teaching of F. D. Maurice and his successors, and

shows that it was a specifically Anglican development, which only
very much later found kinship with a somewhat similar development
taking place in the Roman Catholic Church. It is a book to be most
warmly commended to all students of Anglican thought, and the
Alcuin Club is more than happy to present it to the public in celebration of its own ninetieth anniversary.

George Timms

Preface

The genesis of this work could be said to have been post-ordination training in the Diocese of Manchester a quarter of a century ago! For a Tutor I was directed to Canon (later Professor) Ronald Preston, and when he asked me about my choice of area for study, I told him that I wanted to discover what happened to the Christian Socialist Movement after the Labour Party victory of 1945. It was during the course of these investigations that I first realized the vital connection which existed between the latter-day followers of F. D. Maurice and the Parish Communion. I can only hope that Professor Preston approves of this long overdue conclusion to those fascinating conversations of the late fifties.

When I came to Liverpool Professor Peter Hennock of Liverpool University taught me how to think as a historian. More recently I am much indebted to those who have provided supervision of my researches at Manchester University. In the first place, the Rt Rev'd Professor Richard Hanson, who started me firmly and confidently on the right road, then the Rev'd Dr Kenneth Stevenson, and finally the Rev'd Dr Richard Buxton. The last-named has been a tower of strength and a wise dispenser of advice and guidance in the later crucial stages.

There is also my debt to the many libraries and Librarians for their unfailing courtesy in dealing with my enquiries, as well as those who kindly assisted me by either answering my letters or producing important documents. Mention must particularly be made of the help and hospitality provided by the Society of the Sacred Mission at Willen Priory, Milton Keynes and the assistance given by Mr Reg Groves, the Rev'd R. H. Martin, the Rev'd Alan Ecclestone, the Rev'd P. J. Jagger, Canon Eric James, the Rev'd Dr Michael Wilson, and the Chaplain-General (the Ven. W. F. Johnston).

The task of preparing this book would have been impossible without the help of the Rev'd Professor Paul Bradshaw of Notre Dame University, Indiana and, nearer home, of the Rev'd Dr Geoffrey Cuming, the Editorial Secretary of the Alcuin Club. I am proud to be among those who have benefited from Dr Cuming's wisdom and scholarship. The Chairman of the Alcuin Club, the Ven. Archdeacon George Timms, has done me the honour of writing a foreword; it is a kindness I appreciate. Financial assistance from the St Aidan's Trustees and the Christendom Trust is most gratefully acknowledged.

My thanks are also due to my staff at Liverpool Parish Church, who endured my preoccupation with this research and even assisted with some proof reading. I am grateful to my son Timothy for the cover design.

Yet it must be my wife Joyce that I must mention as the last, but certainly not the least, person who has been involved in this work. Not only has she typed and re-typed each draft and re-draft of these pages and compiled the index, but has patiently allowed so much of our spare time to be absorbed by the research for this work. That was only possible because she shared the conviction that the Eucharistic worship of the Church is at the very centre of its life and mission.

Donald Gray

Corpus Christi, 1986
Liverpool

Abbreviations

ACC	Alcuin Club Collection.
CA	Church Army.
CR	Community of the Resurrection.
CSL	Church Socialist League.
CSU	Christian Social Union.
DECH	S. L. Ollard, Gordon Crosse, Maurice F. Bond, eds, *Dictionary of English Church History.*
DNB	*Dictionary of National Biography.*
GSM	The Guild of St Matthew.
ICF	Industrial Christian Fellowship.
LC	Liturgical Commission.
LKG	League of the Kingdom of God.
OCM	Order of the Church Militant.
ODCC	F. L. Cross and E. A. Livingstone, eds, *Oxford Dictionary of the Christian Church.*
ODQ	*Oxford Dictionary of Quotations.*
RAChD	Royal Army Chaplain's Department.
SPCK	Society for Promoting Christian Knowledge.
SSJE	Society of St John the Evangelist.
SSM	Society of the Sacred Mission.
TLCAS	*Transactions of the Lancashire and Cheshire Antiquarian Society.*

Introduction

The necessity to keep religion and politics in separate watertight compartments has never lacked its advocates; equally, those who argue for the inseparability of these major concerns of life are never without eloquent prophets and preachers. Hitherto the effect of this continuing debate on the development of liturgical patterns in the Church of England has not been examined, and yet an awareness of the vitality of that school of sacramental socialism which owes its origins to the preaching, teaching, and writing of Stewart Headlam and Henry Scott Holland in its earliest stage, and Conrad Noel, Percy Widdrington, Jim Wilson, and many others in its second, should have alerted others to this possibility. All these stalwarts were united in acknowledging that they in their turn looked back to F. D. Maurice for their fundamental theological inspiration, despite being no doubt aware that Maurice's liturgical interests were meagre and that a fairly restrictive diet of Prayer Book worship with no frills or fancies easily satisfied all his needs in these matters.

It would be foolish to suggest that every Christian Socialist in the Church of England was an Anglo-Catholic, but it would be nearer the truth than suggesting that every Anglo-Catholic was a Christian Socialist. For this purpose, at least, two clear divisions can be seen in the Anglo-Catholic party, divisions which run through and cut across all the other separations and differences. The categories into which Reg Groves places these high-churchmen seem to be pertinently accurate. Groves calls one 'authoritarian and sacerdotalist' and the other he defines as 'social democratic'.[1] The result of these divisions has had a decisive effect on the way in which the Church sees itself in every aspect including its worship.

In believing the Church to be a fellowship pledged to strive for God's Commonwealth of social justice and righteousness, the social democrats were in open conflict with those Anglicans to whom the Church was an exclusive club concerned only with the spiritual exercises necessary to secure for its members reserved places in a heaven above the clouds. In seeing ceremonial as the outward, dramatic expression of the gospel and life of the divine commonwealth for which they were striving, the social democrats were in conflict with the Ritualists, to whom ceremony was a professional performance of mysteries comprehensible only to the clerisy, mysteries of an unseen

---

[1] Reg. Groves, *Conrad Noel and the Thaxted Movement, An Adventure in Christian Socialism* (*cit.* Groves, *Noel*) 1968, p. 37.

spiritual life which had to avoid contamination by remaining inside the church, having nothing to do with life outside the holy temple.[2]

Groves' analysis is basic and gets right to the root of the problem, defining an antithesis which continues to exist to this day in the Church of England without being now confined merely to one ecclesiastical party.

The liturgical developments which will be examined began to emerge during the period in which the Church of England was facing the greatest possible challenges to its pastoral policies. These arose, first of all, from the continuing growth of urban and industrial society at the end of the nineteenth century, which was too soon followed by the awful calamities and catastrophes of the First World War. Both these events posed urgent and basic questions for the Church which it could not easily answer, and there were particular challenges which arose to test the Church. One of these concerned a growing awareness among some churchmen that there was in the secular world a craving for fellowship. These same churchmen realized that this was an area in which the Church had something to offer, the fellowship of the Lord's Table. Chaplains from the front and priests in urban parishes urged the Church authorities to support them in developing a form of worship which would be, at one and the same time, true to the primitive concepts of the Eucharist, expressive of *Koinonia*, and would also make the point that the Eucharist is an extension of the incarnational concerns of the Gospel in the workaday world.

Unfortunately, even those Bishops who had at one time demonstrated a sensitivity to these issues were content to allow the Prayer Book Revision debates of the 1920s to be used as an attempt to construct an ecclesiastical compromise which would serve the disciplinary requirements of the Church rather than be an enabling of its evangelical mission. Yet even so, without, rather than because of, episcopal encouragement, the seed continued to grow secretly. Without any detectable borrowing from the comparable Roman Catholic Liturgical Movement which was developing on the Continent of Europe, the idea of the Parish Communion began to take root in the 1920s and 1930s. The evidence exists that this type of service commended itself, in the first place, to priests who had an awareness of the need of the Church to identify with the hopes, aspirations, frustrations, and pains of the community in which it was placed, those who were not content with a separation of the Church from the body politic in every sense.

[2] *Ibid.*

These are the real origins of the Parish Communion. It is not merely a new, original, and somewhat more attractive way of ordering the Holy Communion Service so that there is a greater element of congregational participation in it and it is also a more convenient service for whole families to attend together. It is not even the possibility of a service held at an hour which allows prospective worshippers longer in bed on a Sunday morning before making their Communion, whether or not they considered themselves restricted by any rules regarding fasting. The real issues involved, those which informed the true origins of the Parish Communion, are far more fundamental and gospel-based than any of these matters, even if they have since been too often forgotten and obscured, despite the comparative shortness of the time since they were first enunciated.

For the sacramental socialists the pattern was quite clear: they were convinced that the *Corpus Christi*, which is the Church, needs to feed together in fellowship on the *Corpus Christi*, which is the Body and Blood received in the Holy Eucharist, in order that it may fulfil its role to be the *Corpus Christi*, the loving hands, feet, and eyes of Christ active and incarnate in his Servant Church. For the God of the Catholic, incarnational Christianity of the authentic pioneers of the Parish Communion was not a God who was absent in heaven, whither his followers aspired to follow him, but was to be recognized as the 'God of earth and altar'.[3]

The production of *The Alternative Service Book* by the Church of England in 1980 was the culmination of a process which had been in progress over many decades. One of the stages in the more immediate preparation was the holding of a series of Liturgical Conferences for the National Assembly of the Church of England. The Conferences had no legislative authority, but were a means of informing the Church Assembly about the progress of liturgical reform. At the first of these in 1966, Canon Arthur Couratin was given the task of explaining to the Conference the background to the thinking of the Liturgical Commission on the subject of a revised order for the Holy Communion.

The Liturgical Commission had been set up in 1954 by the Archbishops of Canterbury and York at the request of the Convocations 'to consider all matters of liturgical concern referred to it by the Arch-

[3] *The Collected Poems of G. K. Chesterton*, 3rd ed. 1933, p. 146. Chesterton was a friend and disciple of Conrad Noel and other Christian Socialists around 1900 (Maisie Ward, *Gilbert Keith Chesterton*, 1944, pp. 121, 133, 142 etc).

bishops and to report upon them to the Archbishops'.[4] By 1966 the
Commission was in a position to present to the Archbishops proposals
for a number of alternative services for experimental use by the
Church which could now run the gauntlet of the ecclesiastical democratic system under the provisions of the newly authorized *Prayer Book
(Alternative and Other Services) Measure*.[5] Those present at the Conference, aware of the long history of eucharistic controversy, were
anxious to hear Canon Couratin's description of the Commission's
modus operandi. He told them:

It might be best if I began by telling you how we started producing this draft.
We were, all of us, thinking in terms of a parish communion, that is to say, a
Sunday Service, with a sermon, and the bulk of the congregation communi-
cating.[6]

The title 'Parish Communion' nowhere appears in the formularies
of the Church of England, so how had it come about that, when
speaking of this proposal which was aimed at producing the first fundamental revision of the eucharistic rite of the Church of England
since 1662, the Commission should so confidently take this model as
the one which would be, at one and the same time, both the most
widely understood model and also the most widely accepted? At no
time in the subsequent debates in Convocation, Church Assembly, or
(eventually) General Synod was this basic assumption challenged on
any grounds whatsoever. In the course of this book the paths by
which the Church of England came to this situation in its Eucharistic
worship will be explored and the reason why Couratin was able to
make this assumption on behalf of the Liturgical Commission and to
make it unchallenged will be examined.

Clearly we have here a way of presenting the Eucharist which had
cut across all party lines and disputes, a major achievement in the
Church of England by any reckoning. Although, as we shall see, the
type of service which developed into the Parish Communion had its
origins in the later outworkings of the Oxford Movement, in recent
years it has begun to influence the pattern of worship in the majority
of Anglican parishes, irrespective of their churchmanship. Colin
Buchanan, an evangelical liturgist, has made the position of many
evangelicals on this matter clear:

[4] *Prayer Book Revision in the Church of England—A Memorandum of the Church of England
Liturgical Commission*, LC 1958/2, 1957, p. vii.
   [5] *Prayer Book (Alternative and Other Services) Measure, 1965.*
   [6] *The Liturgical Conference 1966, Report of Proceedings*, 1966, pp. 70–71.

The Lord told his people to "do this", and the dominical sanction is therefore unequivocal. The social perspective bulks large in the New Testament, and it is the sacrament which binds and holds the people of God in one. To the apostles there could never have been two categories of Christians—communicants and non-communicants—all were equally communicants once they were baptised, and if not they were self-excommunicating.

It is a slight jump from these New Testament principles to assert the propriety and necessity of a weekly main communion. It is well arguable that a once-a-month communion which in fact was the only communion service of the month would equally well fit the principles. Such a communion would be the great meeting-point of the local church. Its place in church life would stand out a mile, and be the subject of teaching in the congregation. But such a pattern is unknown in any parish in the Church of England, and as an alternative to a weekly communion it remains a wholly theoretical hypothesis. The actual outworking of the biblical principles is to be found in the Parish Communion.[7]

Against such a background of increasing consensus across the churchmanship divide, the end result of twentieth century liturgical revision in respect of the Holy Communion in the Church of England has been to produce an order which is suitable for the Parish Communion defined as:

A celebration at 9, 9.30, or 10 (the time has tended to get steadily later) with hymns and sermon, and with everyone communicating.... In the conduct of the Parish Communion great importance was attached to the participation of the laity, who were encouraged to join in some of the prayers hitherto said by the celebrant alone, to make responses to the various petitions in the Prayer for the Church, to bring up the elements at the Offertory, and to assist with the Chalice.[8]

Having in mind that it is the roots of such a corporate, communicating, participatory eucharist that is being sought, it will be neces-

---

[7] Colin Buchanan, *Patterns of Sunday Worship*, Grove Booklet on Worship No. 9, 1972, p. 8. Buchanan's comment about a once-a-month only pattern being 'unknown in any parish in the Church of England' is almost certainly true of the twentieth century. Firm evidence of prevailing patterns of worship in the eighteenth century are sparse, but even if any parish did have a once-a-month only service of the Holy Communion, it was certainly not designed as the central feature of parochial life. See J. Wickham Legg, *English Church Life*, 1914, pp. 31–33; Norman Sykes, *Church and State in England in the XVIIIth Century*, 1934, p. 255; Arthur Waine, *Church and Society in Eighteenth-Century Devon*, 1969, p. 145, W. K. Lowther Clarke, *Eighteenth-Century Piety*, 1944, p. 11; S. C. Carpenter, *Eighteenth-Century Church and People*, 1959, p. 189.

[8] G. J. Cuming, *A History of Anglican Liturgy* (cit. Cuming, *History*) 2nd ed. 1982, p. 194. Cuming is writing in a period in which the pressures of fasting communion are off, and hence a later time for the service becomes possible.

sary first of all to look at the influence which the Oxford Movement
had on the celebration of the Eucharist in the Church of England
from the early part of the nineteenth century through to the beginning of the twentieth. Then, next, at the progress of the process of liturgical revision from the 'watershed' date of 1904.

PART ONE

FALSE TRACKS

1   The Oxford Movement and the Eucharist

In the popular mind adherents of high-church ways, those influenced by the nineteenth-century Oxford Movement, can easily be detected by the elaborateness of their ceremonial, particularly that surrounding the Eucharist and indeed, their whole emphasis on that sacrament as the most important and fundamental for Christians so that it must always be given primacy of place. This was certainly the outcome of that movement which traces its origins to Keble's sermon on 14 July 1833,[1] but it was not one of the movement's original aims. However, any campaign which started from a 'high' view of the church and its sacraments was almost bound to generate practical action which would result in the Eucharist being restored to a central and pre-eminent place in the life of the Church and would, at the same time, gather to itself ceremonies and customs which would visually emphasize this point.

However, in the 1830s and 1840s the situation was far from the ritual and ceremonial controversies of a later period. There was a primary task for the early Tractarians, that of asserting the authority of the church in the face of the encroachments of rationalism and secularism. Although the Keble sermon has been hailed as the beginning of the Oxford Movement it was at the meeting that H. J. Rose called at his Rectory at Hadleigh from 15–19 July 1833 that they began to work out the details of their campaign. It was here that it was resolved to defend 'the apostolical succession and the integrity of the Prayer Book'. The *Tracts for the Times*[2] which commenced publication on 9 September 1833 were by no means pre-occupied with liturgical subjects. Of the ninety *Tracts* published between 1833 and 1841 only ten (3, 9, 13, 24, 37, 39, 63, 84, 86, 87) are concerned with any kind of liturgical matter.

In *Tract No. 3* Newman addressed to the clergy his 'Thoughts on the Alterations in the Liturgy'. He counselled the clergy to petition the Bishops to resist any alterations. He was anxious lest silence would be interpreted as acquiescence in change.

We know not what is to come upon us; but the writer for one will try so to acquit himself now, that if any irremediable calamity befalls the Church, he

---

[1] 'The following Sunday, July 14th, Mr. Keble preached the Assize sermon in the University pulpit. It was published under the title of "National Apostasy". I have ever considered and kept the day as the start of the religious movement of 1833'. John Henry Newman, *Apologia pro Vita Sua*, 1864, Everyman ed. (n.d.), p. 56.

[2] *Tracts for the Times by Members of the University of Oxford*, 1833 ff.

may not have to vex himself with the recollections of silence on his part and indifference when he might have been up and alive.[3]

In *Tract No. 9* R. H. Froude[4] wrote critically of those who complained that the services of the Church were too long, while in *Tract No. 13* Keble[5] explained the principles of selection in the Sunday lessons and advised no change. It is this spirit of 'no change' which is reflected in all the liturgical contributions to the *Tracts*, and there is a good deal of evidence that the early Tractarians were more concerned to encourage the full use of the provisions of the Book of Common Prayer than to modify, curtail, or add to it. They had a 'high' view of the Prayer Book to the extent that Isaac Williams's *Tract No. 86* was entitled 'Indications of a Superintending Providence in the Preservation of the Prayer Book and in the changes which it has undergone'.[6] Belief in such a superintending providence gave confidence to the Tractarians in the 1830s and 1840s to stand for what they called 'Church Principles' which included the use of those parts of the Prayer Book which had fallen into neglect in the recent years. A lack of any enthusiasm for Prayer Book reform was a continuing characteristic of early Tractarians, because any suggestions in that direction seemed to be coming from those animated by a latitudinarian and Erastian spirit.[7] Härdelin has emphasized:

The conviction that Prayer Book revision ought to be rejected, so often expressed in the documents of the early stages of the Movement, must thus be understood first of all as a consequence of the definite anti-liberal and anti-Erastian views of the Oxford men.[8]

It was the formation of the Cambridge Camden Society which added to the Oxford Movement the dimension of 'ecclesiology' with its interest in the design and furnishings of churches, the vestments of the clergy and their assistants.[9] The spirit of the Oxford Tractarians had now reached the other ancient English University, which was now poised to make its own particular contribution to the ecclesiastical ferment of the time.

[3] *Tracts, op. cit.*, vol. 1 for 1833–1834.

[4] *Ibid.*, 31 October 1833.

[5] *Ibid.*, 5 December 1833.

[6] *Ibid.*, 1840, vol. v for 1838–1840.

[7] R. C. D. Jasper, *Prayer Book Revision in England 1800–1900* (*cit.* Jasper, *Prayer Book*), 1954, pp. 12–26.

[8] Alf Härdelin, *The Tractarian Understanding of the Eucharist, Studia Historico-Ecclesiastica Upsaliensia—8* (1965), pp. 259–260.

[9] James F. White, *The Cambridge Movement: The Ecclesiologists and the Gothic Revival*, 1979, *passim*.

One of the first to discern the complementary nature of the
Universities' role was Dr Francis Close, the Vicar of Cheltenham,
who preached a sermon to which he gave the title *The Restoration of the
Church is a Restoration of Popery; proved and illustrated from the Authentic
Publications of the Cambridge Camden Society*. In this diatribe Close thun-
dered:

It will be my object to show that as Romanism is taught analytically at
Oxford, it is taught artistically at Cambridge—that it is inculcated theoretically at one University and it is sculptured, painted and graven at the other.[10]

The original authors of the *Tracts* were concerned first of all for the
defence of ecclesiastical and sacramental principles and doctrine
which would be worked out in terms of worship; whereas the Ecclesiologists started from a concern for the decoration, ritual, and structure of churches and believed that this could affect the way in which
men worshipped. So they redesigned or reordered the buildings and
added various items of ecclesiastical furnishings.

Among the Bishops who had initially joined the Cambridge Camden Society was Bishop Charles James Blomfield of London, and he
was also the first Bishop to resign from the Society because he disapproved of its literature. Nevertheless, as Owen Chadwick puts it,
'without the smallest intention to provoke, he precipitated the first of
the ritual controversies'.[11] Blomfield knew that he could not prevent
any tampering with the Prayer Book by a high churchman unless he
also put restrictions on the low churchman who failed to observe its
full provision. So it was that in his 1841 Charge to the Diocese of
London he supported the strict observance of the rubrics of the Book
of Common Prayer by all clergy, high and low:

Every clergyman is bound, by the plainest obligations of duty, to obey the
directions of the Rubric. For conforming to them in every particular, he
needs no other authority than that of the Rubric itself. We ought not to be de-
terred from a scrupulous observance of the rites and customs prescribed or
sanctioned by our Church by a dread of being thought too careful about
externals of religion. If we are not to go *beyond* her ritual, at least we ought not
to *fall short* of it, not make her public services less frequent nor more naked
and inexpressive than she intends them to be.[12]

[10] Quoted in Kenneth Clark, *The Gothic Revival*, 2nd ed., 1962, pp. 166–167; Michael
Hennell, *Sons of the Prophets*, 1979, p. 118.

[11] Owen Chadwick, *The Victorian Church*, 1966, I, p. 215.

[12] Alfred Blomfield (ed.), *A Memoir of Charles James Blomfield DD Bishop of London with
selections from his correspondence*, 1863, II, p. 33.

Blomfield believed that, far from questioning the right of the clergy to observe the rubrics in every particular, it was their duty to be completely loyal to them. In his Charge Blomfield particularly mentioned the administration of public baptism at the time prescribed (i.e. at Matins or Evensong), the reading of the Offertory Sentences, the use of the prayer for the Church Militant when there was no Communion to follow, and the observance of Holy Days. He also spoke of the Daily Offices, and the frequent celebrations of the Holy Communion.[13]

The Bishop also ventured into other areas. He said he disapproved of the decorating of the Communion-table with flowers:

Especially when that decoration is varied from day to day, so as to have some fanciful analogy to the history of the saint who is commemorated. This appears to me to be something worse than frivolous, and to approach very nearly to the honour paid by the Church of Rome to deified sinners.[14]

On an even more contentious subject he took what some would have regarded as the High Church view, in that he approved of the wearing of the surplice rather than the gown at a morning service.[15]

The effect of Blomfield's Charge was eventually widely felt. At first only the vast diocese of London was influenced, with some clergy refusing to obey, while others obeyed but only 'in bounden duty'. Others, again, complied with enthusiasm and inspired their people with their own enthusiasm for the offertory, for daily services and more frequent communions. The full text of the Bishop's Charge appeared in the *Quarterly Review*,[16] and in each diocese a few conscientious clergymen wondered anxiously whether they were being as faithful to their ordination oaths as they ought to be.[17] They were thrown into even greater turmoil when in 1845 Blomfield (and Bishop Phillpotts of Exeter, who had delivered a similar charge) withdrew their directions because of opposition from both laity and Low Church clergy.[18] One priest who was confused by the Bishops' change of mind was Frederick Oakley, who wrote in retrospect 'It was too evident that the Bishops proceeded on no fixed principle, but were uncertain, capricious and impulsive.'[19] It was this kind of con-

---

[13] *Ibid.*, p. 34.

[14] *Ibid.*, p. 36.

[15] *Ibid.*, p. 38.

[16] *Quarterly Review*, vol. LXXII, May 1843, pp. 237 ff.

[17] D. C. Gray, 'The Influence of Tractarian Principles on Parish Worship 1839–1849', *Alcuin*, 1984, pp. 2–3 and *passim*.

[18] Jasper, *Prayer Book*, p. 54.

[19] F. Oakley, *Historical Notes*, p. 68, quoted Härdelin, *op. cit.*, p. 262.

cern that preoccupied the early days of the Oxford Movement, and it was only slowly that the more outwardly florid items began to be added. Although Keble and Newman preached in black gowns and celebrated the Holy Communion in surplice and hood at the north end of the altar,[20] it was the fact that they were teaching a doctrine of the Eucharist and the Real Presence which demanded a greater reverence for the altar and all that surrounded it, that brought with it other developments.[21]

As we have seen, the Cambridge Camden Society was forthright in encouraging churchman to look to the glories of the past, but they maintained that they took their examples from Church of England traditions. In what J. F. White, the historian of the Cambridge Camden Society, has described as 'perhaps the most important scholarly work published under the auspices of the Society'[22] they argued:

It was never the intention of the compilers of our present services that their work should be considered as a new fabrick, but as a reformation of the present system. Consequently many things then in actual use, and always intended to be retained, were not expressly commanded, any more than they were distinctly forbidden, in the new rubric. This general consideration will serve to explain why the existing rubrics do not mention many of the usages and ceremonies which the *Hierurgia Anglicana* will describe.[23]

The authors of *Hierurgia Anglicana* hoped, that from the illustrations which they gave, their readers would gain a much clearer idea of what the Anglican Church had allowed. They also hoped to convince those 'who have distrusted the late improved feeling on these points' that the various items of ceremonial which they advocated are 'entirely compatible with the most dutiful allegiance to our own Communion'.[24]

While the study of ceremonial went on in the universities, its practical results were to be found chiefly outside their confines and continued apace over the next decade. While the more active ecclesiastical politicians were involved with Bishop Hampden and his

---

[20] H. P. Liddon, *Life of Edward Bouverie Pusey*, 1894, II, pp. 476–477.

[21] Härdelin, *op. cit.*, pp. 268–271 on the significance of Newman's design of his church at Littlemore.

[22] White, *op. cit.*, p. 67.

[23] *Hierurgia Anglicana or Documents and Extracts Illustrative of the Ritual of the Church of England after the Reformation edited by Members of the Ecclesiological late Cambridge Camden Society*, 1848, p. 1.

[24] *Ibid.*, p. ii.

alleged heterodoxy (1847),[25] Mr Gorham and baptismal regenera-
ton,[26] and the fear of the establishment of the Roman hierarchy in
Britain and the so-called 'Papal Aggression' (1850),[27] the High
Church influence on the parochial scene continued to increase.

It was given a further fillip by the Denison case, which limped on
from 1853 to 1858. This case concerned Archdeacon George Anthony
Denison, Vicar of East Brent in Somerset and Archdeacon of Taun-
ton in the Diocese of Bath and Wells, who taught that all who come to
communion receive the body and blood of Christ, worthy as well as
unworthy. This doctrine was, for Denison, of one piece with the doctrine of the real presence, and stood or fell together with it.[28] After
many legal complications the Archbishop of Canterbury's court
found Denison's doctrine repugnant to Articles xxviii and xxix, and
he was deprived.

Later the prosecution was found to be invalid on a legal point, to
the great delight of the Tractarians. In defence of Denison, Keble
wrote a book *On Eucharistical Adoration*, Pusey published a volume
entitled *The Real Presence*, and Robert Wilberforce wrote on *The
Doctrine of the Holy Eucharist*. 'Meanwhile', wrote Owen Chadwick,
'younger men in the parishes were translating this high sacramental
language into external symbols and ritual.'[29] The controversies had
passed beyond arguments about the surplice and offertory.

Outward honour to God's presence within the sacrament was in question:
vestments, genuflections, candles, ornaments of the altar.[30]

It is to this working out in the parishes that we now turn and try to
discover what attempts were made, not merely to give the Eucharist
its primary place in the worship of the Church and to surround it with
all due dignity and honour, but also to make this service available to
as wide a cross-section of the parishioners as possible and to see it as
an act of offering by the whole parish—in other words, to what
extent, if at all, they were sowing the seeds of what later became the
Parish Communion.

How far W. J. E. Bennett's introduction of a weekly celebration following Morning Prayer at eleven o'clock at St Paul's, Knightsbridge

[25] Chadwick, *op. cit.*, I, pp. 237 ff.
[26] *Ibid.*, pp. 250 ff.
[27] *Ibid.*, p. 271.
[28] Härdelin, *op. cit.*, pp. 168–176; Joyce Coombs, *George Anthony Denison: The Firebrand, 1805–1896*, 1984, pp. 124 ff.
[29] Chadwick, *op. cit.*, I, p. 495.
[30] *Ibid.* See also Owen Chadwick, *The Founding of Cuddesdon, 1954, passim.*

in 1846 would stand up to this test is doubtful.[31] It might at first sight look like a move in the right direction. There was a great deal of dignity about the service; the celebrant stood at the north side of the altar and the Epistoler and Gospeller at the south.[32] There was a surpliced choir,[33] and two candles were lit on the altar.[34] It was the only celebration of the Eucharist on a Sunday and there was general communion. However, by 1848 Bennett had diluted the effect by introducing an additional early celebration at 7.45 a.m., although the idea of this early service being for communion and the later service for worship had not as yet appeared on the scene.[35]

Although Bennett's service had a surpliced choir, only a small part of the service had been sung. It is generally alleged that the first fully sung Communion of the period started at Margaret Street Chapel in 1847. This chapel had begun to take on its particular role in 1839 with the licensing of Frederick Oakley as Minister.

This must be regarded as the inauguration of the system which has logically developed, and of the principles which have consistently prevailed from that time to the present, in Margaret Chapel and All Saints' Church. It marks the first attempt to exhibit in London the practical application in worship of the principles of the Oxford Movement. It is this fact which entitles the church in Margaret Street to its particular glory as the pioneer in London of the Catholic revival in worship and work.[36]

Further evidence for this fully sung service is contained in a letter that Benjamin Webb, one of the founder members of the Cambridge Camden Society, wrote to John Neale who had been leader of the original Ecclesiologists in 1847. Webb reported that at Margaret Street Chapel:

They have now got up a complete musical Mass; the Commandments, Epistle, Gospel, Preface etc., all sung to the ancient music. I venture to assert that there has been nothing so solemn since the Reformation.[37]

---

[31] F. Bennett, *The Life of W. J. E. Bennett, Founder of St. Barnabas, Pimlico and Vicar of Froome-Sellwood and of his part in the Oxford Church Movement of the Nineteenth Century*, 1909, p. 40.

[32] *Ibid.*, p. 141.

[33] *Ibid.*, p. 40.

[34] *Ibid.*, p. 41.

[35] *Ibid.*

[36] W A. Wordsworth (compiler), *Quam Dilecta: A description of All Saints' Church, Margaret Street with historical notes of Margaret Chapel and All Saints' Church*, 1891, p. 37.

[37] Webb to Neale letter, 31 December 1847, quoted E. H. Fellowes, *English Cathedral Music*, 5th ed. revised by J. A. Westrup, 1969, p. 31.

2 The Question of Fasting Communion

During this early period of the Anglo-Catholic revival, as has been
seen, there was still an assumption that all who were qualified to do so
would communicate at any celebration of the Holy Communion if
they so wished. The insistence by Anglo-Catholics that Communion
should only be received fasting developed a few years later. H. A.
Bully of Brighton bore witness to this fact in a letter to the Church
newspaper *The Guardian* in 1909:

It was not the practice or intention of the pioneers of the Anglo-Catholic revival to make fasting communion compulsory. In my young days I remember a
good many midday communicants at St. Mary Magdalene's, Munster
Square when Rev'd Edward Stuart was one of the first to restore choral celebrations, with lights, incense, and vestments on loyal prayer-book lines. The
rigorist theory is of comparatively recent introduction amongst us.[38]

Yet this is what happened. The Anglo-Catholics taught that Holy
Communion must be received fasting. The 'Holy Food' of the
Eucharist must not be preceded by ordinary food, and the discipline
of fasting produced an attitude of mind which prepared the worshipper for the Holy Communion. With these principles in mind they developed a pattern of worship to accommodate this. They had an early
'Mass' (or Masses) before breakfast for the receiving of Communion,
and then the faithful returned to church after breaking their fast to
'worship' at the High Mass which was held at 10.30 or 11.00.[39] At
this service there would be no communicants; or if there were, very
few, and they had fasted up to that time like the officiating priest.
Increasingly many parishioners only attended this later service, and
so there came about a revival of that category of worshipper which
was condemned in the 1552 Prayer Book and reviled as being no more
than 'gasers and lookers'.[40] By the time of the publication of the 1662

[38] *The Guardian*, 9 June 1909, p. 917. (Stuart crossed swords with the Archbishop of
Canterbury over his activities at St Mary Magdalene's, see R. T. Davidson and W.
Benham, *Life of Archibald Campbell Tait, Archbishop of Canterbury*, 1891, I, pp. 219–222.)

[39] For the large numbers making their communion at services at 5 a.m., 6 a.m. and
8 a.m. in well-known Anglo-Catholic churches in London, 1859–1872, see H. P. Liddon, *Evening Communion contrary to the Teaching and Practice of the Church in All Ages*, 1876,
p. 25 and pp. 35–36.

[40] The Boke of Common Prayer, and administration of the Sacraments and other
rites and Ceremonies in the Churche of Englande, in F. E. Brightman, ed., *The English
Rite, being a synopsis of the sources and revisions of the Book of Common Prayer*, II, p. 669.

Prayer Book, the custom of the attendance of non-communicants has vanished. As T. W. Drury argued of the 1662 service to the 1906 Royal Commission:

The service contains no express prohibition of the presence of non-communicants; but its whole emphasis rests on actual Communion and no mention is made of attendance apart from it.[41]

The first Tractarian actually to advocate non-communicating attendance was Robert Wilberforce.[42] His intention in doing this was not to deprive worshippers of the eucharist, rather was he giving them more than they had been accustomed to receiving in the recent past, when all that they were offered when they went to Church was the ante-communion service.[43] Wilberforce acknowledged that perfect participation in the Eucharist implied that worshippers should avail themselves of both its purposes, that is, what he speaks of as 'the feast' and 'the offering'. He contended that there was nothing contrary to either natural piety or to any express command in joining in the sacrifice without going on to the Sacrament, or in partaking of the Sacrament without having been present at the oblation. In this latter statement Wilberforce was also defending the right to receive Holy Communion from the Reserved Sacrament.[44]

In the last quarter of the nineteenth century there was a growing concern in many places about the increasing insistence by many Anglo-Catholics on a strict rule of fasting before receiving Holy Communion. Percy Dearmer recalled:

Bewildered people in one parish after another were told that they ought not to communicate at noon, but must come to the newly invented "early celebration" at eight in the morning, an hour which to the great majority of our people is almost impossible. This was because of the introduction of fasting-communion, which has now been taught with great and insistent earnestness for two or three generations, till even at Evangelical gatherings an early Celebration has come to be taken for granted.[45]

Many High Churchmen maintained that it was a grave sin to communicate after taking food. For instance F. N. Oxenham, in a sermon

[41] T. W. Drury, 'Notes on Attendance at Holy Communion without Communicating' *Royal Commission on Ecclesiastical Discipline, Record of Commissioners' Attendances, Appendices, Index and Analysis of Evidence* (Cd. 3072) 1906, iv, p. 61.
[42] David Newsome, *The Parting of Friends*, 1966, pp. 372 ff.
[43] Härdelin, *op. cit.*, p. 287.
[44] R. I. Wilberforce, *The Doctrine of the Holy Eucharist*, 1853, p. 449.
[45] Percy Dearmer, *The Truth about Fasting with special reference to Fasting-Communion*, 1928 (*cit.* Dearmer, *Fasting*) p. 3.

which was printed and widely circulated, spoke of communicating after food as doing that 'which God has forbidden', and starkly stated that such a service would be 'a service which you have good reason to fear He will never accept'.[46] But there was not complete unanimity on the subject, as will be shown.

The teaching was widespread, and Bishop Moberly, Bishop of Salisbury, in his Visitation Charge of 1873 felt it necessary to condemn priests who spoke of those who represented communion after food, even after moderate and necessary food, as mortal sin as 'unkind and cruel'.[47]

Bishop H. T. Kingdon, who came from a sound Tractarian background,[48] wrote a lengthy book in 1875 to counterbalance the teaching of 'rigorist priests' who were 'insisting on Fasting Communion as a necessity even under pain of committing mortal sin'.[49] Kingdon lists three grounds upon which those who were teaching fasting communion based their case: the first was greater reverence to the Sacrament, the second was the obligation of the Canons of the Church, and the third the assimilation of the Church of England's rule to that of other churches. Commenting on the first point Kingdon drew attention to other uncondemned acts of irreverence, such as smoking before communicating, and suggested that 'recollectedness of mind and devout reverence of spirit must be of more importance than accidental disposition of body'.[50] To the second he devoted three hundred closely argued pages, riddled with authorities, and comes to the opinion that 'there is no precept of the English Church binding the conscience to this devotion'.[51] The third point Kingdon dismissed with a fine turn of phrase:

It may be doubted whether any course of action which is likely to hinder

---

[46] F. N. Oxenham, *The Duty of Fasting Communion*, 1873, p. 20.

[47] Francis John Jayne, *Anglican Pronouncements upon 1—Auricular Confession collected mainly by Bishop Dowden (1907) to which are affixed the opinions of Dean Hook (1851) and Bishop Moberly (1873). 2—Fasting Communion, and some other points of disquietude*, 1912, p. 66.

[48] On the title page of his book he is described as 'Late Vice-Principal of Salisbury Theological College'. This college was founded by Bishop Walter Kerr Hamilton of Salisbury, 'who abandoned himself whole-heartedly to the influence of Dr Newman and the Tractarians', Dora H. Robertson, *Sarum Close, A History of the Life and Education of the Cathedral Choristers for 700 years*, 1938, p. 286.

[49] Hollingworth Tully Kingdon, *Fasting Communion historically investigated from the Canons and the Fathers, and shown to be not binding in England*, 2nd ed. 1875, p. 2.

[50] *Ibid.*, p. 5.

[51] *Ibid.*, p. 359.

many from the Sacrament of Union in England would be likely to forward
union.[52]

It will not be a matter of surprise that Kingdon's book did not go
unchallenged by the advocates of fasting communion. The following
year an English Church Union publication, although accepting that
a strictly rigorist theory while so many have no access to anything but
a midday Communion was unrealistic, regretted that Kingdon could
not fully support this act of reverence which they believed enhanced
'the dignity of that holy mystery'.[53]

Kingdon's work came in for more criticism a few years later when
Fr F. W. Puller SSJE addressed the Confraternity of the Blessed Sacrament. The resulting publication *Concerning the Fast before Communion*
became the standard work for those seeking support for the rule of
fasting communion and went through several editions. Fr Puller
believed that:

The primitive rule of fasting before Communicating was in the first place an
expression of the Church's mind concerning the august dignity of the Blessed
Sacrament of the Altar; it was also a witness to the needs of careful preparation on the part of intending communicants and it was a practical safeguard
hindering certain forms of sacrilegious Communion.[54]

Puller relies heavily on a treatise by the Rev'd Frederick Hall entitled *Fasting Reception of the Blessed Sacrament*, published in 1882. This
book was heavily criticized by Dearmer, who condemned it in no uncertain terms, writing that:

It illustrates the great influence which one small book has had in building up
the idea of fasting communion among Anglicans. Mr. Hall's work showed
little sign that he understood the documents he was dealing with, or was in
any sense a historian. One is driven to conjecture that he had derived his
material, directly or indirectly, from Roman Catholic Text Books, and had
taken it as he found it.[55]

---

[52] *Ibid.*, p. 6.

[53] W(illiam) B(right), '*A Postscript on some points in Mr. Kingdon's work on Fasting Communion*', attached to Liddon, *op. cit.*, p. 48. Bright is identified as author in Dearmer,
Fasting, p. 29. Dearmer also notes Bright's change of heart on the subject in 1895, *ibid.*,
p. 114. On Bright see also *DNB, 1901–1911*, 1912, pp. 224–225.

[54] F. W. Puller, Mission Priest of the Society of St John the Evangelist, Cowley, *Concerning the Fast Before Communion: A Paper read before the Confraternity of the Blessed Sacrament
on its Festival, May 18th 1891*, 2nd ed., 1895, p. 1.

[55] Dearmer, *Fasting*, p. 30.

Despite all this criticism the teaching continued, no doubt heavily influenced by the fact that the attitude of the Roman Catholic Church was unbending, and those Anglo-Catholics who took their disciplinary norms (when it suited their convenience) from that Church advocated no other approach. Many High Churchmen accepted the discipline as being helpful to some but refused to support it as a universal rule. Bishop John Wordsworth wrote:

It is good that the body should take part with the soul in its preparation, yet fasting must not be pressed as if it were a part of the Gospel to the injury of weak consciences or to the neglect of Communion on the part of those who find attendance at an early celebration difficult or impossible: nor must it be allowed to foster an attitude of contempt on the part of the physically stronger towards the physically weaker brethren.[56]

Another Anglo-Catholic scholar, Charles Gore, wrote in the same year about the problems produced by an insistence on fasting communion.[57] Like Wordsworth he was willing to describe it as 'a very ancient and venerable custom', but thought it unfortunate that the difficulty had not been seriously faced 'by any considerable body of people who are prepared equally to insist upon all the elements necessary to a right solution'.[58]

Presumably Gore did not consider Convocation as being 'a considerable body of people', despite the fact that both the northern and southern Convocations had produced reports on the subject in the recent past. For instance, in 1899 the Lower Convocation of York asked the Bishops of that province to give definitive guidance on the subject. When the Upper House came to discuss the subject, they decided that

[56] John Wordsworth, *The Ministry of Grace: Studies in Early Church History with reference to present problems*, 1901, p. 321.

[57] Nor would Bishop Edward King of Lincoln, the episcopal hero of the Anglo-Catholics, have sided with them on this issue. Archbishop Benson recorded in his diary for 19 March 1893: 'The Bishop of Lincoln slept here to preach at St. James's. He is a truly sweet person and immensely beloved. He holds exactly what I do about Fasting Communion—that it is good for those for whom it is good, and to be recommended if people can bear it. But he greatly deprecates the language and practices used and enforced about it by a certain party. He says that Canon Carter, Liddon, Bishop Webb most strongly, and others on that side have all held the same. There is nothing "deadly" in taking food before it. At Ordination he himself always beforehand takes tea and dry toast. I write this within two or three hours (and am certain of every word) because he is sure to be counted on the other side.' Arthur Christopher Benson, *The Life of Edward White Benson, Sometime Archbishop of Canterbury*, New ed. abridged, 1901, pp. 469–470.

[58] Charles Gore, *The Body of Christ: An enquiry into the Institution and Doctrine of the Holy Communion*, 1901, p. 276.

all its members should comprise the Committee which would deliberate on the subject. On 3 May 1899 the Bishops adopted the resulting
report unanimously. In their report the Bishops stated that they were
not impressed by a report on fasting which the Upper House of the
Convocation of Canterbury had produced in May 1893. In the Canterbury report it had been granted that fasting communion was
observed by many as a reverent and ancient custom and as such commended by several of the church's (i.e. Church of England's) eminent
writers and divines down to that present time. In contrast the Northern Bishops were quite adamant in saying that they believed that
there were grave reasons from the history of the church, from the history of the custom 'and from its essential character' against making
fasting one of obligation.[59]

Not surprisingly neither the Anglo-Catholics in the north nor their
brothers in the south were in the least impressed by this kind of statement, with the result that this dispute rumbled on well into the twentieth century and continued to affect, in many places, the availability
of the Holy Communion, and arguably prevented the Parish Communion from emerging in its full force for many years. In 1939 J. S.
Bezzant was arguing that fasting communion also weakened the
social significance of the Eucharist.[60] Many High Church parishes
were unable to disentangle themselves from adherence to this rule
with the result that either they mounted an opposition to the Parish
Communion on the grounds of the problem of fasting, or those who
did adopt the service found themselves restricted to using a narrow
time-band for their services between 9.00 a.m. and 10.00 a.m., with a
9 a.m. or 9.30 a.m. start being the commonest, in order to accommodate fasting communion. Many Anglo-Catholics were only released
from these restrictions by imitating the changes that the Roman
Catholic Church made, first of all in the Apostolic Constitution *Chris-
tus Dominus* of 6 January 1953, and in subsequent further pronouncements on the Eucharistic Fast.[61]

Because of the restrictions imposed by the rule of fasting communion there needed to be a related justification of the practice of non-
communicating attendance at the Eucharist. In order to bolster his

[59] 'Fasting Communion Report', *York Journal of Convocation*, vol. 11, Sessions 3 May
and 4 July 1899, p. 106. cf. 'Appendix on Fasting Communion' in Evan Daniel, *The
Prayer Book: its History, Language and Contents*, 26th ed., 1948, pp. 403–405.

[60] To the ICF Swanwick Conference on the Social Significance of Worship, cf. p.
211, *infra*.

[61] International Commission on English in the Liturgy, A Joint Commission of Catholic Bishops' Conferences, *Documents on the Liturgy, 1963–1979, Conciliar, Papal, and Curial
Texts*, 1982, paras 2116–2118, pp. 667–669.

case W. J. Sparrow Simpson, in a catalogue of evidence supporting the practice, gave many examples of Tractarian writers who advocated non-communicating attendance, but placed particular emphasis on the testimony of the Rev'd George Rundle Prynne because he was not writing from the standpoint of the professed theologian, but from that of the parish priest, confronted with the practical problems of devotion, 'thoroughly conscious of the miserable failure of past methods'.[62] Prynne who was Vicar of St Peter's, Plymouth around 1847[63] wrote:

It is sometimes said that to encourage such a practice is to lead people to substitute attendance at the Sacrifice for Communion. This theory has surely been sufficiently tested during the last two or three hundred years. Christian people have been, practically, driven out of the Church at the commencement of the chief and only divinely appointed act of Christian worship. But has this practice had the effect of leading our people to set a true value on the Holy Eucharist, and to become communicants? Non-communicating England is the reply. Not one in a hundred, probably, of our people are communicants. Nay, further, the great mass even of churchgoers simply ignore the one distinctive act of Christian worship altogether, and satisfy their consciences by attending at Matins and Evensong, and listening to sermons. What they have never seen or joined in, they have learned to forget. It is believed by an increasing number of English Churchmen that a different and a better result may be obtained by returning to a more Catholic practice: and that, if our people can be led to remain and worship their Incarnate Saviour in the Blessed Sacrament of the Altar, they will not long rest until they have also feasted upon their sacrifice, and tasted and seen how gracious their Lord is.[64]

We see now that there is a situation developing in which although the High Churchmen are working hard to restore the Eucharist to its rightful position at the centre of the Church's worshipping life, they are at the same time producing 'communionless' congregations. The maintenance of the rule of fasting before Communion was believed by these Anglo-Catholics to be more important than that the congregations should receive Holy Communion. Although the Lord's Table was now surrounded with all due dignity and honour and the worship

---

[62] W. J. Sparrow Simpson, *Non-Communicating Attendance*, 1914, p. 204.

[63] H. Miles Brown, *The Catholic Revival in Cornish Anglicanism: A Study of the Tractarians of Cornwall 1833–1906*, 1980, p. 40.

[64] A. Clifton Kelway, *George Rundle Prynne, A Chapter in the Early History of the Catholic Revival*, 1905, pp. 224–225. Kelway, *ibid.*, p. 223 states that it was part of Prynne's *Eucharistic Manual* first published in 1865.

conducted with considerable care and attention to details, it was 'hedged' and defended in such a way that one basic aspect of that worship and fundamental purpose of the Lord's Table was commonly neglected by the Anglo-Catholics until it was restored to its rightful place by the Parish Communion pioneers.[65]

3 Worship officially examined

By the end of the nineteenth century a stranger coming unprepared to Anglican diversity would have been amazed at the bewildering array of different forms and styles of worship available within the Church of England. He would have discovered that the variety on offer ranged from the plain and simple to the frankly exotic. He would have found that the spectrum revealed started from the straightforward tradition of the Prayer Book service celebrated at the north end of the Table with celebrant dressed in surplice, academic hood, and black scarf, and progressed through various stages with a series of rites in which the bare bones of that Prayer Book service had been added to and subtracted from until, in what emerged, the original affinity with the Prayer Book was barely recognizable. But even yet our stranger would not have reached the climax of this display of liturgical anarchy—he had still to experience those churches where any pretence at using anything that might in any way resemble Prayer Book custom was so overlaid with the use of ceremonies, vestments, and devotional objects culled from the Church of Rome that the possibility of discerning even a little of the work of Cranmer had long since been completely obscured by great clouds of incense or had been drowned in gallons of holy water.

If this situation was bewildering for the stranger it was also certainly confusing for many of those who believed themselves to be 'of the Church'. Years of protest, demonstration, and even prosecution had been of no avail to those who objected to forms of worship which were different from those which they personally practised. At the same time for those who found the strait-jacket of 'legal' Anglicanism frustrating, but who were not disposed to desert and join another denomination, there needed to be some signs of a sensitive apprecia-

---

[65] Although, as it will be seen, even Gabriel Hebert had a high regard for the practice of fasting communion, cf. A. G. Hebert, ed., *The Parish Communion, A Book of Essays* (cit. Hebert, *Parish Communion*) 1937, p. 29.

tion of their spiritual appetites and needs. In an earlier decade the only answer that responsible authority seemed capable of making was by means of the sledge-hammer of legal.harassment,[66] so that the answer of 1904 was not only surprising but also welcome, and its outcome happier than many could have reasonably expected.

However difficult it might be for a present generation containing only a decreasingly small proportion of anything like active church people to imagine it, it is a fact that in 1904 the Government of the day decided that it was its solemn duty to set up a high-powered Royal Commission on Ecclesiastical Discipline. The task of the Royal Commission would be:

To inquire into the alleged prevalence of breaches or neglect of the Law relating to the conduct of Divine Service in the Church of England and to the ornaments and fittings of Churches; and to consider the existing powers and procedures applicable to such irregularities and to make such recommendations as may be deemed requisite for dealing with the aforesaid matters.[67]

The history of the Church of England in the nineteenth century is besmirched with the stories of Ritual Riots,[68] court cases and imprisonments.[69] The Royal Commission was an attempt to deal once and for all with the question of the limits of what was and what was not permissible in the worship of the Established Church. Evidence was brought before the Commission by three groups. A considerable amount of material was produced by agents of the Church Association which had been formed in 1865 by several leading Evangelical Churchmen to maintain the Protestant ideals of faith and worship in the Church of England.[70] Then there was the evidence accumulated by the Joint Evidence Committee of The Church of England League and the National Protestant Union, which had been specially formed to collect evidence for presentation to the Commission. One of the witnesses on their behalf was Lady Wimborne, who said that the vast majority of the members of the organization she had formed (The

---

[66] James Bentley, *Ritualism and Politics in Victorian England, The Attempt to Legislate for Belief*, Oxford Theological Monograph, 1978, *passim*.

[67] *Report of the Royal Commission on Ecclesiastical Discipline* (Cd. 3040) (*cit. Discipline Report*) 1906, p.v.

[68] M. Reynolds, *Martyr to Ritualism*, 1965. Joyce Coombs, *Judgement on Hatcham. The Story of a Religious Struggle 1877-1886*, 1969. L. E. Ellsworth, *Charles Lowther and the Ritualist Movement*, 1982.

[69] Bentley, *op. cit.*

[70] *ODCC*, (ed. 2) p. 289.

Church of England League) were 'persons of station and education in the country who are equally with ourselves devotedly attached to the Church of England'.[71] The third batch of material was produced by the Rev'd the Hon. W. E. Bowen.

Bowen was the first of 164 witnesses to appear before the Commission. At their first session on 2 June 1904, although Bowen denied that he had ever said that he believed that the breaches or neglect of the law in the conduct of services were an evil which had 'permeated the whole system', he nevertheless stated that he wished to put in evidence material which would cover 1500 churches in England and Wales, that is 10.5% of the churches in England and Wales.[72] In actual fact, he eventually only gave specific evidence about 111 services in 107 churches. The examples of 'lawlessness' that he produced varied from the use of the lavabo and mixing the chalice at one end to the use of the Roman Canon and services of Benediction at the other.

The Archbishop of Canterbury[73] himself gave evidence to the Commission for three days. It was a long and masterly statement in which His Grace also answered, with great skill, many questions put to him. Early in his evidence the Archbishop quoted from one of his own Charges which he had delivered in 1899 when he was Bishop of Winchester. In the Charge he had dispelled any illusions about there having been some past ideal age of uniformity:

We may say with reasonable certainty, that there never was a single year in the history of the Church of England when, in the conduct of Divine Service, the "use" was absolutely and rigidly uniform in every parish throughout the land. The sentence in Cranmer's Preface that "now from henceforth all the whole Realm shall have but one use", or the phrase, "and none other or otherwise", in Queen Elizabeth's Act of Uniformity—important, deliberate and definite as they were—seem always to have been so interpreted as to cover the deviations which custom sanctioned, or which temporary conditions made necessary, and it has often been pointed out how considerable a variety is possible, even under the letter of our rubricism with respect to the details of several of our prescribed services. No doubt, as years pass, and the social conditions of life change, and populations increase, these deviations have, *ipso facto*, even apart from religious questions, a tendency to grow wider, and the religious sympathies and "trends" at different periods differ very greatly. Then it comes about that local customs, unquestioned perhaps for

---

[71] *Minutes of Evidence taken before the Royal Commission on Ecclesiastical Discipline at Church House, Westminster*, vol. 1 (Cd. 3069) (*cit. Minutes*) 1906, I, p. 248, para. 3848.

[72] *Ibid.*, p. 1, para. 4.

[73] Randall Thomas Davidson, 1903–1928, *DECH*, p. 96.

generations, stiffen into rules, and an attempt to revive the unmistakable provisions of some long disregarded rubric has many a time been resented as a
lawless innovation.[74]

The Archbishop also used the diocese of Winchester to illustrate the
great changes that had come over the Church of England during the
century just ended. In 1829, under Bishop Sumner,[75] of the 319
parish churches in the diocese of Winchester divine service took place
twice on a Sunday in 158 churches and in only 11 churches were there
three services on a Sunday. There are no statistics as to the frequency
or infrequency of celebrations of the Holy Communion, but in his
Charge of that year Sumner had earnestly urged that each parish
'should look forward to arrangements, if possible for having at least
one celebration of Holy Communion every month'. Whereas seventy
years later Davidson could state that the Holy Communion was celebrated monthly (or more often) in 557, fortnightly (or more often) in
512, weekly (or more often) in 404, daily in 12.[76] Unfortunately there
are no details provided of the types of service that these celebrations of
the Holy Communion comprised.

After their first meeting the Commission issued a statement in
which they stated that they would be prepared to receive applications
from 'persons desiring to give evidence of breaches or neglect of the
law relating to the conduct of Divine Service in the Church of
England' and in the selecting of the witnesses special consideration
would be given to 'those who are, or have been Church officers in any
parish or are qualified to speak from wide or special knowledge'. In
their final report the Commission had to admit that the announce-
ment had produced little response from Church officers or other persons having special connection with particular churches: 'nor has any
great portion of the evidence which we have recorded come to us from
such persons'.[77]

Though the Report of the Commissioners could eventually con-
clude by stating that complaints had only been made to them from a
small proportion of the churches in the country and that in the large
majority of the parishes the work of the Church is being 'quietly and
diligently performed by clergy who are entirely loyal to the principles
of the English Reformation as expressed in the Book of Common
Prayer';[78] none the less their report does give us an impression of

[74] *Minutes*, para. 12846, V, p. 341.
[75] Bishop of Winchester 1895–1903, *DECH* p. 667.
[76] *Minutes*, II, p. 307, paras 13256–13257.
[77] *Discipline Report*, p. 1, para. 4.
[78] *Ibid.*, p. 76, para. 402.

wide divergence in ways of worship within the Church of England. In fact it provides what Cuming has described as 'an authoritative picture of worship at the turn of the century'.[79]

Of the breaches and neglects of the law which their report catalogues the Commissioners are anxious to distinguish between two categories. They said that one comprised breaches of no significance, having been adopted by parishes on the grounds of convenience (e.g. shortening the words of administration or the omitting of the exhortation); or practices which have resulted from negligence or inadvertence (e.g. the omission of the daily services of Morning and Evening Prayer or a service on Ascension Day or on other Holy Days); or other practices which had become common (e.g. the omission of the whole or part of the Ante-Communion when another service follows it, or a congregational response after the reading of the Gospel).[80] The Commission takes a more serious view of a second category which contained what it views as breaches of the law 'having significance', particularly those which are 'significant of teaching contrary or repugnant to the articles or formularies of the Church of England'.[81]

Thus they deal with eucharistic vestments (worn, it is reported, in 1,526 out of the 14,242 churches in England and Wales in 1902, but on the increase according to evidence given by the Secretary of the English Church Union); the *Confiteor* and Last Gospel; the ceremonial mixing of the chalice at the offertory; use of wafer bread; the lavabo; the hiding of the manual acts in the prayer of consecration; the sign of the cross; the ringing of a sanctus bell; burning of incense; carrying of lighted candles; candles on the altar; sprinkling of holy water; the blessing of palms; the singing of *Tenebrae* in Holy Week; the washing of altars on Maundy Thursday; the lighting of the Paschal Candle; the erecting of Stations of the Cross; and the observance of non-Prayer Book Holy Days.[82]

Of even greater concern to the Commission are certain illegal practices directly connected with the Holy Communion. They particularise these as: celebrations without communicants (including Children's Eucharists); the use of the Canon of the Mass from either the Roman or Sarum Use; omission of the invitation to the Confession; omission of the Creed and the Gloria at a Requiem; the Elevation of the Host; genuflexions; the singing or saying of the *Agnus Dei*; Reservation of the

[79] Cuming, *History*, p. 163.
[80] *Discipline Report*, pp. 12–15, paras 50–74.
[81] *Ibid.*, pp. 15–18, paras 75–87.
[82] *Ibid.*, pp. 15–31, paras 75–185.

Blessed Sacrament; the Mass of the Pre-Sanctified on Good Friday; Benediction.[83]

Some of these additions and elaborations the Commission condemned out of hand, others they obviously had some sneaking regard for; other matters they seem to think as almost beneath their dignity to consider: 'silly' is almost the word they use.

The result of listening to this great mountain of evidence both oral and written was that this wide divergence in the ways of worship within the Church and the obvious inadequacy of the Book of Common Prayer to provide a form which was generally acceptable impressed itself upon the Commissioners, and in their summary they came to the conclusion that:

The Law relating to the conduct of Divine Service and the ornaments of churches is, in our belief, nowhere exactly observed; and certain minor breaches of it are very generally prevalent. The Law is also broken by many irregular practices which have attained lesser, and widely different, degrees of prevalence. Some of these are omissions, others err in the direction of excess.[84]

They realized that the situation was brought about not simply by lawless clergy and came to the conclusion that 'the law of public worship in the Church of England is too narrow for the religious life of the present generation':[85]

It needlessly condemns much which a great section of Church people, including many of her most devoted members, value, and modern thought and feeling are characterised by a care for ceremonial, a sense of dignity in worship, and an appreciation of the continuity of the Church, which were not similarly felt at the time when the present law took its present shape.[86]

However the Commission was not willing to allow a liturgical *laissez-faire*. They admitted that 'the machinery for discipline has broken down' and suggested that:

The law should be reformed, that it should admit of reasonable elasticity, and that the means of enforcing it should be improved, but, above all, it is necessary that it should be obeyed.[87]

In order that there should be a standard of liturgical practice

[83] *Ibid.*, pp. 32–44, paras 187–262.
[84] *Ibid.*, p. 52, paras 292–293.
[85] *Ibid.*, p. 75, para. 399.
[86] *Ibid.*, pp. 75–76.
[87] *Ibid.*, p. 76, paras 400–401.

against which this kind of judgment might be made, the report made
this important and historic recommendation:

> Letters of Business should be issued to the Convocations with instructions:
> (a) to consider the preparation of a new rubric regulating the ornaments
>   (that is to say, the vesture of the ministers of the Church, at the times of
>   their ministrations), with a view to its enactment by Parliament; and
> (b) to frame, with a view to their enactment by Parliament, such modifica-
>   tions in the existing law relating to the conduct of Divine Service and to
>   the ornaments and fittings of churches as may tend to secure the greater
>   elasticity which a reasonable recognition of the comprehensiveness of the
>   Church of England and of its present needs seems to demand.
>
> It would be most desirable for the early dealing with these important sub-
> jects that the Convocations would sit together, and we assume that they
> would take counsel with the House of Laymen.[88]

In August 1906 the Archbishop of Canterbury approached the
Prime Minister of the day, Sir Henry Campbell-Bannerman, drawing
his attention to the Royal Commission's recommendation that Letters of Business should be issued to the Convocations. There is a note
of reluctance in the Prime Minister's reply,[89] but he says that if the
Archbishops of Canterbury and York were to submit a request he
would take it to the Crown. The Archbishops made their request,[90]
but in his letter of acknowledgement Campbell-Bannerman made it
quite clear that:

> His Majesty's Government must hold themselves entirely free to judge for
> themselves the course that they ought to adopt both in regard to the Royal
> Commissioners' proposals for legislation and in other respects, whatever view
> may be taken by the Convocations.[91]

Despite this cold water, the Letters of Business were issued from the
Home Office under the Royal Sign Manual on 10 November 1906.[92]
The way was now open for the debates to take place, and Davidson
issued a letter to the Canterbury Convocation and its House of Laymen in which he made it clear that he was of the opinion that only a
responsible attitude to the process of revision would produce suggestions which were realistic and capable of achievement.
The Archbishop wrote:

It has become abundantly clear that to secure the exact observance, in the

---

[88] *Ibid., Recommendations,* p. 77, no. 2.
[89] G. K. A. Bell, *Randall Davidson, Archbishop of Canterbury,* 3rd ed. 1952, pp. 647–648.
[90] *Ibid.,* p. 648.
[91] *Ibid.,* p. 649.
[92] *Ibid.,* pp. 649–650.

twentieth century, of detailed rubrics drawn up in the sixteenth and seventeenth centuries, is neither possible, nor, from any point of view, desirable. Rules clear in principle and yet elastic in detail we do absolutely require, if the Church, in its manifold activities, is to be abreast of modern needs and yet loyal to ancient order.[93]

Davidson was always aware of the possibility of parliamentary difficulties ahead. Speaking to a full Synod of Canterbury three days after the formal issue of the Letters of Business he warned them:

The task before us ultimately will be how to find a mode of securing the Parliamentary sanction which will be necessary if, and only if, the change of any rubric is recommended—how to secure that without involving discussions which would be quite obviously and manifestly unsuited to Parliament if they necessitated discussions there upon the details either of worship or of doctrine.[94]

The process of producing a Reply to the Royal Letters of Business occupied a considerable amount of Convocation time over the next twenty-one years culminating in the 1927 Prayer Book. Along the way considerable confusion was created by the fact that the Upper and Lower Houses of both the Convocations of Canterbury and York each had their own separate debates on liturgical matters. Further complications were added when the Upper House of the Canterbury Convocation passed the following resolution on 6 July 1911:

That the Archbishop be requested in conjunction with, if possible, the Archbishop of York, to arrange for the appointment of a Committee of scholars of acknowledged weight, whose advice can be sought with regard to liturgical and other proposals with which Convocation is now dealing, and that Committees of this house be instructed to ask for such advice in all appropriate cases.[95]

This 'Committee of Experts', as it became known,[96] was only given cautious recognition in the Northern Province. The Archbishop of Canterbury's Chaplain wrote to the Bishop of Exeter, who was the

---

[93] *Ibid.*, p. 650.

[94] *Ibid.*, p. 652.

[95] *Minutes of the Advisory Committee on Liturgical Questions Appointed at the Request of the Upper House of the Convocations of Canterbury*, 1st meeting, Lambeth Palace, Tuesday 22 October 1912, MS 1642 (*cit.* Jenkins Papers) f. 79, Lambeth, Palace Library.

[96] Archbishop of Canterbury's letter to Bishop of Exeter, 30 April 1915, Jenkins Papers, f. 46.

Chairman of the Committee of Experts, to tell him that the Arch-bishop of York had written to Lambeth to say that after consulting with the Bishops of the Convocation of York he had to report to His Grace that the Northern Bishops did not want to take an official posi-tion in regard to the Committee,

as it was not under their auspices in any way. But at the same time they desired the Archbishop of York to say that they would be most willing to avail themselves of this advice if any occasion for consultation should arise.[97]

North–South rivalry dies hard, even in the matter of liturgical revision!

The confusion about areas of responsibility and how any particular recommendation was to be fed into the system was prophesied by Dr Claude Jenkins who was appointed as Secretary to the Committee. Writing, in an undated letter,[98] Jenkins observed to the Archbishop of Canterbury's Chaplain:

As far as Convocation is concerned there is apparently going on indepen-dently in each of the 4 houses of the Convocations a revision of the Prayer Book.

Constitutionally the Lower Houses will have to send their suggestions to the Upper Houses for consideration. Meanwhile the Upper Houses are pro-ducing schemes of their own. The Upper House of Canterbury has sent to Advisory Committee suggestions approved as to
  i) an alternative form of Morning Prayer,
  ii) an alternative form of Evening Prayer,
  iii) the first rubric of the litany.
These will be considered, presumably by the Advisory Committee on 22 October. The Advisory Committee having no official knowledge of the exis-tence of the Committee of the Lower House (apparently) will some day find itself confronted with similar alternative schemes either referred to it by that body when each becomes aware of each other or else the Upper Houses in recognising the Lower Houses' suggestions. The result will be if not confusion at any rate much waste of time . . .

. . . The position of the Advisory Committee ought to be clearly understood and it apparently is not. It is so far as the Southern Convocation is concerned a quasi-independent body appointed by the Archbishop to which the Lower

---

[97] J. V. Macmillan letter to Bishop of Exeter, 20 May 1912, Jenkins Papers, f. 69.

[98] Internal evidence shows that it must have been written between the announce-ment of the composition of the Committee in February 1912 and the first meeting in October 1912.

House could send direct and without consultation with the Upper House or is it a body in close relation to the Upper House to which the Upper House will send the Lower House suggestions as a whole when it received them?

If whole services are going to be sent to the Advisory Committee that body ought to have before it any suggestions whether of Upper or Lower House in regard to a particular service. Having considered these together it would present to Convocation or to the Archbishops the result of its deliberations on them for consideration or rejection by *Convocation*. The ultimate form would be determined by Convocation and would be Convocation's scheme after it has at any rate been subject to criticism even if the criticism be not accepted.[99]

This extraordinarily clumsy procedure, which contrasts vividly with the way in which the Liturgical Commission which was formed in 1954 operated,[100] developed exactly as Jenkins predicted. The Bishops of the Canterbury Convocation originally formed three committees: one to study the ornaments of the Minister, a second to consider the legal procedure to be adopted in giving effect to such proposals as should be made in the reply to the Royal Letters of Business, and a third to discuss the changes needed in the rubrics. The first committee produced its report in 1908[101] and the third in 1909.[102] To add to the complication, in that same year (1909) the Lower House of Convocation began to discuss a report produced by their own committee.[103]

As the first Committee (on the ornaments of the Minister) had made no recommendation as to action it meant that the Bishops could concentrate their attention on the necessary changes in the rubrics. They completed these deliberations in May 1911,[104] while the Lower House needed until November 1912 to produce their revisions in *Report No. 466*.[105] It is important to note that during this time the high points of this controversy had changed. Although vestments were still a delicate issue for many and the question of the use of the Athanasian Creed could produce heated arguments from many High Churchmen, it began to emerge that the Reservation of the Blessed Sacrament was to be the crucial issue, as indeed it proved to be some fifteen years later when these matters eventually arrived before Parliament.

By this time the additions and emendations to the Book of Common

---

[99] Claude Jenkin's letter to J. V. Macmillan. Carbon copy in Jenkins Papers, f. 5.
[100] See pp. 3–4, *supra*.
[101] *Report 416, Chronicle of Convocation*, NS vol. XXV, 1908.
[102] *Report 427, ibid.*, NS vol. XXVI, 1909.
[103] *Report 466, ibid.*
[104] *Report 427 revised, ibid.*, NS vol. XXVIII, 1911.
[105] *Report 466 revised, ibid.*, NS vol. XXIX, 1912.

Prayer which the report contained had increased considerably, but
they were mainly by way of such things as a greater amount of variations in the Lectionary, the provision of a late evening service, and
other fairly marginal issues. The Holy Communion Service was at
this juncture little changed, although both the Lower Houses of Canterbury and of York made proposals for a rearrangement of the
Canon. A suggestion was eventually approved by the Upper House of
Canterbury but in York 'the bishops were adamantly opposed to anything of the sort'.[106] However, by now the Committee of Experts had
arrived on the scene, and they produced their own criticisms of *Report
427* which were incorporated into a new report numbered *481*.[107] At
this stage action was taken to bring together the proposals of both the
Upper and Lower Houses of the Convocations of Canterbury and
similar action was taken in the Convocation of York. The Canterbury
'harmonized' report[108] was discussed in detail by the Committee of
Experts. Dr Claude Jenkins' very full minutes are preserved at
Lambeth Palace Library, but their meetings were over-shadowed by
a stern warning as to the advisory nature of the deliberations from the
Archbishop of Canterbury. Writing to the Chairman the Archbishop
said that he should:

invite members to consider whether any of the recommendations seem to
them to call for protest as being liturgically faulty to such a degree as would
make the reconsideration of the question in Convocation desirable.[109]

but then went on to make himself abundantly clear:

I am anxious, however, to make it clear that I am not inviting the Advisory
Committee to take in hand a revision of all our work. This would constitute
your Committee a new House of Convocation or even a Tribunal Appeal. All
I am anxious for is that if, in the view of those who have given learned consideration to these subjects, something which Convocation has previously said
or done is markedly at variance with what your experts regard as liturgically
right, you should kindly call my attention to the point with a view to the possible reconsideration of the recommendation in question.[110]

The Committee gave its detailed advice on all the matters con-

---

[106] Cuming, *History*, p. 168.
[107] *Report 481 revised*, *Chronicle of Convocation* NS vol. XXI 1914.
[108] *Report 487B*, NS vol. XXXII, 1915.
[109] Archbishop of Canterbury's letter to Bishop of Exeter, *op. cit.*
[110] *Ibid.*

tained in the report. At the same time they took the opportunity to
express a good deal of dissatisfaction because they thought that there
were also a number of what they judged to be other important points
of Prayer Book revision about which they had not been asked for their
advice. W. H. Frere led a protest of eminent liturgists on this issue at
the meeting of the Committee held 19–23 October 1915[111] and persuaded them to include a list of fourteen points on which 'this Committee would be glad to offer their advice'. They were:

1. Principles of Psalter-recitation and of the Lectionary at Morning and
   Evening Prayer.
2. The use of the *Quicunque Vult*.
3. The use of an alternative Order of Holy Communion.
4. The use of a general alternative Order for Burial.
5. The restoration of some form of Holy Unction.
6. The provision of an alternative and briefer formula for use by the Bishop
   at Confirmation.
7. The Lectionary of the Holy Communion.
8. The provision of psalmody for the Holy Communion.
9. The correction of the misplaced words in the Preface.
10. The restoration of 'Holy' in the Nicene Creed.
11. The use of Antiphons in the Occasional Offices.
12. The provision of a substitute for *Te Deum* in Lent.
13. Processionals for the Great Festivals.
14. The Order for the Consecration of Churches.[112]

This offer was not taken up with sole exception of the recommendation on the use of the Athanasian Creed, and to no one's great surprise
the Committee was not summoned again.[113]

As will be noted later, both the Convocations, York in 1902 and
then Canterbury in 1906, discussed patterns of worship which included 'Parish Communion-type' Services,[114] but the Convocations
seemed able to keep these debates in a water-tight compartment quite
separate from its discussions on liturgical revision, as if those con-
siderations were not about real services in real parishes. Again, during
the War the Canterbury Convocation discussed the necessary prep-
arations the Church would need to take in its worship in order to cope
with the needs of returning servicemen.[115] Even this did not impinge

[111] R. C. D. Jasper, ed., *Walter Howard Frere. His Correspondence on Liturgical Revision and Construction*, ACC No. xxxix, 1954, p. 53 (*cit.* Jasper, *Frere*).
[112] *Report of the Advisory Committee on Liturgical Questions upon the Resolutions of the Joint Committee* (4878B) pp. 22–23.
[113] Jasper, *Frere*, p. 55.
[114] See pp. 166–167 and 169–170, *infra*.
[115] *Ibid*.

upon liturgical revision. With hindsight how extraordinary it appears that no-one saw the need to connect these two issues together. Further proposals for revision were made by the Convocations in 1917 and in 1918, despite the fact that the nation as a whole was by now engaged in a catastrophic war. It must be admitted that no less a person than the Archbishop of Canterbury saw the folly in this. Writing to Charles Gore about the Reservation controversy, which was one of the issues involved, he said in June 1915:

This particular juncture in national life is quite extraordinarily unfortunate as a moment for our launching upon the Church what would probably be the gravest controversy of our generation. Must it be pressed forward now?[116]

Nevertheless, while thousands were being killed, with or without the ministrations of the church, the official church bodies were engaged upon the minutiae of rubrical revision of liturgical forms which it will be seen were in many cases tried, tested, and found wanting in the trenches of France and Gallipoli.

4   The First World War Chaplains and Worship

The provision of Chaplains to serve the spiritual needs of servicemen was already well established in Great Britain before 1914.[117] However, the greatly increased size of the Army and Navy in this war[118] meant that there was an almost immediate need to recruit additional clergy to provide adequate chaplaincy cover. So it was that many priests went from the security and predictableness of English parochial life into the dangers and arbitrariness of the Front. There they were called upon to represent God and the Church to thousands of men, most of whom, they discovered, had little or no knowledge of the Christian faith and this despite, by then, over forty years of universal education in which the Church of England had a large stake. Indeed, the Church had been involved in popular education through the National Society since 1811[119] but now its results proved gravely disappointing.

In that same period of time the Church of England had also been

[116] Bell, op. cit., p. 808.

[117] John Smythe, In this Sign Conquer: The Story of the Army Chaplains, 1968, passim.

[118] In 1914 the ration strength of the army was 164,000 men, in 1918 it was 5,363,382. 'Sir John Steven Cowans (1862–1921)' DNB 1912–1921, 1927, p. 138.

[119] Paul A. Welsby, A Short History of the National Society 1811–1961, 1961, passim.

very active in improving its standards of worship and pastoral care.
Indeed it could perhaps be described as the Golden Age of the parochial ministry in England. There was a high level of activity, diligent
parochial visiting, many parish organizations and clubs. Parish
priests were inspired by the example of their famous and 'successful'
brethren and read their books of counsel avidly.[120]

Vigorous parochial life there certainly was, and what is also true is
that by 1914 there were also the contrasts in worship between different
parishes which have already been mentioned, and much ceremonial
and liturgical variation existing side by side in the Church of
England. Horton Davies has suggested that some might have thought
that there were three Churches of England, not one.[121] One of those
'Churches' would have been characterized by 'the bare and even
bleak interiors' of the Evangelical parishes. This would have contrasted starkly with the ceremonial and furnishings of the moderate
Anglo-Catholics of the Percy Dearmer school, which in its turn would
have seemed to have little connection with the Baroque and Rococo
altars of the more extreme Anglo-Papalists of the Society of SS Peter
and Paul.[122]

In order to make his point Horton Davies wrote of these three contrasting styles, but many parishes did not fit easily into these categories. There was still a mainstream Anglican tradition which was not
bleak and bare, but neither was it extravagant. It had absorbed many
things, almost without noticing, from the Oxford Movement,[123] and
it was now increasingly more influenced by Dearmer, the Warham
Guild, and the Alcuin Club than it realized,[124] but it provided the
majority of Anglican parishioners with what they would recognize as
the Church of England and its worship. Still, at this time, Mattins
reigned supreme as the typical Church of England service, with the
fair certainty, at least in town parishes, of an 8.00 a.m. celebration of
the Holy Communion on each Sunday. The occasional sung celebration could be found in some parishes, but in general this was a

---

[120] E.g., Peter Green, *The Town Parson: His Life and Work*, Pastoral Theology Lectures,
Cambridge, 1914, 1919; Clement Rogers, *Principles of Parish Work*, 1915; C. F. Garbett,
ed., *The Work of a Great Parish*, 1915.

[121] Horton Davies, *Worship and Theology in England. The Ecumenical Century 1900–1965*,
v, p. 284.

[122] All this is fully described and illustrated in Peter F. Anson, *Fashions in Church
Furnishings 1840–1940*, 1960. Marcus Donovan argues for a very early date (1860
onwards) for the parting of the two streams of Anglo-Catholicism (*After the Tractarians*,
1933, pp. 129–131).

[123] Owen Chadwick, *The Mind of the Oxford Movement*, 1960, p. 58.

[124] Roger Lloyd, *The Church of England in the Twentieth Century*, 1946, pp. 162–163.

post-1918 development. Evensong was still popular, and a reasonable proportion of worshippers would attend church twice on a Sunday.

In these parishes the service would be according to the Book of Common Prayer, with such shortenings of the service as were allowed in *The Act of Uniformity Amendment Act* of 1872 (generally known as 'the Shortened Services Act').[125] Music would be a general feature with versicles and responses, psalms, and hymns sung. The dress of the priest would be modest, a stole at the Holy Communion would be the only one of the controversial eucharistic vestments that would be worn in such a church. It will be seen that what might be described as a 'parish communion' type of service had scarcely appeared at all. All this added up to 'The Church of England' for the average Englishman who took any interest in these matters as he went off to the War, and this is what he saw his Chaplain as representing. But there were also large areas of complete ignorance.

Priests coming from the new industrial area had already had some warning of the alienation of the working class from the Church, but to many it came as a great shock and surprise to discover the extent of the ignorance of the majority about basic Christian doctrines and ways of worship and devotion.

In a carefully researched inter-denominational project sponsored by no fewer than eleven Churches and organized under the auspices of the YMCA, thousands of questionnaires were distributed to everyone from front-line soldiers to the Chaplain-General to find out the degree of understanding (or misunderstanding) that existed in the armed forces.[126] A thick book containing the results, *The Army and Religion*, included many which were startling. From the evidence that was accumulated it was estimated that the Churches had failed to attract four-fifths of the young men of the country.[127]

In the middle of the war the Church of England suddenly decided to put all its energies into the National Mission of Repentance and Hope. Archbishop Davidson asked Canon Armitage Robinson to bring together a group which might find ways of bringing good out of the obvious evil of the War.[128] Roger Lloyd described it as 'a vast and adventurous undertaking—the most considerable act of the Church

[125] Cuming, *History*, p. 156.

[126] Albert Marrin, *The Last Crusade, The Church of England in the First World War*, 1974, pp. 203–204.

[127] *The Army and Religion. An enquiry and its bearing upon the Religious Life of the Nation*, 1919, p. 122.

[128] David M. Thompson, 'War, the Nation, and the Kingdom of God: The Origins of the National Mission of Repentance and Hope, 1916–19', in W J. Shields, ed., *The Church and War*, Studies in Church History, vol. 20, 1983, pp. 339–340.

of England during the War'.[129] It was carefully prepared for in many
dioceses with special training courses for the clergy. How successful it
was is a matter of debate. Thirty years afterwards Maurice Reckitt in
his Scott Holland Memorial Lectures for 1946 said:

The National Mission was widely accounted afterwards to have been on the
whole a failure. It is a little difficult to know by what standards it could have
proved itself a success; judged by the aims which they necessarily set before
themselves all missions must be in some measure a failure, and the wider the
scale of the effort, the more disparate will ideal and achievement appear.
Moreover, to found a national mission, to a people convinced of the
righteousness of its cause and suffering for its conviction, upon a call to repentance is to court misunderstanding, essential as such a call may be.[130]

By contrast, Roger Lloyd's judgement was more cautious:

Whether the National Mission as a whole failed or succeeded, there is no
doubt that the preparation of the clergy for it gave to them a spiritual power
which at the least saw them through the bitter, dark years of the war that
were still to come. In point of fact it is impossible cavalierly to write off the
National Mission as a total failure, though it has become customary to do
so.[131]

One positive result of the National Mission was a decision to set up
five Committees of Enquiry to examine the character and manner of
the Church's teaching; the worship of the Church; the evangelistic
work of the Church; the discovery of removable hindrances to the
Church's efficiency; and the bearing of the Gospel on the individual
problems of the day.

For our purposes we need to examine the Report of the Archbishop's Second Committee of Enquiry entitled *The Worship of the
Church*.

The terms of reference of the Committee are given in a letter from
the Archbishops:

To consider and report upon ways in which the public worship of the Church
can be more directly related to the felt needs of actual life at the present time.
It is desired that this Committee should pay special attention:
(a) to a recent Report of Convocation and its Committees on the Revision of
the Prayer Book.

---

[129] Lloyd, *op. cit.*, p. 226.
[130] Maurice B. Reckitt, *Maurice to Temple, A Century of the Social Movement in the Church
of England*, Scott Holland Memorial Lectures, 1946 (*cit.* Reckitt, *Maurice to Temple*),
1947, p. 159.
[131] Lloyd, *op. cit.*, p. 228.

(b) to opinions and desires expressed by Chaplains in the Navy and in the Army.[132]

From this ('the felt needs of the present time') it can be seen that a more realistic wind was now blowing through the discussions rather than the *recherché* liturgical deliberations of the Convocations. Yet the Committee was not absolved from studying the crop of Reports which those tortuous debates had produced.

The Dean of Christ Church (the Very Rev'd Thomas B. Strong) was the Chairman, and there were seven lay as well as fourteen clerical members, yet only one Bishop. Just two ex-members of the Committee of Experts were chosen: Dr W. H. Frere and Dr Guy Warman.[133]

From the outset of its work the Committee was 'confronted . . . with the grave fact that the instinct for worship has seriously diminished in the people as a whole'.[134] They were willing to admit that some of the blame for this could be quite reasonably laid at the door of the Church, being directly connected with the public worship, of the Church and its existing performance of that worship but there were other factors at work, they believed. The day had long gone when there was any statutory or legal obligation to attend church laid upon an Englishman, and now an entirely new approach was necessary:

The habit of attendance lasted longer in the villages than elsewhere, while the rapid growth of town populations in the eighteenth and nineteenth centuries in areas inadequately provided with opportunities of worship ended in the formation of large districts in which no such tradition existed. Even where the habit existed it steadily lost its force and by the beginning of the present century very little of such a habit survived. It may be no great loss that churchgoing as a mere conventional custom has disappeared; but in such circumstances it is urgent that a better sense of obligation should be re-established which may rest not upon law or convention but on devotion and a sense of spiritual need.[135]

Like so many committees, before and after it, they were convinced that part of the solution to the problem lay in better religious educa-

[132] *The Worship of the Church being the Report of the Archbishops' Second Committee of Enquiry*. Published for the National Mission by SPCK with foreword by the Archbishop of Canterbury, 1918 (*cit. The Worship of the Church*), p. 5.

[133] *Cf.* Jasper, *Frere*, p. 26 and *The Worship of the Church*, p. 2.

[134] *The Worship of the Church*, p. 6.

[135] *Ibid.*

tion for the young. Although there needs to be a prior recognition of the paramount claim of God upon our lives which will produce an instinct for worship, yet while this instinct, which lies at the root of all devotion, is 'untrained it remains a crude instinct'.[136] So, more important than the revisions of existing services or the provision of new ones was the need to improve the idea and practice of religious instruction. The Committee is of the opinion that:

Present educational conditions are not only definitely unfavourable to the development of a really religious impulse but even tend to sterilize it in the young.[137]

Having improved the standards of religious education, which would not be limited to 'religious knowledge' but would bring children 'into direct and conscious relation with the Christian Society and with God', the Committee believed that they could then be led to organized Christian worship 'that can offer that full and varied response to man's religious need which the Christian faith has brought within his power'. At the same time they see the need to provide 'at any rate under present conditions' services for the uninstructed which they can understand.[138] These services would be half-way houses meant to lead people on from the simplest stages to full worship of the Church. The Report recognizes that the conditions of modern industrial society had had an adverse effect on the traditions of public worship, particularly by alienating 'the poorer classes', who have felt that they have no place in the Church.

The idea of the Church as an institution governed by and administered for comparatively small circles of the well-to-do classes steadily took root in the mind of the people, and completed the process of alienation which the industrial system began.[139]

The answer to this situation which the Committee produced is not educational or liturgical but practical and sociological:

The Committee, therefore, is convinced that, while even under such conditions many individuals among these classes, by noble effort of will, may continue steadfast in the duties of religious worship, yet only by removal of

[136] *Ibid.*, p. 7.
[137] *Ibid.*, p. 8.
[138] *Ibid.*, p. 9.
[139] *Ibid.*, p. 14.

the worst features of our social and industrial system, or even by a radical change in the system itself, will the way be made clear for the return of the people to the public worship of the Church.[140]

In this important passage it would seem that the Committee has absorbed some of the basic teaching of the Christian Socialists and to be anxious to apply it to patterns of public worship. It could have marked a milestone if it had been acted upon.

Before detailing their suggestions in regard to the Book of Common Prayer the Committee emphasized that it would not be by merely making changes in the Prayer Book that people will be recalled to the practice of worship but by the kind of programme they have already outlined and which they summarized thus:

It desires to emphasise the conviction already expressed that not in such things as defects in the Prayer Book or in the rendering of Church services lie the deeper causes of the alienation of the people from public worship, but rather in the lack of religious education, in the failure to use the gifts of the laity, and in those perverted conceptions of life among all classes which it is the duty of the Church to correct, and those social and industrial wrongs which it is the duty of the nation to redress.[141]

With this important rider the report turns next to the subject of revision of the Prayer Book, with one eye, consistent with its terms of reference, on the Convocations' discussions on the answer to the Royal Letters of Business. The Committee reports that it has received a large number of suggestions, a large proportion of which are already contained in the Convocations' documents. They also report that a large section of opinion deals with the Communion Service. This must be given particular attention.

It is almost universally felt that the Communion Service has fallen out of its proper place in the scheme of worship. Church-going has largely come to mean attendance at services such as Matins and Evensong, and the Holy Communion has been driven into the position of an exceptional service requiring certain definite convictions and special efforts such as are not expected of the average member of the Church. It is clear that this is a serious misfortune.[142]

That its primary place in church order ought to be restored is argued under three heads. First that the Sacrament of the Lord's Supper is definitely ordained by Christ and has therefore a greater

[140] *Ibid.*
[141] *Ibid.*
[142] *Ibid.*, p. 15.

claim on Christians than any other source than can be devised. Secondly, that the Communion Service 'makes less demand for intellectual effort and satisfies more directly the spiritual impulses than such services as Morning and Evening Prayer'. The third point is that the whole tradition of the Church is in favour of making the Eucharist 'in some way central'.[143]

Although the Committee did not make any definite recommendations, which should apply to all churches without exception, they did offer some suggestions. They said that they had evidence of valuable results being obtained in parishes where the Holy Communion 'somewhat elaborate in its features' was celebrated every Sunday and at which comparatively few persons communicated. In others, they observed, a special Communion Service was held at regular intervals which the Committee very interestingly described as being 'a corporate parish celebration at which a large number of parishioners would communicate'; while in some parishes a choral celebration was held every Sunday at 8 a.m. or 9.30 a.m. meeting, they believed, 'the best desires of those who wish to communicate and of those who do not'.[144]

They also noted that although there were those who argued that a Children's Eucharist provided a valuable training ground for worship, they realized that others believed it preferable for the family to worship together. It can be seen here that many of the features of what became known as the Parish Communion are receiving their first recognition in an official document of the Church of England. The Report does not come down solely in favour of a presentation of the Holy Communion which would be completely recognizable as a Parish Communion, yet it is firmly convinced about the centrality of the Eucharist in the Church's worshipping life:

The Committee is unanimous in holding that the act of Communion is the true centre of all Christian worship and the bond of union between communicants, and as such is the duty of all Christian people. These facts have been obscured in recent times, and one of the most pressing necessities of the day is that they should be brought vividly into the consciousness of the Church. The need will have to be met in various ways according to the requirements of the parish; and the changes involved will cause considerable alterations of English practice in hours and methods.[145]

---

[143] *Ibid.*

[144] *Ibid.*, p. 16. See also Thompson, *op. cit.*, p. 343 where he quotes from the papers of Canon A. W. Robinson and reports that the original planning group had advocated Eucharists 'at an hour at which the largest number of communicants can be expected'.

[145] *Ibid.*

The terms of reference which were given to the Committee by the Archbishops at the outset of their work also counselled them to 'pay special attention to the opinions and desires expressed by Chaplains in the Navy and in the Army'. It is an important fact to note that the whole of the published 'opinions and desires' of Chaplains, whether it be in reference to this particular report or whether it be other documents, consists entirely of responses made by Army Chaplains. Why should this be? It seems reasonable to suggest that it is because the Chaplains serving in the Army at the front with the soldiers could say with awful sincerity:

We have felt the purgatorial fires. And we Chaplains, not least, have moved where the flames are hottest and have seen the pure metal dropping apart from the dross.[146]

This is a quotation (indeed a justification for the title) from a book produced by seventeen temporary Church of England Chaplains who were at the time serving on the Western Front. It was entitled *The Church in the Furnace*, and it was published about the same time as the report *The Worship of the Church*. Three of the seventeen contributors, Archdeacon H. K. Southwell, Canon F. B. Macnutt and the Rev'd Neville S. Talbot were the Chaplains who supplied a statement to the Archbishop's Committee which is published as an appendix to that Report.[147] The Committee says that it has taken the Chaplains' opinions into consideration in producing their main report. However, this statement 'out of the furnace' ought to be given individual attention as representing the opinions of those who had been attempting to use the church's official formularies amidst the turmoil of active service.

Southwell, Macnutt, and Talbot state that in preparing their special contribution they have sought the views of a considerable number of Chaplains 'who have, we believe, a right to speak owing to their experience and work with the men'.[148] The Chaplains say that they find it very hard to come to clearly defined conclusions which they can pass on with complete confidence. They realize the dangers in making generalizations about what they call 'the lay mind', which they believe is at many stages of development.

Very few generalisations about it can cover the gulf which divides the more or

---

[146] F. B. Macnutt, ed., *The Church in the Furnace. Essays by seventeen Temporary Church of England Chaplains on Active service in France and Flanders*, 1918 (*cit. The Church in the Furnace*) p. ix.
[147] *The Worship of the Church*, Appendix, p. 33.
[148] *Ibid.*

less unthinking and sentimental mass from the lively-minded and impatient few, or the scarcely-attached and ignorant majority from the instructed and faithful minority.[149]

That they write as men who 'long for great though sensible changes' is a basic admission, changes necessary if the alienation of 'the minority of men of all classes who are some real degree mentally and spiritually alive' is not to continue. One of the constantly repeated themes of Chaplains and others who write from the Front is that, although among the majority of soldiers it is possible to discover only a few who have any real time for or real knowledge of organized Christian religion, it is equally possible to discern what was called 'the religion of the inarticulate'. An influential advocate of this concept was Donald Hankey. Hankey writing under the pseudonym of 'A Student in Arms' contributed a series of articles to *The Spectator* in which, as the Editor put it:

He proved an inspired interpreter of the private soldier. He was worthy to be named liaison officer between the nation and its Army.[150]

Percy Dearmer thought that at that particular time, Hankey had 'more theological influence than nearly all the bishops and doctors put together'.[151]

In an article entitled 'The Religion of the Inarticulate' Hankey wrote from his own experience of how he discovered that soldiers were

Men who believed absolutely in the Christian virtues of unselfishness, generosity, charity, and humility, without ever connecting them in their minds with Christ; and at the same time what they did associate with Christianity was just on a par with the formalism and smug self-righteousness which Christ spent His whole life in trying to destroy.[152]

The tragedy, Hankey believed, was that this fact was unrecognized even at first by the Chaplains.

The Chaplains as a rule failed to realize this. They saw the inarticulateness, and assumed a lack of any religion. They remonstrated with their hearers for not saying their prayers, and not coming to Communion, and not being afraid to die without making their peace with God. They did not grasp that the men really had deep-seated beliefs in goodness, and that the only reasons why they did not pray and go to communion was that they never connected

[149] *Ibid.*
[150] Donald Hankey, *A Student in Arms*, Preface by the Editor of *The Spectator*, 1916, p.5. Hankey was a member of CSU at Oxford *c.f.*, K. G. Budd, *The Story of Donald Hankey*, 1931, p. 42.
[151] Percy Dearmer, *The Art of Public Worship*, 1919, p. 76.
[152] Hankey, *op. cit.*, pp. 112–113.

the goodness in which they believed with the God in Whom the Chaplains said they ought to believe. If they had connected Christianity with unselfishness and the rest, they would have been prepared to look at Christ as their Master and their Saviour. As a matter of fact, I believe that in a vague way lots of men do regard Christ as on their side. They have a dim sort of idea that He is misrepresented by Christianity, and that when it comes to the test He will not judge them so hardly as the chaplains do. They have heard that He was the Friend of sinners, and severe on those who set up to be religious. But however that may be, I am certain that if the chaplain wants to be understood and to win their sympathy he must begin by showing them that Christianity is the explanation and the justification and the triumph of all they do now really believe in. He must make them see that his creeds and prayers and worship are the symbols of all that they admire most, and most want to be.[153]

Hankey is equally hard on the so-called educated Christians and he blames himself, and others like him, for their inability to convey the essentials of their faith to the seeker. 'If the working man's religion is often wholly inarticulate', he writes, 'the real religion of the educated man is often wrongly articulated'.[154]

This point of view began to influence many of the Chaplains. Unfortunately, Hankey did not survive to serve the Church in its post-war planning. He was killed on the Somme on 12 October 1916.[155] Alan Wilkinson records that when the report *The Army and Religion* was being drawn up, particular sorrow was expressed that Hankey would be unable to take part in its preparation.[156]

The three Chaplains writing their statement for the Archbishop's Committee were fearful lest the Church would go back into its old pre-war grooves which would have no room for inarticulate searching. They believed that 'a large fringe of intelligent but vaguely-perplexed and dissatisfied men' could greet with delighted surprise the fact that 'the old church was willing and able to revise and adapt her old equipment', yet they are not for wholesale change, believing it best to 'build upon what we already have of Prayer Book cultus and Anglican liturgical tradition'.[157] In the event, as will be seen, little or no account was taken of this in the subsequently proposed revision of the Prayer Book.

Like the main report, the Chaplains' statement is convinced of the

---

[153] *Ibid.*, pp. 113–114. A recent assessment of the work of Chaplains has been made in Michael Moynihan, *God on our Side: The British Padre in World War I*, 1983.

[154] Hankey, *op. cit.*, p. 115.

[155] *Ibid.*, p. 5.

[156] Alan Wilkinson, *The Church of England and the First World War*, 1978, p. 160.

[157] *The Worship of the Church*, pp. 33–34.

need to restore the centrality of the Holy Communion in the life of the Church, but they are even more definite about how that would manifest itself. Although they record the disappointment felt by many Chaplains about the neglect of the Holy Communion by the majority of men at the Front, they feel confident to say that:

We think that almost all Chaplains will return home anxious to make this service the main, corporate, family congregational act of fellowship.[158]

This is plain speaking and is obviously born of deep conviction. There was a breed of Army Chaplains who were not afraid of speaking their mind, and among them were the authors in the book of essays which has already been briefly mentioned, *The Church in the Furnace*. The two essays on 'Worship and Services' are obviously of importance to this study. The first of them is by the Rev'd Eric Milner-White who had proved himself a courageous Chaplain, having been recommended for the highest award for bravery, the Victoria Cross, but in the event being awarded the next highest, the Distinguished Service Order.[159] Milner-White believed that worship could never be the same after the experience of the war:

Three years we have spent in sheds and barns and fields and orchards and schoolrooms and dug-outs and mine-craters, hastily adorned, or merely tidied, or *in puris naturalibus*; a new church every Sunday and most weekdays; new services in them; and new ideals as to the scope and wealth of public devotion.[160]

These facts would have to be taken into account by bishops, liturgiologists, clergy and people, 'for it spells change when those who for three years have almost forgotten the ordered progress of the Prayer Book return to their altars'. In a moving passage Milner-White declares:

We are a new race, we priests of France, humbled by much strain and much failure, revolutionaries not at all in spirit, but actually in fact; and while often enough we sigh for the former days, the procession of splendid offices and the swell of the organ, these will never again content us unless or until the great multitude also find their approach to God through them.[161]

---

[158] *Ibid.*, p. 35.
[159] Philip Pare and Donald Harris, *Eric Milner-White*, 1965, p. 18.
[160] *The Church in the Furnace*, p. 175.
[161] *Ibid.*, p. 176.

Although he came from a background of carefully ordered Prayer Book services,[162] Milner-White's wartime experiences had revealed to him that it was not always the best vehicle for worship and devotion:

Fitness for place and use has become in these days the standard by which men and things are judged; and even the Prayer-book, august and beloved ever, stands for judgment. For while our tribes have wondered, dwelling in tents and holes of earth, it has been at best semi-used and semi-usable; and we have come to look upon it from the unfamiliar distance.[163]

After dealing with the inadequacies of Morning and Evening Prayer to provide 'popular' services and the failure of the Prayer Book Burial Office, Milner-White turns his attention to the Holy Communion. 'The problems surrounding the Eucharist are educational', he states, and asks, 'How shall the vast unsacramental multitude learn the service, learn to understand it, learn to love it?'[164] It is the same question that G. A. Studdert Kennedy soliloquized on:

I wonder why we did not succeed, we who teach, in making the Sacrament mean to you all that we believe it was intended to mean. I think it is quite evident that in a large number of cases we have not succeeded. I wonder why.[165]

Milner-White has a two-fold programme of action, first to make the liturgy fully intelligible, and secondly to guarantee that it is wholly accessible.

By making the liturgy intelligible he does not mean a simplifying away of all its mystery nor a modernizing of its ancient dignity, rather he is hoping for more thorough teaching of 'its meaning, its course and its evangelical action'.[166] Milner-White is not concerned at this time to argue liturgical points, although he himself was a highly competent liturgist and skilled author of collects and prayers, a fact recognized among other ways by his inclusion in the original membership of the Liturgical Commission in 1954. Rather is he anxious that the church should learn from the facts and lessons of France. After listing four minor simplifications which might be introduced he then turned to the matter of the rewording of archaisms distinguishing between those which are dignified and those which add an unsympathetic

[162] Pare and Harris, *op. cit.*, p. 16.
[163] *The Church in the Furnace*, p. 177.
[164] *Ibid.*, p. 182.
[165] G. A. Studdert Kennedy, *The Hardest Part*, 1918, p. 121.
[166] *The Church in the Furnace*, p. 201.

tinge. He believed that at certain points the Prayer Book is too purely ecclesiastical, at others too aristocratic.[167]

In order to introduce an element of what he describes as 'home-liness' Milner-White suggests that this can most easily be done by way of enrichment and lists various national as well as family occasions which could be provided with their own collect, epistle and gospel. But even this, he acknowledges, goes nowhere near tackling the main problem.

So far we have scarcely touched the fringe of our new task. The incredible ignorance of officers and men alike with regard to the Lord's own service, its foreignness hitherto in their religious experience—this it is the Church must rouse herself with furious energy to dispel. For three years we priests of France have watched it aghast. And it is so tragic because men do approach the Holy Communion wistfully as a thing divine and wonderful; with honest hope that the love and strength of God will somehow there be mediated to them. And first they are baffled by their ignorance of the service itself. The shyness that this causes during its progress is painful to priest and congregation alike, and often robs both of any feeling but awkward discomfort.[168]

The second part of Milner-White's programme was to tackle the problem of accessibility to the Sacrament. He admits that hitherto the Church has only provided for those who keep normal hours or can freely leave home, not for those who work all night or start work at dawn or who are tied to the house until evening. To tackle this Milner-White, although a convinced Anglo-Catholic, admits that in France he and others,

frankly and gladly, 'for their sake' accepting the situation have come now to afternoon, evening, and night Communion'.[169]

But he is obviously not fully happy about this development and fears that it will 'minister disastrously to the Englishman's laziness in things religious'.[170] To some extent he salves his conscience by advo-cating that some of these non-morning communions could be made from the Reserved Sacrament. Yet he returns to the problem at the end of his essay pleading that:

Search be made with new-opened eyes to find whether or not there are not

---

[167] *Ibid.*, p. 202 Milner White quotes a nonconformist who said, 'Your Prayer-Book smacks of the court, not of home' as an illustration of its aristocratic nature, and the remoteness of the Adult Baptism service as an example of an incomprehensible eccle-siastical office.

[168] *Ibid.*, pp. 203–204.

[169] *Ibid.*, p. 208.

[170] *Ibid.*, p. 209.

sections, even classes, of people for whom the morning provision is useless or unreasonably hard; and that, if so, other provision be publicly made; and we priests be less bewildered by conflict between church order and the people's need, and hurried into practices, often overrash, always too individual. We return to the same plea, that even here in the Holy of Holies the home Church fear not to experiment, so only the flock, the whole flock, be fed.[171]

The war-time Chaplains were convinced of the need to build up many into the fellowship of the Church. The statement drawn up by the three Chaplains for inclusion at the end of the report *The Worship of the Church* also had attached to it an 'additional statement' whose author was Neville Talbot.[172] In his addition he pleaded for the Holy Communion to be celebrated at an hour which would ensure that the service was available to all, not just to what might be called the 'officer class'. Talbot later published a fuller version of his ideas for the post-war Church to which he gave the title *Religion Behind the Front and After the War*. Although what he writes about worship is in no way completely adequate as a description of the full aim and purpose of a Parish Communion, it is a plea that the Church might re-find one of its constituent elements which many say they find lacking—fellowship. Talbot thought that if this element in worship could be strengthened it would help to provide the fertile ground in which aspects of a full church life could eventually grow. Looking to the future, Neville Talbot wrote:

As the church must call men to worship so that they may ever and again renew their relationship with God, so she must call them into fellowship that they may be reinforced by and in the love of the brethren. Worship and fellowship are mentally necessary for the health of either. No fellowship had nor has to be made. It is in existence as part of God's gift to the world in Christ. The Body of Christ is in the world and very many are already in it. It is there to be turned to better use than heretofore.[173]

It was towards such a church fellowship that Talbot and his colleagues of the trenches looked forward with high hope and expectation because they had come to realize that there was 'a great wealth of unappropriated, unattracted vitality'[174] in those who had not hitherto thought that there was likely to be a welcome for them in the

---

[171] *Ibid.*, p. 210.
[172] F. H. Brabant, *Neville Stuart Talbot 1879–1943, A Memoir*, 1949, p. 67.
[173] Neville S. Talbot, *Religion Behind the Front and After the War*, 1918, pp. 107–109.
[174] *The Worship of the Church*, p. 40.

Church of England. The clergy who had gone as Chaplains[175] must have contained among them a large proportion of those who have been involved in 'The Golden Age of parochial work in the towns of England', as Archbishop Lang called the period from 1890–1914.[176] They had been roused by men like Maurice, Kingsley, Headlam, Gore, and Scott Holland to an attitude of social consciousness. If that heightened sensitivity received some hard knocks in the War, if the wartime experiences had made it painfully clear to them that the impact of the Church's mission had been far less effective than they had optimistically understood it to be, there still remained enough of the idealism to want to make the Church as well as the nation 'fit for heroes to live in'.[177] This was increasingly understood by their generation as full welcome into the heart of the Church, and at that heart was the Eucharist. The various ramifications of the developments of a social consciousness in the Church of England and the 'eucharisticizing' of that growing insight have yet to be explored in this work, but suffice it to say at this point, that as the vision of the Divine Society loomed larger in the overall consciousness of the Church the fact that the characteristic rite of that Divine Society was the Eucharist became inescapable.[178] How far these idealisms were able to influence the official mind of the Church must now be investigated.

5   The official Church plans for worship after the 1914–18 World War

It has already been noted that the work on preparing the answer to the Royal Letters of Business went on unabated throughout the war.[179] However, by the end of hostilities the emphasis of these discussions had begun to change. Whereas previously the debates had been preoccupied with rather insubstantial and uninteresting additions to and subtractions from certain parts of the Book of Common Prayer, while carefully leaving the Holy Communion Service severely alone, there

[175] The total number of clergy of the Church of England commissioned as Chaplains during the War was 3030 (Bell, *op. cit.*, Note p. 850).

[176] J. G. Lockhart, *Cosmo Gordon Lang*, 1949, p. 155.

[177] David Lloyd George in a speech in Wolverhampton 24 November 1918, 'What is our task? To make Britain a fit country for heroes to live in', *ODQ*, 1st ed., p. 246a.

[178] Lloyd, *op. cit.*, p. 271.

[179] See p. 35, *supra*.

now came a new emphasis. As Archbishop Davidson's biographer comments,

With the War, however, there came a considerable change. The Eucharist became more and more prominent in the worship of Churchmen, and so more and more prominent in public discussion on the Prayer Book.[180]

Even though the movement for a modification of the Prayer Book Office for the Holy Communion began to gain pace, it received no encouragement from the Archbishop of Canterbury who said he could not bring himself to stress the points of liturgical reform and a change in the Canon.[181] Yet with or without archiepiscopal approval the work went on after the war.

In October 1918 a conference was arranged consisting of all four houses of the Convocations, which managed to reach agreement on all the points put to it with the exception of the proposals for the re-arrangement of the Eucharistic Canon. This matter had assumed an increasing place of prominence on the agenda of the Church of England ever since a meeting of the Lower House of the Canterbury Convocation which had been held in February 1914. From then on, Eucharistic revision 'came to the very front in the Revision Movement'.[182]

Since the issue of the Letters of Business to the Convocation in 1906, there had been an important development in the system of Church government in England. With the passing of the *Church Assembly (Powers) Act 1919* it became obviously tactful that any liturgical proposals should be discussed by this new 'church parliament'. Indeed, while the legislation which created the Church Assembly was passing through the House of Lords, Archbishop Davidson had given their Lordships an assurance on this particular matter.[183] What no one expected was that this decision would prolong the process to the extent that it did. After already fourteen years of debate it was assumed that all the issues had been dealt with exhaustively, but with 'the ardour and unwisdom of youth'[184] the Assembly insisted in doing the work all over again.

By now there had appeared a series of counter-proposals, three sets of which needed to be given serious consideration by the Assembly. The first of these came from the Anglo-Catholics. Known as 'the

---

[180] Bell, *op. cit.*, p. 1326.
[181] Bell, *op. cit.*, p. 815.
[182] Jasper, *Frere*, p. 58.
[183] Bell, *op. cit.*, p. 1328.
[184] Dom Gregory Dix, *The Shape of the Liturgy*, 1945, p. 698.

Green Book' it was the product of the Prayer Book Revision Committee of the English Church Union.[185] The Church Union decided that they would print a model Prayer Book *in extenso*.[186] In the early stages the Anglo-Catholics had shown little or no enthusiasm for the Prayer Book revision project. As they perceived that the demand for revision derived originally from an attempt to suppress many of their greatly loved practices, this was hardly surprising. It has already been shown that in the early days of the Oxford Movement there was what could be called a type of 'Prayer Book Fundamentalism' with High Churchmen believing that the Prayer Book was on their side;[187] and even if at the turn of the century there was a growing number of Anglo-Catholics who would have preferred some modifications, it was generally recognized that the net result of any revision would probably be to their disadvantage. In 1899 Darwell Stone, a doctrinaire Anglo-Catholic liturgical scholar, had written,

There are many good reasons which make Churchmen unwilling at the present time that steps should be taken in the direction of the revision or alteration of any part of the Book of Common Prayer. In the present circumstances of the Church in England, it is a wise course to use every effort to maintain the Prayer Book unaltered. If the years that are coming see a solid growth in the acceptance of sound church principles, there is no good reason that a task which it would be unwise at present to undertake should not be entertained and successfully carried out.[188]

Speaking to a meeting of the English Church Union in 1906, Stone said that to revise the Book of Common Prayer along the lines of the principles involved in the first Recommendation of the Royal Commission would be 'to court the gravest disaster that could befall the English Church'.[189] In this attitude the Anglo-Catholics for a number of years shared a common ground with most of the Evangelicals over against the opinion of the Central Churchmen.[190] However, towards the end of the war it became increasingly obvious that a Reply to the Royal Letters of Business could not be delayed much longer and consequently in 1917 the English Church Union made a decision,

[185] *English Church Union, Report of the Committee on Prayer Book Revision*, 1922.
[186] *A suggested Prayer Book being the text of the English Rite altered and enlarged in accordance with the Prayer Book Revision proposals made by the English Church Union*, 1923, p. iii.
[187] See p. 10, *supra*.
[188] Darwell Stone, *Holy Baptism*, 1899, p. 187.
[189] Cross, *op. cit.*, p. 166.
[190] *Ibid.*, p. 167.

which was effectively an abandonment of its anti-revisionist policy. At the same time they asked a group of liturgiologists 'to prepare and publish a detailed statement of the alterations in the Prayer Book which we ourselves would approve'.[191] The Anglo-Catholics were encouraged to come to this position by a decision of the Convocations that the text of the 1662 Prayer Book should remain unchanged and that all alterations should only take the form of 'permissive alternatives'. The English Church Union now took an increasing part in the ensuing debates, and when the proposals contained in the Church Assembly's Report[192] were made public in 1922 the English Church Union thought the mood of the Church was moving towards a decision which would mean that opportunity would be given to the various groupings in the Church of England to pursue a path of liturgical experimentation which might reasonably satisfy their ambitions. In anticipation of this, the work which resulted in the 'Green Book' was put in hand under the principal guidance of Darwell Stone and N. P. Williams.[193]

The second important set of revision proposals emerged from the Alcuin Club. When the Club had been founded in 1897, at a meeting of four Anglican laymen, they had decided that:

The object of the said Club be to promote the study of the history of the Book of Common Prayer.[194]

In 1912, after a couple of false starts,[195] the Alcuin Club embarked upon a programme of publications which were intended to spread:

Sound knowledge upon liturgical subjects and the consequent growth in the mind of the English Church of a high and consistent ideal of worship.[196]

The consequent booklets were to be entitled *Prayer Book Revision Pamphlets*. Eventually there were fourteen pamphlets in the series, of which the last three (XII–XIV) consisted of a survey of the various

[191] *Ibid.*, p. 168.
[192] *The Second Report of the Prayer Book Revision Committee of the National Assembly of the Church of England, NA 60*, 1922.
[193] Cross, *op. cit.*, p. 172; Eric Waldram Kemp, *N. P. Williams*, 1954, p. 58.
[194] Peter J. Jagger, *The Alcuin Club and its Publications. An Annotated Bibliography 1897–1974*, 1975, p. 4 (*cit.* Jagger, *Alcuin*).
[195] *Ibid.*, p. 5.
[196] 'Note by the Committee' in T. A. Lacey, *Liturgical Interpolations and the Revision of the Prayer Book*, Alcuin Club Prayer Book Revision Pamphlets, 1912, p. iv.

proposals that had been made for the Alternative Prayer Book. Because of the colour of the soft-backed editions of these pamphlets, they were collectively known as 'The Orange Book'.[197] The Alcuin Club Committee was anxious that their motives in producing these pamphlets should not be misunderstood and stated carefully that the Club 'takes no side in the discussion as to the advisability at this time of Prayer Book Revision'.[198]

After this cautious start there eventually followed a whole flurry of activity. By October 1923 the Alcuin Club Committee had recognized that the situation was now so critical that they decided that the Committee should meet on a fixed day every month for the next six months.[199] At that time Bishop Gore was President of the Club, with A. S. Duncan-Jones, F. E. Brightman, T. A. Lacey and Christopher Wadsworth as Vice Presidents. Brightman and Duncan-Jones were members of the Publication Committee, along with W. H. Frere, Stephen Gaselee, J. H. Srawley, R. M. Woolley and E. G. P. Wyatt.[200]

The main burden of the work was shouldered by Frere although other members of the Committee assisted,[201] notably Duncan-Jones who was at that time Vicar of St Paul's, Knightsbridge.[202] The pamphlets reflected Frere's point of view that a number of alternatives and variations should be permitted and that there should follow ordered experimentation which should be on a broad rather than on a narrow basis.[203] The Alcuin Club's aim was to survey all the proposals and not to be tempted to produce a solution of their own. They explained:

The final outcome of our Survey is not to add one more to the schemes already put forward, but on the contrary to indicate how these schemes can be simplified and combined.[204]

The schemes that this refers to were the official proposals,[205] the work of the English Church Union (the 'Green Book') and another

---

[197] Jagger, *Alcuin*, p. 5.

[198] 'Note by Committee', see note 196.

[199] Jagger, *Alcuin, ibid.*

[200] *A survey of the Proposals for the Alternative Prayer Book, Part i: The Order of Holy Communion Occasional Offices*, Alcuin Club Prayer Book Revision Pamphlets XII (*cit. Survey* pt i), 1923, p. i.

[201] Jasper, *Frere*, p. 95.

[202] S. C. Carpenter, *Duncan-Jones of Chichester*, 1956, p. 68.

[203] Jasper, *Frere, ibid.*

[204] *Survey*, pt. 1, p. 6.

[205] NA 84.

publication which was the work of those who were involved in the Life and Liberty Movement.[206] This publication was also popularly known by the colour of its cover, in this case the 'Grey Book'.[207]

The 'Grey Book' was mainly the work of Percy Dearmer, Russell Barry, and R. G. Parsons. Barry's biographer records that:

> Russell was also invited to join an informal group of able young parsons, all of whom had seen war service and were anxious to bring pressure to bear on the committee which had already got to work on the revision of the Book of Common Prayer. His interest in revision had been aroused when he had to conduct impromptu services for the troops on the Nile in 1916 and after the War, for the highly critical students at Knutsford. Although he had a great reverence for the language of Cranmer, he was convinced that revision was long overdue. The book which this group produced in 1923, and became known as 'the Grey Book' on account of the colour of its cover shows the mark of Russell's hand throughout.[208]

In the Foreword which he contributed to this particular set of proposals William Temple, then Bishop of Manchester, explained that he himself had had no hand in framing the suggestions but states that they are:

> the work of men drawn from all 'parties' in the Church, well versed in liturgiology, experienced in the spiritual work of parishes, and eager to help in making worship the worthiest that can be offered to God as well as the most strengthening for the life of Christian discipleship.[209]

Temple further claimed that the proposals had been seen by 'men of very different ecclesiastical traditions', and that they had expressed a preference for this set of proposals over against others that had been put forward. This led Temple to believe that it was possible that these texts were capable of producing an agreed solution of this 'specially delicate and important problem'.[210]

What was now being sought, it will be recalled, was an alternative to the Book of Common Prayer, not a new Prayer Book. This policy

---

[206] F. A. Iremonger, *William Temple Archbishop of Canterbury His Life and Letters*, 1948, pp. 220–240.

[207] *A New Prayer Book. Proposals for the Revision of the Book of Common Prayer and for additional Services and Prayers drawn up by a Group of Clergy together with a foreword by William Temple, D. Litt., Bishop of Manchester*, 1923 (*cit. A New Prayer Book*).

[208] Frank H. West, *'FRB'—A Portrait of Bishop Russell Barry*, 1980, p. 34.

[209] *A New Prayer Book*, p. iii.

[210] *Ibid.*

had been adopted for two reasons, first as being only fair to those who wanted no liturgical change at all and secondly in order to take seriously the views of those who wanted changes but wished to make trial of them experimentally before making them final.

The Alcuin Club supported the idea of broad-based experimentation. They suggested that this should be over a period from five to ten years, particularly for the Communion Service, and then the Church should return to uniformity of rite 'so far as it proves possible or desirable'.[211]

It was now the turn of the House of Bishops to consider the matter. Between October 1925 and the beginning of 1927 the Bishops met for a total of forty-five days to discuss the Prayer Book Revision proposals.[212]

At this stage it is possible to review the situation in which the Bishops found themselves in 1925. They presumed that they must now be approaching the end of a long process which had commenced as a result of the recommendations of the 1904 Royal Commission. That, in itself, was the culmination of years of confusion and liturgical anarchy caused by either neglect of the Prayer Book by some churchmen or a desire to add to or subtract from its provisions by others. Their actions suggest that the Bishops were little aware that they were now living in an entirely new era, both in terms of the secular world and the ecclesiastical scene. Europe was only slowly recovering from the effect of the War and those who had been caught up in that searing experience were convinced that things could never be the same again. For some that conviction was characterized by a complete indifference to all serious theological and philosophical discussion. Instead they were engaged in a hectic search for excitement, glamour, and sheer fun. Alternatively, for others it involved a profound questioning of many of the previously easily accepted religious norms, in particular for those who were committed to a conception of the Church as the instrument of God's work in the world. Such churchmen were deeply concerned that the Church should be well-equipped for such a high task. Those who had seen the Church being tried and tested in the furnace of war were anxious that the pure metal would drop apart from the dross.[213] The Church had begun to order its forces at an organizational level with the coming of the Church Assembly and the Parochial Church Councils but what it still needed, many of the veterans of the trenches were convinced, was a form of

[211] *Survey*, pt. 1, pp. 2–3.
[212] F. R. Barry, *Mervyn Haigh*, 1964, p. 85.
[213] *The Church in the Furnace*, p. ix.

worship in the parish churches of England which was freed from the antiquities, confusions, and controversies of the immediate past generations conducted in language which did not seem to be preoccupied with the 'hereafter' rewards of the heavenly Jerusalem, or be trapped in the thought-forms of a feudal, rural, agrarian society. The evidence is that the Bishops of the Church of England, as they engaged in their liturgical debates between 1925 and 1927, were unable to face up to and meet these challenges; they were, unfortunately, still pre-occupied with the conception of using liturgical revision to enforce discipline. One of the Bishops involved recognized this, at least retrospectively. Bishop Henson of Durham confessed:

The restoration of discipline and the revision of the formularies were excellent objects, but in the actual circumstances of Modern England not easily harmonized. The one was an insistent popular demand, but the other commended itself to few outside the small company of liturgical scholars. I soon perceived that in pursuing a twofold quest the Bishops were endangering the success of their honest and laborious effort. Perhaps it would not be excessive to say that the ultimate failure of Prayer Book Revision had its root in the well-intentioned but intrinsically irrational attempt to serve two conflicting policies, of which the one was designed to satisfy the popular demand for order in the Established Church, and the other aspired to revise the system which was to be enforced.[214]

An insight into the various nuances and cross-currents which led to the Bishops' decisions is available in the reminiscences of Mervyn Haigh, who was at that time Domestic Chaplain to the Archbishop of Canterbury.[215] Haigh recorded that:

Notwithstanding the tolerance and mutual understanding shown by the bishops to each other during these debates, in spite of sharp differences of opinion and conviction between them, listening to these debates was for me a most disappointing experience. Most of the bishops, many of whom had taken part in the early discussions of Revision in the Convocations between 1906 and 1914, seemed weary of the subject before they started this, as it was hoped, final consideration of it. All had before them a specially prepared book of about five hundred pages, on each of which were three columns, one showing what the Assembly Committee had proposed when reporting to the Assembly, another giving the amendments to those proposals approved by

[214] Herbert Hensley Henson, *Retrospect of an Unimportant Life*, 1943, II, p. 152.
[215] In succession to Davidson's biographer, G. K. A. Bell, who had left Lambeth to become Dean of Canterbury. Ronald C. D. Jasper, *Bishop Bell, Bishop of Chichester*, 1967, p. 54.

the House of Clergy, and yet another giving the similar or different amendments approved by the House of Laity. But there was no column reminding
the bishops of the text of the Book of Common Prayer. It was a great mental
strain to have three sets of suggestions in front of one and to be also constantly
referring to the Prayer Book as it still was. Undoubtedly this proved too great
a strain for some bishops, and the almost inevitable effect of having so much
'official' material under their eyes was largely to limit the outlook of the
bishops to what, or something like what, was before them. Few took much, if
any, notice of the Green, Grey, and Orange Books with which they were also
supplied; and few indeed seemed to have any vision of a Book of Common
Prayer which, while remaining in essence its own glorious self, would yet be
more appropriate for use by, and better adopted to the needs of, people living
not in the seventeenth but in the twentieth century.[216]

The Bishop of Gloucester, A. C. Headlam, wrote to a friend after
the opening meetings in October 1925:

The discussions were often irrelevant, and whenever we got to a difficult point
we postponed it. By the end of the third day it had become quite clear to me
that if we were to continue in the present process, we should none of us be
alive when the Revision was complete.[217]

In July 1927 the Assembly passed the Deposited Book[218] by 517
votes to 133, despite concerted opposition from some Anglo-
Catholics.[219] That December the Book reached Parliament for the
first time and was carried in the House of Lords after a three-day long
debate by 214 to 88, but suffered a narrow, but decisive, defeat in the
House of Commons on 15 December, by 238 votes to 205.[220] It was a
debate which produced, experienced observers agreed, 'as fine a display of oratory as any which Parliament has heard this century'.[221]
Bell writes of the high oratory of Sir William Joynson-Hicks, who in
only the second speech in the debate 'kindled the first sparks of the fire
which was to consume the new Book in the fire of the fear of Rome'.[222]
Taken with the 'simply ultra-protestant harangue' of Rosslyn
Mitchell,[223] some parts of the debate recalled the kind of evidence

[216] Barry, op. cit., pp. 86–87.

[217] Headlam, letter to Maynard Smith, 23 October, 1925, quoted R. C. D. Jasper,
Arthur Cayley Headlam, Life and Letters of a Bishop, 1960, p. 183.

[218] 'Deposited Book' because it had been deposited with the Clerk of the Parliaments.
Bell, op. cit., p. 1339.

[219] Cross, op. cit., pp. 189–196.

[220] Jasper, Frere, p. 138.

[221] A. J. P. Taylor, English History 1914–1945, The Oxford History of England XV,
1965, p. 259.

[222] Bell, op. cit., p. 1345.

[223] Ibid., p. 1346.

that the Rev'd the Hon. W. E. Bowen and Lady Wimborne had produced twenty years earlier at the sessions of the Royal Commission.
This proved that such prejudice had not been one of the victims of the
World War and was still very much alive. There seemed to be evidence that the spirit of the war-time dream of Hensley Henson was
still a long way off:

The English protestant, at home perhaps a 'Wycliffe Preacher', or some other
manner of itinerant gospeller, sees R.C. priests and nuns moving about amid
the scenes of death on blessed ministries of comfort and mercy, and learns for
the first time that the 'Confessional' and the 'Mass' are instruments of that
same Divine compassion which he had always held to be the core of the
Gospel. How could the 'crucifix' ever become again to him an exasperating
symbol of popish superstition after he has seen it standing forlornly besides
peasants' war-wasted fields or erect as if in solemn triumph in the ruined
churches or lovingly clasped in dying soldiers' hands?[224]

The Anglican liturgical scene was now thrown into complete confusion. The 'result of twenty years of careful and unremitting work …
a work on which so much labour has been spent'[225] looked to have
been in vain. Yet there was the curious fact that the Division list of the
House of Commons clearly revealed that there had been a marked
majority amongst those members who represented English consti-
tuencies in favour of the Book, and so on 23 December the Archbishops issued a statement in which they said that the House of
Bishops had resolved to reintroduce the Measure into the Church
Assembly as soon as possible with 'such changes, and such changes
only, as may tend to remove misapprehensions and to make clearer
and more explicit its intentions and limitations'.[226] This they did, but
at the cost of losing the support of some of the less extreme Anglo-
Catholics without in any way pacifying the Evangelicals. Among
those who now withdrew support was the influential, if at times
hesitant, Walter Frere, by now Bishop of Truro. Fr Keble Talbot,
Superior of the Community of the Resurrection, applauded Frere's
decision, feeling that the Catholic side had been 'a ragged army'
which had needed a strong voice other than that of the more extreme

[224] H. H. Henson, 'The Church after the War' in F. J. Foakes-Jackson, ed., *The Faith
and the War. A series of essays by members of the Churchman's Union and others on the religious
difficulties aroused by the present conditions of the world, 1915*, p. 251.
[225] A. C. Headlam, *The New Prayer Book, being a Charge delivered to the Clergy and Churchwardens of the Diocese of Gloucester on the occasion of his second visitation, 1927*, pp. 2–3.
[226] Bell, *op. cit.*, p. 1347.

Darwell Stone.[227] Others were now unhappy for different reasons. Among some there was a feeling that the changes that were being proposed had been thought up for the sake of satisfying the House of Commons; they were suspicious of them because 'mixing religious questions with political ones has so often been the undoing of the Church and nowhere more so than here in England'.[228]

Frere told the Upper House of Canterbury in March 1928 that the proposed Book was too narrow to allow the growth and development of worship in the Church, and prophesied that things would soon be back to the same position as they had been in before the 1904 Royal Commission. At these meetings of the Convocations, although the Prayer Book Measure still received majorities in all four Houses, they were reduced majorities. When subsequently the Measure was considered by the Church Assembly, it was clear that many who had previously supported it had decided to abstain at that stage. Nevertheless the majorities in favour were still large.

In preparation for the re-submission to the House of Commons the Archbishop of Canterbury had joined the many others who put pen to paper on this controversial subject. In the House of Lords debate in 1927 Davidson had struck a personal note and had reminded his hearers, 'I am an old man'.[229] By the time of the 1928 debate the Archbishop was eighty years old and so could justifiably emphasize this aspect again in his booklet. He wrote:

I am an old man, and we are told that old men dream dreams. My dreams for the world I shall soon be leaving are rich in hope. I can descry among the sometimes bewildering channels of thought to which I referred at the outset many facts and many tendencies which reinforce my faith. The confused and tumbled questionings of average people are not hostile to the old Faith wherein we stand, though it is looked at from different angles and in a good many novel ways. My heartfelt prayer is that ere I say my *nunc dimittis* I may somehow—and not least by our new Book—be helpful to the younger folk whose pathway gleams with promise.[230]

His object in writing at this juncture, the Archbishop explained, was to make sure that the endeavours of those involved in introducing

---

[227] Jasper, *Frere, op. cit.*, p. 152; Darwell Stone, *The Prayer Book Measure and the Deposited book—The Present Situation: a Plea for an Agreed Book*, 1928.

[228] Canon A. G. Robinson, letter to Frere, quoted Jasper, *Frere*, p. 161.

[229] Bell, *op. cit.*, p. 1343.

[230] The Archbishop of Canterbury (R. T. Davidson), *The Prayer Book: Our Hope and Meaning*, 1928, p. 41.

a new Prayer Book should 'in the midst of comment and criticism be fairly understood'.[231] But his advocacy was too late. Bell says of the booklet that although it was straightforward and disarming, it did not influence votes.[232] In the event no one was very surprised when on 14 June 1928, this time after two days of debate, the House of Commons rejected the Prayer Book Measure by a slightly larger majority (266 to 220) than it had done the previous year, even though the speeches of the supporters were given more attention than in 1927.[233]

It was a crisis of no mean proportions. There were many cries of 'disestablish', and Church-State relations were strained to near breaking point. In the light of this defeat the Bishops agreed the following bold statement unanimously:

It is a fundamental principle that the Church—that is, the Bishops together with the Clergy and the Laity—must in the last resort, when its mind has been fully ascertained, retain its inalienable right, in loyalty to our Lord and Saviour Jesus Christ, to formulate its Faith in Him and to arrange the expression of that Holy Faith in its forms of worship.[234]

This was followed over the next four months by a nation-wide consultation conducted by Bishops with their respective Diocesan Conferences. The Conferences supported their Bishops in recognizing that worship in 1928 could not be brought back strictly into the limits of the 1662 Book of Common Prayer and so the Bishops agreed that 'during the present emergency and until further order be taken' they would not:

regard as inconsistent with loyalty to the principles of the Church of England the use of such additions or deviations as fall within the limits

of the proposals as set forth in the 1928 Prayer Book.[235]

This 'emergency' lasted effectively for thirty-six years until the *Prayer Book (Alternative and Other Services) Measure* of 1965 came into force, because as a result of the parliamentary veto:

---

[231] *Ibid.*, p. 9.

[232] Bell, *op. cit.*, p. 1350.

[233] Lockhart, *op. cit.*, p. 308.

[234] Bell, *op. cit.*, p. 1351. Dom Gregory Dix commented, 'Readers of the New Testament may be startled by this statement. Our Lord did not say ... And unto God in the last resort the things that are God's. But even with this qualification this was the bravest thing on the subject which had been said by English Bishops since 1559', an acid and brilliantly witty remark (Dix, *op. cit.*, p. 709).

[235] *Ibid.*, note, pp. 1358–1359.

the laborious procession of revision covering a quarter of a century came to a sudden enforced stop.[236]

6   The Failure and Limitations of the 1928 Prayer Book

The question needs to be asked, why did the 1928 Prayer Book fail to win approval? In the first place the proposals proved to be a victim of the notorious disunity of the Church of England. As has already been noted, there was an 'unholy alliance' between the most conservative Evangelicals and those belonging to the 'Western' wing of the Anglo-Catholic party. These Evangelicals were unwilling to accept any change in the Prayer of Consecration or the suggestions for the Reservation of the Blessed Sacrament. Both of these matters, together with the prospect of the authorization of eucharistic vestments, only heightened their fears that the Church of England was in danger of betraying its Protestant heritage. Meanwhile the Anglo-Catholics of the more extreme school were unwilling to accept a new Eucharistic Canon which broke with the Western tradition of a 'Moment of Consecration' associated with the Dominical Words of Institution by introducing an Eastern-type *Epiclesis* after these words.[237] They also thought that they detected an intention to use the new service to destroy the atmosphere and ethos of the Anglo-Catholic Mass.

The Anglo-Catholics were further convinced of an impending introduction of a policy which would use the new Book to curtail their activities by placing severe restrictions on the mode of Reservation, being particularly suspicious of the strict episcopal control that was envisaged in the regulations. This category of High Churchman was also considerably apprehensive about some elements of what they called 'liberalism' in, for example, the permission to omit the imprecatory verses in the Psalter, the variation in the rules governing the use of the Athanasian Creed, the softening of the reference to original sin in the Baptism service, and even the equalizing of the vows in the Marriage service. Bearing in mind the fact that the High Church Party had produced many of the leading liturgiologists of the day, it is not surprising that they very much objected to the fact that the whole process of revision had not been initiated by liturgiologists for the general enrichment of the church's worship and devotion, but

[236] *The Alternative Service Book: A Commentary by the Liturgical Commission*, 1980, p. 11.
[237] Buxton, *op. cit.*, p. 204 and *passim*.

by the Bishops.[238] And the Bishops' only purpose in being involved in the subject at all, they were convinced, was in order to control, discipline, and curtail the liturgical activities of the Anglo-Catholics. Bell, who was not of their party, was in effect agreeing with them when he wrote:

A revision of worship, of common prayer, which is intended from the start to be used as an instrument for stopping disobedience is at any rate not likely to produce the happiest results in the realm of worship! And side by side with this, the recommendation of the Royal Commission to consider the preparation of a new Ornaments Rubric 'with a view to its enactment by Parliament'—and to frame modifications in Church services 'with a view to their enactment by Parliament'—started all on a false track.[239]

Reviewing the situation before embarking upon its own daunting task thirty years later in 1958, the newly appointed Church of England Liturgical Commission identified three other reasons for the 1928 Book's failure. They were 'the latent Protestantism and anticlericalism of the British people';[240] the fact that many of those outside the Church, in the Commons for instance, who might have been expected to support the Measure failed to do so, because they were not completely convinced that the 1928 Prayer Book represented what the vast majority of the members of the Church wanted by way of alternative services; and lastly, the great lack of real conviction about the whole subject displayed by Randall Davidson, the Archbishop of Canterbury. Bell is most revealing on the Archbishop's attitude:

The Archbishop could not bring himself to believe that the revision of the Prayer Book was in fact a vital matter to the Church. Not believing it himself, he lacked the fire to convince others, and especially the House of Commons. To acknowledge this is not to say that the Archbishop was wrong, because of this lack of interest or conviction. His religious interests were of a more general, even a broader character. But his inability to devote his best mind to what was first the Rubrics and then the Prayer Book question, prevented him from giving a decided lead to the Church itself, and from pressing for a swifter and much less ambitious revision—when this was possible, in the earlier stages before the War.[241]

---

[238] A low estimate of the Bishops' competence in liturgical matters lingered on. Gregory Dix said in 1945 that 'the Bishops as a body are not equipped for composing a liturgy' (Dix, *op. cit.*, pp. 719–720).

[239] Bell, *op. cit.*, p. 1357.

[240] *Prayer Book Revision in the Church of England, op. cit.*, p. 12.

[241] Bell, *op. cit.*, p. 1356.

Being wise after the event, many churchmen realized that it had been a grievous mistake to allow Parliament to arbitrate on the Church's differences. Although there might be no objection to asking the State to sanction any measure of Prayer Book Revision on which the Church was substantially agreed, ecclesiastical arbitration was not a Parliamentary role.[242]

Much that was very good was lost in the defeat of the 1928 Prayer Book. E. C. Ratcliff may not always have been consistent on the point,[243] but in 1932 he could write of parts of the book that they were intended to 'meet new needs and to make use of liturgical knowledge for improvement and enrichment'.[244]

W. H. Frere was unswerving in his support of the 1928 Eucharistic Canon and in his last published work stated that he was convinced that it 'represents ... the best mind of the Church of England of the day.'[245] The Swedish theologian Yngve Brilioth wanted to go much further, and said he believed that if the 1928 Prayer Book had come into official use the Church of England would have possessed 'one of the noblest of all evangelical eucharistic liturgies'.[246]

Thus are opportunities lost, but, with the benefit of hindsight, we can now see that the rejection was not the block to all liturgical progress that it might have seemed at the time, because the Church of England had not by then worked out its pastoral and parochial policy in regard to the Eucharist, and although the strait-jacket restrictions of the Book of Common Prayer made life difficult for those attempting to introduce a Parish Communion, at least it did mean that the various experiments of these pioneers were able to establish patterns which were eventually crucial in shaping the *Alternative Service Book* to accommodate them.

The history of the programme of liturgical revision undertaken by the Church of England as a result of the recommendations made by the Royal Commission on Ecclesiastical Discipline in 1904 has been examined again to show that at no stage did either those who were actively involved in preparing the drafts for discussion or those debat-

[242] W. K. Lowther Clarke, *The Prayer Book of 1928 Reconsidered*, 1943, p. 86.

[243] A. H. Couratin, 'E. C. Ratcliff as Liturgist', in A. H. Couratin and D. H. Tripp, eds, *E. C. Ratcliff: Liturgical Studies*, 1976, p. 11 ff.

[244] E. C. Ratcliff, 'The Choir Offices' in W. K. Lowther Clarke, ed., *Liturgy and Worship: A Companion to the Prayer Books of the Anglican Communion*, 1932, p. 269.

[245] W. H. Frere, *The Anaphora or Great Eucharistic Prayer: An Eirenical study in Liturgical History*, 1938, p. 205.

[246] Yngve Brilioth (trans. A. G. Hebert), *Eucharistic Faith and Practice Evangelical and Catholic*, 1930, p. 227.

ing them in the legislative bodies seriously consider them in the context of the growing need in many parishes for a eucharistic Sunday
morning service which would be the one main act of worship for that
parish, around which all other parochial activities for the week would
be gathered. The question why they did not, remains.

As a result of the Oxford Movement, as has been shown, the
Church of England's worship had become much more eucharistic-
centred. Horton Davies, writing about the growing importance of the
Eucharist in the Church in the twentieth century, has said that for
High Churchmen and Low Churchmen alike it became:

the chief means of grace, the application of the benefits of Christ's Passion and
Resurrection to His people, and the inspiration and solace of the Christian
life.[247]

The Oxford Movement, as Chadwick has said, 'changed the external face, and the internal spirit of English religious life'.[248] Chadwick
argues that the proposed 1928 Prayer Book represented the prevailing
theology of many instructed Anglicans and that the influence on that
revision of the Oxford Movement can be seen to be stronger than any
other in suggesting changes from the 1662 book. However there is no
sign in the 1928 revision proposals that the Church had begun to ab-
sorb the ideas of the 'Sacramental Socialists' who were that part of the
Anglo-Catholic tradition which was inaugurated by the publication
of *Lux Mundi* in 1889 and for which Athelstan Riley coined the phrase
'Sub-Tractarian'.[249] Nor were the revisers willing to acknowledge the
experience gained by the Service Chaplains and quite significantly
absorbed by the Worship Committee of the National Mission. Perhaps the Church of England needs a longer period of gestation before
an idea can be taken fully into its system.

It is sad that although the ideas that were going in the near future
to lead to the emergence of the Parish Communion as a powerful force
in the Church of England's worship were beginning to bubble up
under the surface in the 1920s they had still not acquired the force to
impinge upon and significantly influence the process of liturgical revision that had been set in motion twenty years before, when the first
few glimmerings of the idea were by no means strong enough to in-

---

[247] Davies, *Worship and Theology*, v. p. 310.
[248] Chadwick, *The Mind of the Oxford Movement*, p. 58.
[249] Athelstan Riley in Introduction to Donovan, *After the Tractarians*, p. 5. Cf. Part
Two, *infra*.

fluence official thought. It would seem that by the 1920s the official process of revision had acquired the impetus of an undeflectable juggernaut set on a path that no one was going to be able to change radically, leading to the inevitable result of a book cast in a '1904'[250] style and mould, even though advancing scholarship had been able to influence some important elements in it, notably the Eucharistic Canon.

There is also the fact that the official process was set in motion in response to a Royal Commission of Ecclesiastical Discipline. It is a fact that contributed to the difficulty of taking a new approach to worship by 'psychologically' naming the purpose of the exercise. As has been observed in the words of G. K. A. Bell, it was not likely to produce the happiest results in the realms of worship.[251]

When the literature concerning the 1928 Prayer Book is examined it is quite clear that the concept of a corporate Parish Communion was not in the mind of either compilers or critics. Nor have those who have written about it subsequently considered it in this light. The eucharistic rites in the three published examples (the Grey, Green, and Orange Books) all concentrated on finding a substitute for the Prayer Book order. They did not visualize any additional congregational participation, nor did they reveal any increased awareness of the need to relate the Eucharist to the work of the church in the world.[252]

In the intervening years a number of accounts of the proceedings have been published. The most extensive is by Dr Jasper and is based upon Bishop Frere's papers.[253] It is established elsewhere that Bishop Frere introduced one of the first examples of a Parish Communion[254] and that he never lost his 'socialist-bent'.[255] However he does not seem to have felt it right or necessary to take these emphases along with him when engaged in discussing liturgical reform. Dr Lowther Clarke reconsidered the 1928 Prayer Book in 1943,[256] and although he made a number of suggestions for ways in which he thought the

[250] Buchanan has said that the 1928 Prayer Book was rejected 'in the interests of keeping one or other of Victorian ways of doing things uppermost' (Buchanan, *Patterns of Sunday Worship*, p. 5).

[251] Bell, *op. cit.*, p. 1357.

[252] With the possible sole exception of the Prayer for the Church Militant in the Grey Book, which sought to relate the prayer to the world and its needs.

[253] Jasper, *Frere*.

[254] P. 154 ff, *infra*.

[255] *Ibid.*

[256] Lowther Clarke, *The Prayer Book of 1928 Reconsidered*.

book might have been improved he did not include any thoughts on its usefulness as a vehicle for a Parish Communion. The 1928 Prayer Book did not, in any way, prepare the Church of England for the emergence of the Parish Communion. Not all the roots of the Parish Communion are not to be found in the Oxford Movement. Others must be sought in a contemporary, but very different, movement, to which we now turn.

PART TWO

THE SACRAMENTAL SOCIALISTS

1   The Beginnings of Christian Socialism in England

Not every anti-capitalist movement is necessarily socialist. It may represent a conservative attitude or an attempt to stabilize an order of things antedating the industrial revolution. So far as Britain is concerned, socialist thinking, properly so called, made its appearance in the 1820s when the urban factory proletariat had begun to form. What had earlier passed for social criticism bore the familiar imprint of tradition: agrarian, clerical, or philanthropic. The solutions proposed would, if adopted, have conserved the ancient order of things. Not surprisingly the class of industrial entrepreneurs was not to be found on the side of such reformers. This is enough to explain why the democratic movement of the 1790s which had formed under the impulsion of events in France obtained so little middle-class support in England.

One exception was Robert Owen, the son of a Welsh ironmonger with an education that began and finished at the village school.[1] Owen was one of the 'new men' who managed to transform Britain in the age of industrial revolution. But unlike most of his fellow employers he had an instinctive humanism which was gradually converted into a form of socialism. After a period as a factory manager in Manchester he went to work out his developing theories at New Lanark in Scotland.

In 1816 Owen put forward his plan. It was that instead of paying out doles the Government should employ the unemployed in 'Villages of Co-operation' (modelled on his own establishment at New Lanark). These would be centres of social life and rational education as well as of productive activity. They would be agricultural as well as industrial centres. They would raise the produce needed for their own consumption and would exchange surplus products with other such centres.[2] G. D. H. Cole has said:

He was putting forward a 'Social Utopia' destined speedily to sweep away capitalism and the competitive system, and to inaugurate for all the world a new era of peace and brotherhood.[3]

At first Owen was listened to with respect and welcomed by a number of people in the upper and ruling classes. But gradually its subversive

---

[1] Robert Owen, *The Life of Robert Owen, 1857–58*, repr. 1965, *passim*.
[2] T. C. Smout, *A History of the Scottish People, 1560–1830*, 1972, p. 383 ff.
[3] Preface to Everyman edition of Robert Owen, *A New View of Society*, 1927.

character became clearer; it was seen that it struck at the root of the whole profit-making system, and that Owen meant it, not as a mere measure of relief for the unemployed, but as the basis of a wholly new industrial order. His supporters fell away and his fellow-employers organized strong opposition to 'The Plan'. As a result Owen went off to the United States of America where he remained for a number of years.[4]

In 1820 the younger generation of intelligent workmen who were growing up within the new industrial order and learning to accept industrialization itself as inevitable, seized on Owen's doctrine of co-operation and founded the Economical and Co-operative Society.[5] In the years 1820–30 the doctrines of Owen, supported by the anti-capitalist deductions from Ricardo's theory of value, entered the wide field of working class agitation and coalesced into a system of social-ism. The word 'Socialist' was used for the first time in England in *The Co-operative Magazine* in November 1827.[6]

The character of the Socialist Movement was marked by the ex-perience of the French Revolution, hence the relationship of socialism to democracy was inevitably viewed in the light of the political con-vulsions France and Europe had recently undergone.

England and France being the twin birth-places of the new move-ment, it was inevitable that national differences should enter into the understanding of what the term 'socialism' signified. Not all those who employed it were committed to the revolutionary ideas which its French adherents had taken over from the men of 1789 and 1793.

In France, Jacobinism for many years remained the dominant mode of thought among what was coming to be known as 'the Left', even though some prominent French socialists were critical of the tradition. To the British it was a foreign import, and Robert Owen's followers in particular tended to disparage it. The association of socialism with democracy took time to establish itself; that of social-ism to republicanism (let alone atheism) was far more difficult to dis-entangle, at any rate for radicals outside France. There was a real need for this, particularly as a school of Christian Socialists developed in England. It was only then that the notion that socialist conclusions

---

[4] G. D. H. Cole, *A Short History of the British Working Class Movement, 1798–1898*, 1927, I, pp. 81–82.

[5] Harold Perkin, *The Origins of Modern English Society 1780–1880*, 1969, p. 235.

[6] In French literature *'Socialisme'* was used on 13 February 1832 in *La Globe*, which was edited by Pierre Leroux; see George Lichtheim, *The Origins of Socialism*, 1969, p. 219.

could be derived from religious precepts began to make some appeal to the philanthropists of the middle class.

However, in its early days socialism was viewed generally with suspicion by organized Christianity. The Anglican Evangelicals, who were otherwise greatly concerned for the deprived and underprivileged, gave socialism no encouragement. A clear example of this is in the writings of William Wilberforce. He wrote that Christianity renders

the inequalities of Social state less galling to the lower orders whose lowly path has been allotted to them by the hand of God.[7]

Wilberforce believed that the poor were to bear the inconveniences of their present state, assured that the peace of mind which religion brings affords more satisfaction than 'all the expensive pleasures which are beyond the poor man's reach.'[8] The rest of the Church of England revealed no greater interest in the new ideas.

As yet the successors of Wesley were equally unenthusiastic. 'The Methodist Movement was not favourable to working class movements', say the Hammonds.[9] There is an irony in that, although the Wesleyan Revival was unfavourable to working-class aspirations, it did actually indirectly serve them. In the first place the Methodist preoccupation with the eternal destinies of individuals and concern for the saving of every soul emphasized in a class-ridden society the value of each individual, however humble, and the spiritual equality of all men.[10] However, souls cannot be separated from the bodies they 'inhabit', and therefore the belief in spiritual equality leads on to the idea of social equality.

Then the close contact of preachers and teachers with the poor in the actual conditions in which they lived and worked eventually awoke a human natural sympathy with their sufferings in the leaders. At the same time the ordinary Methodist 'man in the pew' learned to read and study the Bible and discovered a fuller and more generous revelation than some of the early Wesleyan preaching had dwelt on.

[7] W. Wilberforce, *Practical View of the Religious System of Professed Christians in the higher and middle classes of this Country compared with Real Christianity*, 1797, p. 213.

[8] *Ibid.*

[9] J. L. and B. Hammond, *Town Labourer*, 1917, p. 270.

[10] N. P. Goldhawk, 'The Methodist People in the Early Victorian Age: Spirituality and Worship', in Rupert Davies, A. Raymond George, Gordon Rupp, eds, *A History of the Methodist Church in Great Britain*, 1978, II, pp. 115–117.

Again, the Methodists gathered together in communities around their chapels and there learnt self-discipline and to value liberty and self-government. It is from this point onwards, from 1815, that the leaders of Methodism can reasonably be counted among the spiritual ancestors of the Labour leaders of the late nineteenth century, but as we shall see there were those in the Established Church who were equally awakening to the fact that Socialist political principles could be reconciled to the basic tenets of Christian teaching.

Samuel Taylor Coleridge (1772–1834) has been called 'the first voice of Christian Socialism'.[11] As an undergraduate Coleridge came in touch with Owen. Coleridge's writing within this area has been described as being important, not so much for what is actually said,

as in its assumption that Christianity contains a social ethic; he wove into the fabric of his Christian thought and outlook that communistic conception of human social life which underlines all Socialism.[12]

In his turn Coleridge was to have a great influence on Frederick Denison Maurice. On going up to Cambridge as a shy and isolated son of a Unitarian minister from Bristol, Maurice was introduced by a young friend John Stirling to The Apostles Club.[13] He had already studied Coleridge's philosophical thinking,[14] and in that debating society he was a keen advocate of it. Maurice wrote:

I, in a small society of which I was a member, defended Coleridge's metaphysics and Wordsworth's poetry against the Utilitarian teaching.[15]

None the less, Maurice did not keep company with Coleridge and Wordsworth in rejecting all the ideas of the Enlightenment. From being enthusiastic supporters of the French Revolution they had changed to become staunch defenders of England's ancient institutions. Such was not the case with Maurice. In his opinion the ancient institutions were just obstacles which had to be swept away. The spiritual life of the nation was not confined to certain classes alone, and since it embraced the whole nation, it was wrong that only certain sections of it were granted privileges. All classes must therefore be endowed with power. Going down from Cambridge, Maurice read

[11] Max Beer, *A History of British Socialism*, 1923, I, p. 137.
[12] G. C. Binyon, *The Christian Socialist Movement in England—An Introduction to the Study of its History*, 1931, p. 41.
[13] Torben Christensen, *Origin and History of Christian Socialism 1848–54. Acta Theologica Danica*, vol. iii, 1962, p. 14.
[14] *Ibid.*, p. 13, note 11.
[15] Autobiographical note in F. Maurice, ed., *The Life of Frederick Denison Maurice Chiefly told in His Own Letters*, 1884 (cit. *Maurice: Life*) I, p. 176.

for the Bar but he did not spend much time at those studies, being more concerned to express his ideas about society and democracy. He did this through journalism. At the beginning of 1828 he became a diligent contributor to *The Athenaeum*, a publication which he actually bought and eventually edited. At the same time he wrote articles in *The Westminster Review*, which was at that time the acknowledged organ of Philosophic Radicalism (as opposed to the Whig *Edinburgh Review* and the Tory *Quarterly Review*). In both these journals his articles still showed the influence of Coleridge, and he was writing that:

individuals for the most part have sufficient sense to pursue their own interests; ... they will pursue them to better purpose than any persons can pursue them on their behalf.[16]

In 1828 Maurice experienced a spiritual crisis. *The Athenaeum* having failed financially, he spent some time at his parents' home. Conversation with his sister Emma, who was dying, forced on him the question of a personal living faith in God. Emma had broken with her father's Unitarian faith and had become an enthusiastic Evangelical Christian. Maurice came to the realization that:

the abyss separating God, as the perfect being of love, from sinful man could only be bridged if God revealed Himself in a human body and dwelled constantly in men through the Holy Spirit, thereby cleansing him from all his evil and conforming him to God's own nature.[17]

The outcome of his spiritual experience was that Maurice was baptized on 19 March 1831 and ordained on 26 January 1834.

For the next fourteen years Maurice seems to lose all interest in political and social problems. He continued to write widely but his writings and his correspondence are of a philosophical, theological, and religious nature. Indeed it is to be speculated as to whether he would have given his mind wholeheartedly to the matter again if it had not been for the influence of John Malcolm Ludlow.

Ludlow was a barrister, born in 1821 in Numack, India, where his father was with the East India Company. When he was two years old, his father died and his mother brought the family back to England but eventually decided to live in France. As a matter of course he received a French education and proved an able and successful pupil.

[16] Christensen, *op. cit.*, p. 18 (footnote).
[17] *Ibid.*, p. 23.

At an early age Ludlow took a keen interest in politics and social issues. Like his family he was a Liberal, but although the political issues in England first took his interest, his experience of the July Revolution in Paris in 1830 made a deep impression on him. 'From this time French politics became all important to me', he wrote.[18] To be living in France in the 1830s was, not surprisingly, bound to excite and stimulate the interest of a politically conscious young man. Additionally, Ludlow was a deeply committed Christian. Raven comments:

There was about his religion nothing affected or shamefaced. Perhaps it was his French education which freed him from the conventional hesitation of the Englishman when he mentions what he called "sacred things".[19]

In Michaelmas term 1842 Ludlow was called to the Bar and in January 1843 took chambers in Lincoln's Inn. A visit to France in 1846 brought to his attention the work of a Lutheran pastor Louis Mayer, who became a kind of father-figure to him.[20] Mayer was organizing young members of the educated classes to serve their brethren among the poor in an organization he called the *Société des Amis des Pauvres*. Inspired by this example he returned to London determined to see how he could initiate a similar scheme and decided that a start might be made among the young barristers at Lincoln's Inn; he was passed on to the Chaplain—F. D. Maurice.

This first meeting was not very propitious. Maurice showed little interest in the project and suggested that the local incumbent might be of more help. Ludlow's comment was, 'A good man, but very unpractical'.[21] Undeterred, Ludlow eventually started the work in the local parish but alone.

In 1848 France's experiment with a constitutional monarchy came to an end, Louis-Philippe abdicated, and a Republic was proclaimed. As Ludlow's two sisters lived in Paris, he at once decided to go there. Once he had assured himself of their safety Ludlow took the opportunity to study the situation at the closest possible quarters. He was very impressed by all he saw. It seemed to be a revolution which had the approval of the whole nation, particularly the working classes, who hoped that it would remove the social evils under which they had

---

[18] A. D. Murray, ed., *John Ludlow, the Autobiography of a Christian Socialist* (*cit.* Ludlow, *Autobiography*), 1981, pp. 15–18.
[19] C. E. Raven, *Christian Socialism 1848–54*, 1920, pp. 65–66.
[20] Brenda Colloms, *Victorian Visionaries*, 1982, p. 29.
[21] *Ibid.*, p. 71.

been suffering. Encouraged by socialist propaganda they hoped to find in Socialism the answer to their problems, and the early proclamations of the government encouraged them in this belief.

Ludlow was much in favour of the developments and believed that God was at work in the events of the Revolution, but was anxious that the new social order should be founded on Christianity so that it might be a universal blessing:

For myself, the sight of all I saw around me in France impressed on me the conviction, on the one hand that this was an essentially socialistic revolution, the principles of which would spread from France throughout the whole world; and on the other hand that socialism must be made Christian to be a blessing for France and for the world.[22]

Returning to England Ludlow tried first of all to raise the capital for a newspaper (*La Fraternité Chrétienne*) to be published in Paris which would preach the Christian message in the revolutionary situation. This venture having failed, he felt a compelling urge to talk over his Paris experiences and the special tasks, as he saw them, of Christians at that hour. He now did what he later described as 'a strange thing' and wrote a letter to Maurice in which he 'unbosomed' himself.[23] This time he found a more sympathetic ear. He discussed with Maurice how the masses of people who had no connection with the Christian faith and were carried away by Chartist propaganda might be approached.

Persistent economic hardship, the virtual collapse of the trade union movement by 1837, and dissatisfaction with the political reforms of 1832–35 had given rise to the working-class Chartist Movement. In 1836 William Lovett formed the London Working Men's Association 'to seek by every legal means to place all classes of society in possession of equal political and social rights'. Seeing political changes as the essential prelude to social reform the Association published in 1838 its People's Charter. It demanded universal male suffrage, annual Parliaments, equal electoral districts, abolition of property qualifications for MPs, payment of MPs, and the secret ballot.[24] Initially enthusiasm for the Charter and for a national petition to Parliament had been widespread. However, division split the movement, especially between moderates favouring peaceful per-

[22] Ludlow, *Autobiography*, p. 112.
[23] *Ibid.*, p. 113.
[24] Alex Wilson, 'Chartism' in J. T. Ward, ed., *Popular Movements c. 1830–1850*, 1970, p. 116 ff.

suasion and those willing to advocate physical violence. There were often widely different regional responses.[25]

1847 was marked in England by a deep economic crisis. The crop failure of previous years weighed heavily on the working classes, and there was widespread unemployment, which brought with it hunger and distress. Social discontent and unrest quickly spread across the country. In this situation there was an attempt to revive the agitation for the Charter. There was little enthusiasm until the beginning of 1848, but with the news of the February Revolution coming through from France there was an added stimulus. What the Chartists had struggled for years to obtain, the Parisian workers had accomplished in three days. In addition the new Democratic Republic in France had guaranteed the right of work to everyone, a most hopeful promise to a working class suffering under economic depression.

Chartist meetings now became crowded, and the demand for the People's Charter became linked with the idea of a socialistic order of society. Excitement grew and the fear of revolution spread among the wealthier classes. At the beginning of April a National Convention was held which decided on presenting a new National Petition for the Charter on 10 April. In the event the Great Metropolitan Demonstration was a fiasco and the whole event an anti-climax.

Among those who were convinced that the Chartists contemplated starting a revolution on 10 April was the young Vicar of Eversley, Charles Kingsley. His love of justice and his compassion for the poor could not but convince him of the justice of many of the Chartist demands. But equally he was convinced that 'physical Chartism', which is what he believed a revolution would be, was sinful. Law and order must be preserved. So on 10 April he went up to London intending to distribute handbills to persuade the Chartists to desist from violent action. On his way he called on Maurice. After admiring Maurice's work from a distance Kingsley had eventually made himself known to his hero. Kingsley's wife added this note to the printed version of the first letter he wrote to Maurice:

During the summer of 1844 he made the acquaintance of Mr. Maurice to whose writings he owed much.[26]

---

[25] See A. Briggs, *Chartist Studies*, 1959, *passim*. 'A new narrative history of Chartism, long overdue, cannot be written ... until local histories have been adequately treated', *ibid.*, p. 2.

[26] *Charles Kingsley: His Letters and Memories of his Life*, ed. by his wife, 4th ed., 1877, I, p. 127.

Kingsley and Maurice talked over the situation and Maurice told him of Ludlow's plans. Armed with a letter of introduction from Maurice, Kingsley set off to call on Ludlow.

Unlike many others Ludlow was calm. He had already experienced two revolutions and he did not believe that the mass meeting planned would lead to revolution. Kingsley, however, was determined to go to the Demonstration with his leaflets, and Ludlow decided to go with him, but they discovered on arrival at Kennington Common that the meeting was already breaking up peacefully.

The meeting and conversation were to prove decisive in the sealing of the partnership between the three pioneers. That evening Ludlow and Kingsley called on Maurice and together planned a poster bearing a proclamation to the 'Workmen of England'. The poster said: 'The Almighty God and Jesus Christ, the poor man who died for poor men, will bring freedom for you, though all the Mammonites on earth were against you', and concluded:

There will be no true freedom without virtue, no true science without religion, and no true industry without the fear of God and love for your fellow citizens. Workers of England be wise, and then you *must* be free for you will be *fit* to be free.[27]

Raven comments of the Proclamation:

It is the first manifesto of the Church of England, her first public act of atonement for a half-century of apostasy, of class prejudice and political sycophancy. And as such irrespective of its contents, it may fairly be described by that much abused word epoch-making.[28]

However the Danish historian Torben Christensen is right in pointing out that Raven is being a little extravagent. Christensen says:

The only novelty lies in its addressing itself directly to the workers. The papers of the various denominations and sections of the Church of England all made it clear that the complaints of the Chartists must be taken seriously and likewise expressed their good will towards the workers.[29]

The next project on which Maurice, Kingsley, and Ludlow embarked was a periodical entitled *Politics for the People*. During that

[27] Raven, *op. cit.*, p. 107.
[28] *Ibid.*, pp. 107–108.
[29] Christensen, *op. cit.*, p. 72.

summer seventeen weekly editions were published. The theme which pervaded all the articles was that religion and politics could not be separated. Somehow or other, the Christian dynamic must be infused into Socialism; if not it would be the worse not only for Socialism but for Christianity. The problem was how to supply this dynamic through a church, mainly exercised in its Evangelical branch with questions of individual salvation, or amongst the Tractarians with Patristic theology. Reformation within the Church, a new emphasis on the social rather than the personal implications of Christianity, a stress on God's intentions for mankind rather than on the short-comings of men must be the first stage in setting things right. Maurice saw that his work as Professor of Theology at King's College, London was of prime importance in this task. The training of a new gene-ration of priests fired with a vision of all men as God's family was essential for the future of the Church.

Maurice saw with a clarity, to which the twentieth century has most tragi-cally witnessed, that religion, philosophy, politics alike grounded on other foundations than God, would "tumble down and leave the most fearful wreck all around them".[30]

The periodical made little impression and was little read by workers. Christensen is quite definite in saying that it failed in its original pur-pose and that his researches do not bear out Raven's contention that it caused a 'storm of protest'. He says,

The paper remained unnoticed by the public at large—its appeal was left unheeded.[31]

Nevertheless during the course of 1848 a small brotherhood of young men grew up, the members of which were bound together by ties of personal friendship, and under the influence of Maurice's Sunday afternoon services at Lincoln's Inn and the Bible reading in his house in Queen's Square on a Monday evening, became a spiritual fellow-ship. Maurice repudiated any suggestions of being their leader, but Christensen has declared:

By his sermons and Bible readings, Maurice had laid the foundation for this unique position. It is necessary to keep this clearly in mind if one is to under-stand the history of Christian Socialism.[32]

Ludlow wanted this fellowship to make contact with the working

---

[30] Florence Higham, *Frederick Denison Maurice*, 1947, p. 61.
[31] Christensen, *op. cit.*, p. 89 (cf. Raven, *op. cit.*, pp. 115–116).
[32] Christensen, *op. cit.*, p. 93.

classes to break down 'those fearful class-estrangements'.[33] A series of meetings was planned at the Cranbourne Coffee Tavern. It was at these meetings that one particular worker, Lloyd Jones, an Irishman who had previously worked in Liverpool and Manchester and had become a zealous Owenite, came to the fore. Jones had participated in the last revival of Chartism, but as an Owenite he considered social reforms to be equally important, and his Socialist convictions had been given a new impetus by the revolutionary events in France.

At the meetings that now took place the workers did not rest satisfied with the knowledge that Maurice and his friends were sympathetic and could assure them that the true principles of Socialism were in conformity with Christianity; they wanted them to bring pressure to bear on the authorities to bring about action. In particular they wanted assistance in removing the legal obstacles which prevented the establishment of Home Colonies. These village communities were the pivot of the Owenite 'New Moral World'.[34] Maurice was unsure about the scheme. He wrote to Ludlow:

I am thankful to be able to connect Church Reformation with Social Reformation—to have one's thoughts tested by their application to actual work and by their power of meeting the wants of suffering, discontented, resolute men.[35]

But despite such a declaration he could not support the scheme, because in the first place it implied the abolition of the sacred right of private property which he believed to be part and parcel of society as constituted by God. Secondly, 'the Communist principle'[36] was not something which had to be made manifest through Home Colonies, since it was already a living reality in the Church as a universal fellowship in which every one shared the common privileges and gifts. For Maurice to be a Church Reformer was to bear witness to this fact.

Many standard works date the foundation of the Christian Socialist Movement from 1848. Christensen has criticized this:

From a historical point of view it is misleading to describe, as tradition does, Christian Socialism as a Movement started in 1848 in answer to the February Revolution and ensuing events. True enough, the events of that year had caused the setting up of a small brotherhood which subsequently became the core of the Christian Socialists, but it was characteristic of its members that, despite being filled with a burning desire to come to the rescue of their dis-

[33] *The Christian Socialist*, vol. 1, p. 75.
[34] See p. 71, *supra*.
[35] Maurice, *Life*, II, p. 8.
[36] Maurice used this actual phrase, see *ibid.*, p. 9.

tressed fellow-men they had but vague ideas about where and how to set to work.[37]

Some vision of 'where and how to set to work' was given to Maurice and his small brotherhood with the arrival in England in 1849 of the French Socialist refugee Jules St André le Chevalier. For the first time they came face to face with contemporary French Socialistic thinking, and it is more realistic to maintain that this encounter caused the emergence of Christian Socialism.

His plausible address, wide knowledge and ready enthusiasm gave him at once a prominent position in their counsels.[38]

Although he had long since ceased to have any connection with the Roman Catholic Church, Lechavalier[39] had no basic objection to religion, yet what he discovered in the Maurice fellowship was a revelation to him. He now discovered that the Socialist ideas he had brought with him from France were identical to Christianity as understood by Maurice. His *'l'économie sociale'* did not attempt to create a new society, but aimed at co-ordinating the existing economic and social forces in order to achieve unity and co-operation, and he saw that the instrument which could achieve that goal was the Church.[40] Thus the fellowship gathered around Maurice, which in the first place had been acquainted with the Owenite Socialism from their contacts with the workers, now had the experience of French Socialism. They fused together these two experiences to produce their Christian Socialism.

The process of development continued. A scheme for a Health League to tackle the need for sanitary reform was still-born, and a scheme for the mass emigration of those who could not be found employment in the inner-city areas was recognized as impracticable. But a plan was adopted to form a Working Association for tailors which could tackle the iniquities of the 'slop-system' by which 'sweaters' distributed work among the lowest-bidding tailors and needlewomen, while they themselves pocketed a considerable part of the money paid by the manufacturers for having the work done.

This practical action was followed by the publication of a series of *Tracts on Christian Socialism.* Maurice was anxious, at times over-anxious, to avoid giving the impression that he and his friends had

---

[37] Christensen, *op. cit.*, p. 108.
[38] Raven, *op. cit.*, p. 143.
[39] He adopted this spelling in England.
[40] Christensen, *op. cit.*, pp. 109–115.

established themselves as a party with a definite programme. He believed that any publications should be addressed to the various classes and groups in English Society to show how 'each in his vocation and ministry' might contribute to restoring order and unity to the nation to the benefit of their fellow-men, but it was time to nail their colours to the mast. He wrote to Ludlow:

I see it clearly, we must not beat about the bush. What right have we to address the English people? We must have something special to tell them, or we ought not to speak. *Tracts on Christian Socialism* is, it seems to me, the only title which will define our object, and will commit us at once to the conflict we must engage sooner or later with unsocial Christians and unchristian Socialists. It is a great thing not to leave people to poke out our object and proclaim it with infinite triumph. "Why, you are Socialists in disguise." "'In disguise'; not a bit of it. There it is staring you in the face upon the title page!"[41]

By calling himself a Socialist Maurice wanted to signify that he agreed with the Socialists in their view that fellowship and co-operation represented the true order of society, whereas competition, selfishness and rivalry were expressions of what he called in the first of the Tracts, 'dividing, destructive principle'.[42] At the same time Socialists were not fighting for a new system of their own devising but for God's established order against the new competitive world which man's selfishness had created. God had constituted a universal fellowship in which men should live and work together. He had pledged Himself to remove their selfish inclinations and make them fulfil the law of His Order.

In the third Tract Maurice wrote:

A brotherhood to be real demands a Father; therefore it is that we speak of Christian Socialism.[43]

In the wake of such propaganda Maurice and his friends built on the foundation of the first Association which they had helped to form for tailors. A number of requests for assistance in forming other Associations were received and it was decided to form a Central Board for the whole work of Associative Labour. In the event it was named The Society for Promoting Working Men's Associations.[44]

[41] Maurice, *Life*, *op. cit.*, II, pp. 34–35.
[42] Christensen, *op. cit.*, p. 136.
[43] *Ibid.*, p. 137 (footnote).
[44] *Ibid.*, p. 142 ff.

As soon as the S.P.W.M.A. had been formed, Ludlow returned to his idea of a newspaper. The first name suggested was *Brotherhood, A Journal of Association*, but it was decided to call it *The Christian Socialist: a Journal of Association*. The first issue appeared on 2 November 1850.[45]

Unfortunately all was not success. It was soon discovered that it was not as easy as they had thought to get workers interested in Associative work. The skilled workers did not feel inclined to give up their relatively well-paid work in order to embark on Associative Production, the prospects for which were at the best doubtful. Petty disputes broke out, there were only scanty successes, and it is tempting to dismiss the whole experiment as fool-hardy and worthless. But Raven warns against making such a judgement. He believed that it is too easy to sneer at the ventures, and suggested that

When [the critic] realises the vast change that has come over our social life ... and discovers the potency of the trifling and apparently futile experiments, he will become convinced that the men who had the courage to act and, in spite of obvious failures and constant disappointments, to go on acting deserve a fuller share of praise than they have yet received. These Associations, whose puny conflicts seem a mere battle of frogs and mice, were not only the forerunners but the forebears of the great co-operation movement, and of the legislation of organised labour.[46]

The next venture of the Christian Socialists was to attempt to open a Co-operative Store in London. Lloyd Jones had himself been part of an early co-operative experiment in Salford and had followed the developments in consumers' co-operation which had developed with the Rochdale Equitable Pioneers. There is a tendency to regard Lancashire co-operation as beginning with the Rochdale Pioneers, whereas in fact there was little that was new or pioneering about them; their society was merely a revival of the Owenite co-operation of the earlier period.[47]

Through these stores, Lloyd Jones convinced the others, workers could obtain unadulterated food and provisions at equitable prices and so increase the purchasing power of their wages; at the same time capital would be accumulated which could be used for promoting Productive Associations. The store was duly opened on 24 October 1850 in the same building as the headquarters of the S.P.W.M.A. at

[45] *Ibid.*, p. 151.
[46] Raven, *op. cit.*, p. 224.
[47] A. E. Musson, 'The Ideology of Early Co-operation in Lancashire and Cheshire', *TLCAS*, vol. LXVIII, 1958, pp. 117–118.

76, Charlotte Street with Lloyd Jones as the manager.[48] Ludlow however, was not happy with the scheme. He saw no morality in the stores, he believed that a successful consumer co-operative would attract middle class people who knew a bargain when they saw it and that in the end it would do nothing to help the working class. Ludlow was still very keen about producer associations and believed that too much energy was being put into the co-operative stores. In this he particularly crossed swords on the issue with Edward Vansittart Neale. Neale was a wealthy barrister who had known Maurice in his Oxford days. He had since become interested in the Socialistic system and had become convinced that co-operation was the best way to help workers to better living conditions. He joined the Council of Promoters of S.P.W.M.A. in 1851.[49] It was at the end of that year that the dispute between Ludlow and Neale came to a head and became so bitter that Ludlow felt he had to resign as editor of *The Christian Socialist* and also from membership of the Council of Promoters. In his last issue Ludlow gave the numbers of types of co-operatives in operation in Britain. There were 35 working men's producer associations and 14 flour-mill schemes, yet there were 145 towns and villages which reported one or more co-operative stores. Brenda Colloms sums up the situation:

In spite of all Ludlow's missionary endeavours, the working classes, especially in Scotland and the north of England, were giving their loyalty and their pennies to the consumer co-operatives, just as Neale had predicted.[50]

A more contemporary commentator, the Chartist and arch-atheist[51] George Jacob Holyoake, writing in 1875 was surprisingly understanding of some aspects of the point of view that Ludlow was taking. Writing of Christian Socialism as a whole he said:

Its Social Creed was very clear. Its watchwords were association and exchange rather than competition and profits. Its doctrine as to Christianity was not so definable. It maintained that Socialism without Christianity is as lifeless as the feathers without the bird, however skilfully the stuffer may dress them up into an artificial semblance of life. Christianity may be true and sacred in the eyes of the co-operator but he cannot well connect the special

[48] Colloms, *op. cit.*, p. 89.
[49] Maurice, *Life*, *op. cit.*, II, p. 75.
[50] Colloms, *op. cit.*, pp. 108–109.
[51] Colloms, *op. cit.*, p. 56: 'Although several Chartists were atheists, some of them indeed professional atheists, like George Jacob Holyoake'.

doctrines of Christianity with those of Co-operation. When Mr. Pitman associated anti-vaccination with co-operation the incongruity was apparent to most persons. Christian Socialism is an irrelevance of the same kind though it sins on the popular side.[52]

In 1852 the Provident Society Act[53] came into force. Ludlow had been instrumental in the drafting of the Bill. It was now no longer necessary for anyone wishing to set up an Association to seek the help of the Council of Promoters of the S.P.W.M.A. They could apply to the Registrar of Friendly Societies for assistance. Halévy believed that:

The Act of 1852 may be regarded as a political and legal seal set upon the influence of the Christian Socialists. It was a powerful influence. They had created a new type of socialism calculated to attract, by reassuring them, those who had been alarmed by some extreme doctrines preached by Owen.[54]

Although they changed the name of the Society to The Association for Promoting Industrial and Provident Societies, stating in its preamble that the Promoters had united to apply Christian principles to trade and society,[55] and Ludlow returned to join the Council of Promoters, they were unable to find real unity in the group and a common zeal. Ludlow was still basically unhappy that the distinctive Christian character of the work had been diluted.[56] A further distraction came in 1853 from Maurice's controversy with the Council of King's College, London. His orthodoxy had come under suspicion when in his *Theological Essays* he had attacked the then currently popular view of the endlessness of punishment in the future life, maintaining that 'eternity' had nothing to do with time.[57] Maurice realized from the outset that he ran the risk of expulsion from King's College.[58]

[52] George Jacob Holyoake, *The History of Co-operation, 1875-7*, revised ed., 1906, 2, p. 538.
    [53] 13 and 14 Vict. cap. 115, *An Act to Consolidate and Amend the Laws relating to Friendly Societies*, Parliamentary Debates, 3rd ser., vol. XCII, pp. 95 sqq. and vol. CXIII, pp. 1017-1018.
    [54] Elie Halévy (trans: E. J. Watkin & D. A. Barker), *A History of the English People in the Nineteenth Century, vol. 4, Victorian Years 1841-1895*, English ed. 1948, p. 268.
    [55] Colloms, *op. cit.*, p. 126.
    [56] Christensen, *op. cit.*, p. 319.
    [57] Gordon Huelin, *King's College, London 1828-1978*, 1978, pp. 22-23.
    [58] Maurice, *Life, op. cit.*, II, p. 164.

He wrote to a friend:

A crisis, I am convinced, is at hand which will bring the question to an issue, whether we are believing in what Dr. Jelf calls religion of mercy (proved to be such because phrases about salvation are to phrases about damnation as 57 : 8—the Bible being a great betting book, where the odds on the favourites are marked as at Doncaster or Newmarket), or whether we believe in a Gospel of deliverance from sin and perdition. We cannot avert this crisis. I do not willingly do anything to hasten it, God knows.[59]

The expulsion duly took place at a special meeting held on Thursday 27 October 1853. They resolved that:

The council feel it to be their painful duty to declare that the continuance of Professor Maurice's connection with the college as one of its professors would be seriously detrimental to its usefulness.[60]

Maurice was now looking for some use of his many talents, and found it in the Working Men's College. This was not an original idea, since Mechanics' Institutes catering for working men had been operating since the 1820s in some parts of the country.[61] The Council of Promoters met in January 1854 at which Thomas Hughes proposed and Lloyd Jones seconded that they framed and planned a People's College in connection with the London Associations. Maurice undertook to prepare a scheme for the College.[62] It would be independent and the teachers unpaid volunteers, and he insisted that theology be taught. 'A College founded by the Christian Socialists which omitted theology would seem like a fraud'.[63]

Not surprisingly Maurice became the first Principal of the College. At a meeting held in the Hall of the Association, when a large number of working men presented him with a testimonial declaring their support after his dismissal from King's, the hope was expressed that he

[59] *Ibid.*, p. 182.

[60] *Ibid.*, p. 191.

[61] Perkin, *op. cit.*, p. 70. Among them was the Manchester Mechanics' Institution founded in 1824 out of which the University of Manchester Institute of Science and Technology has developed. *150 years of Progress. An account of the development of the Institute from its origin as the Manchester Mechanics' Institution*, 1974.

[62] Maurice, *Life, op. cit.*, II, pp. 232–233. Thomas Hughes acquired lasting fame as the author of *Tom Brown's Schooldays*, 1857. He is less well known as the biographer of the second Bishop of Manchester. See Thomas Hughes, *James Fraser, Second Bishop of Manchester: A Memoir 1818–1885*, 1887.

[63] Colloms, *op. cit.*, p. 144.

would not find it a fall to cease to be a professor at King's College and to become Principal of a Working Men's College. Maurice was well content with the outcome.[64]

2   The Second Stage in the Life of the Christian Socialist Movement

It is generally agreed that 1854, the year of the foundation of the Working Men's College, sees the end of the first stage in the history and development of Christian Socialism. However, this could not be said to be the end of the Christian Socialist Movement altogether. To suggest that Maurice and his followers put the whole matter of social righteousness completely out of their minds and occupied themselves with other matters is quite untrue and would suggest that their efforts over the previous quarter of a century had all been somewhat spurious. The fact is that for the next twenty-three years there did not exist a body which had a specific concern for Christian Social matters. Yet organizations are not the only way in which ideas can be propagated, and Maurice, Neale, Hughes, and Ludlow continued to work for both socializing Christianity and christianizing Socialism. Maurice worked on the first and the other three on the second. It was a period in which, as Maurice Reckitt put it, the seed was growing secretly.[65] One of the seeds which was growing was the social awareness of some of those who had been dubbed 'Ritualists' or 'Puseyites'. From the cloistered saintliness of Tractarianism they were moving out into the slums of the industrial cities and towns and revealing a self-denying heroism that was to impress many who had little time for their excessses of ritualistic worship. In many cases priests went to work in the unattractive places of the fast-growing industrial towns from choice, but it is also a fact that in the early days some newly-ordained men found that these parishes with their mission districts were the only places in which they could find employment. A later development again was when young High Churchmen sought out the slum parish clergy house as the only 'real' place to work for a 'Catholic' priest.

The slum priests, as they became known, began to convince those of their critics who would take the trouble to consider the matter, that they were providing their parishioners not only with the opportunity

---

[64] Maurice, *Life, op. cit.*, II, p. 221.
[65] Reckitt, *Maurice to Temple*, pp. 94ff.

to give glory to God in ways of splendour and beauty which contrasted starkly with the hideousness and degradation of their background, but were also at the same time bringing sustenance to the starved souls of those to whom they ministered and understanding to their minds in the only possible way in which this could reach them. It has been well said:

The "Ritualists" were teaching not only through the ear but through the eye—even in "extreme" cases through the nose—an illiterate race of social outcasts who could learn only with difficulty by more intellectual means amidst the hideous and odoriferous squalor of such places as London Docks and Miles Platting. The worship of God in which they joined was, by the violent contrast to all else in their lives, at once a vindication of the otherworldliness of their faith and an implicit condemnation of the filthy environment amid which the social sin of an acquisitive and complacent ruling class had condemned them to live. So regarded, the ritual, which mainly centred round the Presence of our Lord amid surroundings more hostile than those of his very Nativity itself, was not "empty" but full of a profound significance; not "meaningless" but clamouring for an interpretation even more far-reaching than most of those who practised it knew how to provide.[66]

(a) The Guild of St Matthew

The new life for the Christian Socialist Movement came from such a background as that just described. It was Stewart Headlam's Guild of St Matthew, founded in the Parish of St Matthew, Bethnal Green, on St Peter's Day in 1877 while Headlam was a curate there. In 1878 Headlam was dismissed from his curacy at St Matthew's, and the Guild moved out from its local beginnings to become a nationally organized propagandist society.[67]

The Guild possessed three objectives:

1. To get rid, by every possible means, of the existing prejudices, especially on the part of secularists, against the Church, her Sacraments and doctrines, and to endeavour to justify God to the people.
2. To promote frequent and reverent worship in the Holy Communion and a better observance of the teaching of the Church of England, as set forth in the Book of Common Prayer.
3. To promote the study of social and political questions in the light of the Incarnation.

---

[66] *Ibid.*, pp. 112–113.
[67] F. G. Bettany, *Stewart Headlam: A Biography*, 1926, pp. 79–96.

In order to carry out these objectives there were also three rules of the Guild. The first was to propagandize both collectively and by personal influence; the second, to communicate as a body on all great festivals and to celebrate the Holy Communion regularly on Sundays and Saints' Days; and the third rule was that they should meet annually in united worship and for business on the Feast of St Matthew (21 September).[68] These objectives and rules fully justify Professor Peter Jones' description of the Guild as the first example of 'Sacramental Socialism'.[69] One of the major figures in the Guild of St Matthew in the early days was W. E. Moll. He joined the Guild in 1878 while serving a curacy in London, although the majority of his ministry was eventually spent in the north of England. He is an important link with later development, as both P. E. T. Widdrington and Conrad Noel were among the curates he trained.[70] Moll's political and theological position can best be understood from a speech he made to the High-Church English Church Union in 1885 when he said:

As a Catholic, I boldly avow myself a Christian Socialist. As a Catholic I believe that the Church is the Body of Christ filled with His Spirit ... As a Catholic I believe that the Church is the Kingdom of Heaven on earth—an organised society for the promotion of righteousness and freedom and truth among the nations.[71]

The Guild of St Matthew ceased to be an active force from 1895 onwards as the Christian Social Union began to take the centre of the stage in Christian Socialist matters.[72] During that year the Guild's journal *Church Reformer* collapsed. In one of its last issues Percy Dearmer, himself a member of the Guild,[73] crossed swords with Headlam over his attitude towards the Independent Labour Party.[74] Many members of the Guild were unhappy about Headlam's willingness to offer assistance to Oscar Wilde at the time of his famous trial,[75] and a

---

[68] *Ibid.*, pp. 79–80.

[69] Peter d'A. Jones, *The Christian Socialist Revival 1877–1914: Religion, Class and Social Conscience in Late-Victorian England*, 1968, p. 88. Professor Jones did his first research into Christian Socialism for a higher degree at Manchester University, *ibid.*, p. 17.

[70] Maurice B. Reckitt, ed., *For Christ and the People, Studies of four Socialist Priests and Prophets of the Church of England between 1870 and 1930*, 1968, p. 141.

[71] Quoted *ibid.*, p. 124.

[72] Jones, *op. cit.*, p. 145.

[73] Nan Dearmer, *The Life of Percy Dearmer*, 1940, p. 35.

[74] Bettany, *op. cit.*, p. 144.

[75] G. F. Maine, ed., *The Works of Oscar Wilde, 1856–1900*, 1948, p. 7 and Jones, *op. cit.*, pp. 145–148.

number resigned their membership. Although Headlam survived an attempt to remove him from the office of Warden, the influence of the Guild declined.

Headlam himself continued to witness to his sacramental social-ism,[76] that same witness that he had made a few years earlier when preaching in Westminster Abbey. To a perhaps surprised congre-gation he had said that when the Eucharist was called the Holy Com-munion this was 'pledging all who partake of it to be sharers of their wealth . · . to be Holy Communists'. He continued:

In the worship of Jesus really present in the Sacrament of the Altar before you, all human hearts can join, and especially secularists, for when you wor-ship Him you are worshipping The Saviour, the social and political Emanci-pator, the greatest of all secular workers, the founder of the great socialist society for the promotion of righteousness, the preacher of a revolution, the denouncer of kings, the gentle, tender sympathizer with the rough and the outcast, who could utter scathing, burning words against the rich, the re-spectable, the religious.[77]

(b) The Christian Social Union

The torch of Christian Socialism which the Guild of St Matthew was in the process of laying down was taken up by the Christian Social Union. It had its origins in a group which called itself the 'Holy Party', which first met in 1875.[78] It consisted of Henry Scott Holland, J. R. Illingworth, E. S. Talbot, and Charles Gore. At that time all were Oxford dons. Scott Holland held a Senior Studentship at Christ Church, Illingworth was a Fellow of Jesus, Talbot was War-den of Keble, and Gore a Fellow of Trinity. In Illingworth's biogra-phy it is said that the Holy Party was the germ of the Christian Social Union, of Mirfield, and of *Lux Mundi*.[79] *Lux Mundi*,[80] which Gore edited in 1889 and to which Talbot and Illingworth contributed, con-tained a development of Tractarian theology which can be said on the one hand to have combined the 'Catholic Church' of Pusey with

[76] *Christian Socialism, A Lecture by the Rev. Stewart B. Headlam*, Fabian Tract No. 42, 1892, 5th reprint August 1907.

[77] Bettany, *op. cit.*, pp. 120–121.

[78] William Richmond in A. L. Illingworth, ed., *Life and Work of J. R. Illingworth MA, DD, as portrayed by his letters and illustrated by photographs*, 1917, p. 133; G. L. Prestige, *The Life of Charles Gore. A Great Englishman*, 1935, p. 25 f.

[79] Letter from J. R. Illingworth to 'M.C.L.' (nowhere identified), September 1901, Illingworth, *op. cit.*, p. 138.

[80] Charles Gore, ed., *Lux Mundi. A Series of Studies in Religion of the Incarnation*, 1889.

the 'Kingdom of Christ' of Maurice,[81] and on the other to have
united the piety and churchmanship of the Tractarians with the critical spirit[82] which had found expression a few decades earlier in *Essays
and Reviews*.[83]

The Christian Social Union was formally set up in 1889. By this
time Scott Holland had become a Canon of St Paul's and the
inaugural meeting was held in the Chapter House there.[84] The stated
aims of the Union were:

1. To claim for the Christian Law the ultimate authority to rule social practice.
2. To study in common how to apply the moral truths and principles of
   Christianity to the social and economic difficulties of the present time.
3. To present Christ in practical life as the Living Master and King, the
   enemy of wrong and selfishness, the power of righteousness and love.[85]

In addition, members were expected to pray for the well-being of the
Union at Holy Communion more particularly on or about the following days: the Feast of the Epiphany, the Feast of the Ascension, the
Feast of St Michael and All Angels. It will be noted that the style of
the Union's aims and rules were very similar to those of the Guild of
St Matthew, but it was less exclusively Anglo-Catholic, though firmly
Church of England, than the Guild of St Matthew. Charles Gore was
quite adamant about this. He believed that only church people could
awaken the Church, and only church people sharing the same sacramental system could awaken their fellow church people to the real
social meaning of their baptism, their confirmation, and their Holy
Communion.[86]

The main difference between the CSU and the GSM was that the
CSU did not declare itself for a particular given platform. It was
organized principally to study and publicize social and economic
problems.[87] Its propaganda methods covered lectures and sermons.

[81] R. Cant art. '*Lux Mundi*' in Alan Richardson, ed. *A Dictionary of Christian Theology*,
1969, pp. 201–202.

[82] Arthur Michael Ramsey, *From Gore to Temple. The development of Anglican Theology
between Lux Mundi and the Second World War 1889–1939. The Hale Memorial Lectures of Sea-
bury-Weston Theological Seminary, 1959*, 1960, p. 11.

[83] *Essays and Reviews*, 1860. 'A collection of essays by seven authors who believed in
the necessity of free enquiry in religious matters', *ODCC* (ed. 2), p. 471; I. Ellis, *Seven
Against Christ, A Study of 'Essays and Reviews'*. Studies in the History of Christian Thought
23, 1980, *passim*.

[84] Stephen Paget, ed., *Henry Scott Holland: Memoirs and Letters*, 1921, p. 169.

[85] Jones, *op. cit.*, p. 177.

[86] Binyon, *op. cit.*, pp. 242–243.

[87] Charles Gore, chapter 'The Christian Social Union' in Paget, *op. cit.*, p. 242.

Indeed the chances of the survival of the new society were tested by the response and attendance at a set of lectures organized at Sion College in 1889 as one of its first activities. Attendance was good, so it continued.[88] In all this type of activity the CSU's methods could be well described as intellectual and Fabian.[89] There were those, nevertheless, who wanted a more radical and practical approach, among them, the Rev'd F. Lewis Donaldson, Vicar of St Mark's, Leicester who led a party of 440 unemployed men out of the Market Square in Leicester singing the hymn 'Lead, kindly Light' watched by a crowd estimated at 100,000.[90] This striking action, reminiscent of Headlam at his most militant, had a wide influence. Maurice Reckitt said of it:

By doing so he turned the march into a pilgrimage, challenged the attention, and often won the sympathy, of the churchmen in the towns and villages through which the procession passed, and reinforced the claims of his fellow-citizens that their plight was no local misfortune but part of the social and economic failure of a nation.[91]

It was Lewis Donaldson who had coined the phrase, 'Christianity is the religion of which socialism is the practice'.[92]

Although G. K. Chesterton could say of the members of the Christian Social Union that they were 'good friends and very gay companions',[93] all was not well with the organization. The aim of the CSU had always been to try and influence the Church, to try and confront it with the challenge of concerning itself with the social problems of the world. Increasingly the leaders of the CSU were disappointed with the response which their preaching and lecturing were arousing, and both Gore and Scott Holland[94] believed that the time was over for mere enquiry into social problems and that Christian Socialists ought to be involved in a more active advocacy of particular reforms.[95] Although the CSU continued until the end of the First World War, it was eventually amalgamated with the Navvy Mission Society to become the Industrial Christian Fellowship,[96]

[88] Paget, op. cit., p. 169.

[89] 'Fabian Society. Originally a group of predominantly middle-class intellectuals . . . established to spread socialist ideas among the educated public'. Alan Palmer, The Penguin Dictionary of Twentieth Century History, 1982, p. 139.

[90] Jones, op. cit., pp. 86–87.

[91] Reckitt, Maurice to Temple, pp. 148–149.

[92] Quoted Jones, op. cit., p. 188; Reckitt, op. cit., p. 151.

[93] Maisie Ward, Gilbert Keith Chesterton, 1944, p. 143.

[94] Gore in Paget, op. cit., p. 250.

[95] Prestige, op. cit., p. 274.

[96] Ibid., p. 282 and Gerald Studdert Kennedy, Dog-Collar Democracy, The Industrial Christian Fellowship, 1919–1929 (cit. Studdert Kennedy, Dog-Collar Democracy), 1982, p. 4.

while a more militant grouping of like-minded churchmen gathered together in the Church Socialist League.

(c) The Church Socialist League

In his biography of Percy Widdrington, one of the founder-members of the Church Socialist League, Maurice Reckitt, himself very much involved for many years in Christian Socialist activities of many kinds, comments:

The CSU leaders had been slogging away at their uphill job not without a certain impact on many in the 'comfortable' classes, but their influence did not go very deep and had little or no effect on the masses, even where the workers still retained any contact with the Church. Neither Gore with his cry for Christian penitence, nor Scott Holland with his attempt to deepen and underpin the social idealism of the day by relating it to the doctrines of the Faith, were deceived by the lack of a satisfying response with which their efforts had met ... Something quite different was plainly needed, and the socialist priests of the industrial north, fresh from the emotions stirred by the Election, knew this and resolved to provide it. Thus in June 1906 was born the Church Socialist League.[97]

The League was created at a conference of Anglican clergy held at the house of Canon Morton in Morecambe on 13 June 1906, the year in which the Liberal Party with its Labour allies won a resounding victory in the General Election.[98] The priests came in response to a letter which Algernon West had sent to a number of acquaintances whom he had thought would be interested:

There is at present no organisation which unites the clergy who are dissatisfied with the present social order and who feel that the Church is making no real attempt to alter existing social and industrial conditions.[99]

The Basis of the new organization was politically uncompromising:

The new League requires its members to be convinced Socialists, in the historical and economic meaning of the word. It is thus a Society within the Church, composed exclusively of Socialists,

the founders declared.[100] They then went on to spell out what they believed this involved, stating as their three Principles:

---

[97] Maurice B. Reckitt, *P. E. T. Widdrington, A Study in Vocation and Versatility*, 1961, pp. 42–43.

[98] *The Optimist, A Review dealing with Practical Theology, Literature and Social Questions in a Christian Spirit. (cit. Optimist)* vol. 4, No. 1, October 1906, p. 63.

[99] *Ibid.*, vol. 8, No. 2, April 1913.

[100] *Ibid.*, vol. 4, No. 1, October 1906, p. 64.

1. The Church has a mission to the whole of human life, Social and Individual, Material and Spiritual.
2. The Church can best fulfil its social mission by acting in its corporate capacity.
3. To this end the members of the League accept the principles of Socialism.[101]

The methods which the League would employ to bring about this 'democratic commonwealth' were also given in the document. They were five in number:

1. To cultivate by the regular use of Prayer and Sacraments the life of brotherhood.
2. Members undertake to help each other in fulfilling the object of the League by speaking and lecturing and in other ways.
3. Members shall co-operate as far as possible to secure the consideration of social questions at their Ruridecanal and Diocesan Conferences, and the election of Socialists on these and other representative bodies.
4. Members shall work for the disestablishment of the Patron, and the substitution of the Church in each parish in conjunction with the Church in the Diocese in the Patron's place.
5. To secure the due representation of the wage-earning classes upon all the official representative bodies of the Church.[102]

There was now a new enthusiasm abroad among Christian Socialists as the CSL harnessed the energies of a growing group of able priests who were unflagging in their devotion to the twin principles of High-Churchmanship and Socialist political action. So it was that the initiative in Christian Socialist circles passed once again to a more Anglo-Catholic clientèle. Among the clergy involved was the Rev'd Conrad Noel who wrote of this time in his autobiography:

We felt the need of an organised Christian Socialist movement, and W. E. Moll, with Percy Widdrington and myself, called a conference at Morecambe to that end. Widdrington was an active Socialist and an able lecturer and had, with myself, emphasized the fact that a society was needed which would be fully Socialist in the ordinary sense understood by the secular Socialist bodies of that time, and yet should have a Christian basis.[103]

---

[101] *Ibid.*, p. 63.
[102] *Ibid.*
[103] Sydney Dark, ed., *Conrad Noel, An Autobiography*, 1945, p. 59. As can be seen, Noel's memory plays him false here, as it does in a number of places in his autobiography. 'This work (edited by Dark) is posthumous and inadequate' (Stanley Evans, *Christian Socialism: A Study Outline and Bibliography*, Christian Socialist Movement Pamphlet 2, 1962, p. 18). The Morecombe Conference was called together by Algernon West.

Noel was clear about the way in which the League would combine the double-sided aims of its founding fathers.

Its basis was the belief that the Catholic Faith, as held and taught by the Church of England, finds its expression and application on the economic side in a Christian Socialism, which is not, as some appear to think, a particular variety of Socialism, milder than the secular brand but economic Socialism come to by the road of the Christian Faith and inspired by the ideas of the Gospel.[104]

Meanwhile Percy Dearmer was still involved in the organization of the ailing CSU, but he sent a message to a meeting of the League held in January 1910, telling them that he hoped to be able to disentangle himself in the near future. He wrote to friends, 'Now I shall soon be free and able to join up with you all'.[105] In 1912 the League launched the journal *The Church Socialist*, at about the time at which Peter Jones believed it reached the peak of its activities.[106] Conrad Noel had become its paid organizing secretary in 1907,[107] and under his energetic leadership there were by 1909 twenty-five branches with about 1,000 active members.[108] The League started in the north of England, as Noel recalled,

We poor Southerners . . . soon found . . . that the North had made its mind up; the socialist clergy of the North and Midlands were not happy in the CSU or the GSM and were determined on forming a new League.[109]

Later it became more and more a London-based federation with seventeen branches in London itself.[110] The Labour Party had come into existence in the same year as the League, 1906, and as Roger Lloyd has put it, the League was attempting to be 'the infant Labour Party's soul'.[111]

As time went by, however, differences of attitude and outlook among the members of the CSL became apparent. During the First World War there was a pacifist and a war-supporting division in the League,[112] but there were other disputes as well.[113] When the

[104] Dark, *op. cit.*, p. 60.
[105] Dearmer, *op. cit.*, p. 171.
[106] Jones, *op. cit.*, p. 261.
[107] Groves, *Noel*, p. 36.
[108] Jones, *ibid.*
[109] *Commonwealth*, vol. xl, No. 1, July 1908, p. 222.
[110] Jones, *op. cit.*, p. 261.
[111] Lloyd, *op. cit.*, p. 292.
[112] *Ibid.*, pp. 273–275.
[113] Groves, *Noel*, pp. 128–132.

National Mission of Repentance and Hope was launched in 1916 Percy Widdrington seized upon the idea with enthusiasm, stating that he could see in it a ray of hope for the Church of England. Widdrington could say this because the Mission had the aim of bringing about a reorientation of the Church's policy. Instead of putting all its efforts into a Church mission to individual souls, it would speak to the Nation and he quoted with approval from the Mission's own literature:

There is a real difference between a converted nation and a nation of converted individuals. All the citizens of a nation might be individually converted, and yet public life be conducted on principles other than Christian.[114]

Rather than being once again in opposition to the Church authorities, and out of sympathy with fellow churchmen, the Christian Socialists and the Church Socialist League in particular could endorse this venture, he was convinced. In this Widdrington was supported by Reckitt but not by Noel,[115] and it seems that this disagreement was the beginning of a more fundamental divide between the two Christian Socialist leaders,[116] so that when the war was over it became almost inevitable that, despite by now being near neighbours, their undoubted energies should be channelled in different directions: Widdrington's into the exposition of Christendom and the Kingdom of God, and Noel's into the more militant stance of The Catholic Crusade.

(d) Widdrington and 'The Kingdom of God'

In 1918 Percy Widdrington left St Peter's, Coventry to become Rector of Great Easton in Essex, sharing the patronage of the Countess of Warwick who had presented Noel to nearby Thaxted in 1910. By the time he arrived in Essex Widdrington was determined to work for the development of what he called a 'Christian Sociology'.[117] This was no new idea for him, for at the time of the setting-up of the CSL he had hoped to persuade his friends that this subject should be part of the Basis.

I was not altogether happy about the Basis. I had a feeling the most important purpose of a Church Socialist League was to elaborate a Christian

[114] Reckitt, *Widdrington*, p. 64.
[115] Groves, *Noel*, pp. 176–177.
[116] Reckitt, *Widdrington*, p. 65.
[117] *Ibid.*, p. 73.

approach to the problems of the new era. So I ventured to plead for the inclusion in the Basis of the adumbration of a Christian Sociology.[118]

He had to wait for almost twenty years for his vision to be recognized and adopted. At the CSL conference in 1923 negotiations aimed at reforming the League broke down, and it was dissolved in 1924. Noel having formed the Catholic Crusade in 1918, it was left to those who took Widdrington's point of view to create a new society, The League of the Kingdom of God.[119]

This new grouping arose out of a shared suspicion of the adequacy of the earlier Christian Socialist movements to demonstrate that the Kingdom of God is the essential character of the Gospel and that the fact that it is part of the Gospel has social consequences. Widdrington was distressed by the knowledge that the influence of organized Christianity on society as a whole was now almost negligible and thought that the disarray of European civilization was caused by the continuing renunciation of God by the nations 'and their repudiation of the Catholic tradition of the vassalage of every nation to the Kingdom of God'.[120] The only answer he believed was for the Church to free itself from its ecclesiastical preoccupations so that, 'aflame with the faith of the Kingdom', it would be 'compelled to adopt towards our industrial system the same attitudes which our missionaries take towards the social order of heathendom'.[121]

The Church's primary role in all this is very plain, and Widdrington made it even plainer with the slogan, 'No Church: No Kingdom'.[122] This is what was meant by 'a Christian Sociology', and another of the pioneers, the Rev'd N. E. Egerton Swann, was able to contend that it stood on three pillars: distributed property, the Just Price, and a guild organization of industry. Swann preferred to call it 'Catholic' sociology and claimed for it that it was:

purely the Church's own programme; and it is perfectly distinctive. It does not involve the Church taking over ready-made opinions from the Labour movement or from any secular philosophy like modern Socialism ... The position sketched out cuts clean across all existing cleavages. It would leave the Church in an attitude of sovereign independence, and might require it to defy alike the Labour movement and the plutocracy.[123]

[118] *Ibid.*, p. 45.
[119] Jones, *op. cit.*, p. 296; Reckitt, *Widdrington*, p. 93.
[120] Reckitt, *Widdrington*, p. 81.
[121] *Ibid.*, p. 83.
[122] *Ibid.*
[123] N. E. E. Swann, *Is There a Catholic Sociology?*, 1922, quoted in Reckitt, *Maurice to Temple*, p. 169.

From this it is clear that Christian Sociology is not what is currently known as Sociology of Religion and studied as such. The question asked at the time was whether Christian Sociology should aim to set forth a distinctively Christian type of living among the faithful or to act upon and dominate a society increasingly non-Christian in theory and practice. The Christian Sociologists believed that the first of these aims should always be part of the Church's programme, and it was the attempt to act upon, and as far as possible dominate, society in general that was the policy they needed to press upon the Church in the name of Christian Sociology.[124]

Widdrington and his friends were optimistic that the League of the Kingdom of God would attract large numbers of Anglo-Catholics into membership, but this did not happen. Reckitt explains it by arguing that many wished to remain aloof because of a dislike of its continuing Socialist associations.[125] Those Anglo-Catholics who were more cautious in social affairs and had perhaps been previously members of the Christian Social Union were more likely to have put their support behind the work of the Industrial Christian Fellowship[126] rather than the League of the Kingdom of God, which was still far from moderate in some of its statements for instance when it declared that 'the Catholic Faith demands a challenge to the world by the repudiation of capitalist plutocracy and the wage-system'.[127] Nevertheless, the Christian Sociologists exerted an influence which was in no way commensurate with the smallness of their numbers. They were the forerunners of the Christendom Group[128] and the Anglo-Catholic Summer School of Sociology,[129] both of which continued to have an influence over the Church of England's social witness until the 1950s.

(e) The Catholic Crusade

As has been seen, Conrad Noel did not share Percy Widdrington's enthusiasm for the National Mission of Repentance and Hope.[130] He

---

[124] John Lewis, Karl Polanyi, Donald K. Kitchin, eds., *Christianity and the Social Revolution*, 1935, pp. 199–200.
[125] Reckitt, *Widdrington*, p. 94.
[126] Studdert-Kennedy, *Dog Collar Democracy*, p. 94.
[127] Reckitt, *Widdrington*, p. 94.
[128] Reckitt, *Maurice to Temple*, p. 178.
[129] Reckitt, *Widdrington*, p. 97.
[130] See p. 96 ff, *supra*.

dubbed it 'the Mission of Funk and Despair', contracted out of the official campaign, and held his own parochial mission in Thaxted.[131] But there were other more basic issues which were causing a chasm to open up between Noel and Widdrington. In the first place Noel was completely sold on an uncompromising Socialist platform whereas Widdrington was moving relentlessly towards his pre-occupation with Christian Sociology.[132] There was also the often uncomfortable fact that Noel had little love for Protestant Nonconformity. In this he saw no ambiguity in combining a broad socialist faith with a narrow, almost sectarian, theology.

For Noel 'Nonconformity' and 'Christo-Capitalism' were synonymous terms of abuse. Christian socialism he regarded as the monopoly of Anglo-Catholics. Nevertheless, his Catholic Crusade, with its religious limitations, was 'radical': it claimed to champion for society at large 'a classless, co-operative world of free men and free nations'.[133]

In contrast with this, Widdrington, while remaining firmly Anglican, was more tolerant towards the other churches. In April 1918 a conference of the Church Socialist League was called to discuss its future. One of the proposals put forward was that the word 'Socialist' should be removed from the League's title. Although this was defeated it was removed from the League's statement of aims and methods. From this point onwards the League was not to be composed of 'people who accept the principles of socialism', and its members were not obliged to

cultivate the life of brotherhood by the use of prayer and sacrament ... to make manifest the social implications of our faith and worship ... To help the advance of Socialism by every means ... to convert Church people to the principles of Socialism, and to promote a better understanding between Church People who are not Socialists and Socialists who are not Church people.[134]

In the light of these decisions it was inevitable that Noel should see that the time had come to form an organization which would 'challenge rather than persuade'.[135]

The decision was taken at a meeting held in Thaxted Vicarage on 10 April 1918.[136] One of those present at the meeting was an ordinand,

[131] Groves, *Noel*, p. 176.
[132] Reckitt, *Widdrington*, pp. 71–85; Lewis, Polanyi, Kitchin, *op. cit.*, pp. 197–200.
[133] Jones, *op. cit.*, p. 301.
[134] Groves, *Noel*, pp. 200–201.
[135] Reckitt, *Widdrington*, p. 67.
[136] Groves, *Noel*, p. 202.

Jack Putterill. He described the new organization in his autobiography:

Towards the end of the first war Conrad Noel launched his Catholic Crusade. It was a movement of Catholic Anglicans, who were socialists and would work through the Church for a new economic society basing itself on the law and principles of the gospels and of the prophets and endorsing the teaching of the great fathers of the church like Ambrose and Chrysostom. The Catholic Crusade gathered quite a lot of members—Conrad Noel had a very attractive personality and many younger and adventurous priests joined. One of the early activities was a series of meetings called in London at Chandos Hall, near Covent Garden, where Conrad welcomed the Russian Revolution.[137]

Few organizations can have had so inauspicious a start. Reg Groves has said:

Less than a dozen people came to a meeting, and of them, only the Vicar, Conrad Noel was known at all outside the little Essex town. The war was in its fourth year; most of the younger men, and the most likely supporters of the new group were away on distant battle fields; and the attention of people at home was fastened on bloody fighting in France, where Allied armies were reeling back before an immense German offensive.[138]

'Catholic Crusade' was what the new society eventually became known as, but its original title decided upon at that inaugural meeting at Thaxted was 'The Catholic Crusade of the Servants of the Precious Blood to transform the Kingdoms of this world into the Commonwealth of God'.[139] Noel was clearly carrying out the advice of his friends who told him to 'form a more definite society at once with the Catholic Creed expressed in the Socialist faith'.[140]

While Widdrington's new League of the Kingdom of God was directing its efforts towards recapturing for the Church its lost and forgotten traditional social beliefs, Noel's Catholic Crusade was engaged in changing the world itself.[141]

The aims of the Crusade were frankly revolutionary. Noel foresaw a revolutionary situation once the war was over, and believed it was

---

[137] Jack Putterill, *Thaxted Quest for Social Justice. The Autobiography of Fr Jack Putterill—Turbulent Priest and Rebel*, 1977, p. 23.

[138] Reg Groves, *The Catholic Crusade: A reprint of its original Manifesto with an introduction and notes*, 1970, p. 2 (*cit.* Groves, *Crusade*).

[139] Groves, *Noel*, p. 203.

[140] Dark, *op. cit.*, p. 107.

[141] Jones, *op. cit.*, p. 296.

vital to have a disciplined, compact, ideologically united group of Catholic revolutionaries who would bear witness to their faith. In his view, this was the one way in which some wholesomeness could be given to the revolution.[142]

The Manifesto of the Catholic Crusade is set out as a series of propositions.[143] For instance the reader is asked:

"IF YOU BELIEVE in the Blessed Trinity and a Divine Commonwealth steeped in the worship of the Social God, in the Blessed Trinity, One-in-Many, Many-in-One, VARIETY IN UNITY, not as a senseless dogma for Sundays only, but as the basis and meaning of all human life; if you believe in recreating the world in the similitude of The Social God, in whom we live and move and have our being; if, in the love of This God you hate the present world which denies freedom, stifles initiative, poisons commonwealth, and will destroy it, or be destroyed in the attempt.

then it is axiomatic that you must 'HELP THE CATHOLIC CRUSADE'.[144] The Manifesto makes plain the revolutionary character of the Crusade by setting out 'the Catholic Doctrine of Revolution'.

Noel said,

If you believe in seizing power from below and not in social sops from above; if you believe in doing things swiftly for yourselves instead of waiting till the rich fling you a few slices of what you want, or the bishops allow you to do what the Church commands you to do, or till the great Slug-God Evolution evolves something, or Progress pushes you down into hell,[145]

then there is only one way to act, and that is to help the Catholic Crusade. And by this he meant helping

shatter the British Empire and all Empires to bits, wrestling against principalities and highly-placed powers; to Create a Free England in a Communion of Free Nations—a Free England.
IN WHICH, in the freedom of the Redeemer,
      the last shall be first and the first last;
IN WHICH, in the Spirit of Saint John the Herald,
      the valleys shall be raised and the hills levelled;

---

[142] Groves, *Noel*, p. 204.

[143] *Manifesto of The Catholic Crusade.* 'Available from The Literature Depot, Sneyd Vicarage, Burslem, Stoke-on-Trent', n.d.

[144] *Ibid.*, pp. 4–5 (capitals as in original booklet).

[145] *Ibid.*, p. 10.

IN WHICH, by the prayers of Saint James,
 the workers shall rejoice in that they are exalted,
 and the plutocrats in that they are brought low;
IN WHICH, in the eager desire of Our Lady,
 the mighty shall be dragged from their seat,
 the hungry filled, the rich sent empty away;
IN WHICH, in the prophecy of Saint John the Evangelist,
 the traffickers in oil and wheat and cattle and
 the bodies and souls of men shall lament, as
 the smoke of their burning cities ascends to
 the heavens;
IN WHICH, in the hope of Saint Cyprian,
 the essentials of life shall not be held by the
 few to the exclusion of the many;
IN WHICH, in the teaching of Saint Ambrose,
 the common property of the people shall be
 restored and all enslaving ownership disallowed;
IN WHICH, following Saint Gregory, who sent us Our Religion,
 the land will be for the workers, and none shall
 be owned by the shirkers.[146]

No wonder Maurice Reckitt can say,

It cannot be questioned that in virtue alike of the vigour and fertility of his mind and the force of his personality, Noel was for two full decades the real leader of the political and ideological Left in the Church of England.[147]

Members came along slowly during the rest of 1918, and though members grew as the Thaxted men, and sympathizers from among other Socialist groups, returned from active service, there were never great numbers of members.[148] There were two other factors which kept the numbers down. The first was the selection process by which membership was attained. A period of probation was enforced on applicants, and only after scrutinizing and debate at the Crusade's annual Chapter could full membership be granted. The second reason why the Crusade only grew slowly was its rule that groups could only be formed in a parish presided over by a Crusade priest. This was because the members were of the opinion that the Crusade made its point

not only, or mainly in words, but in the life of the church and parish, in cere-

---

[146] *Ibid.*, pp. 10–11.
[147] Reckitt, *Maurice to Temple*, p. 181.
[148] Grove, *Crusade*, p. 2.

mony as well as socialism, in sacrament as well as sermon, in plainsong as well as politics.[149]

Unfortunately few livings were held by Crusade priests. Bishops were hostile, to the priests' Socialism or Catholicism, and quite often to both. 'I know you are doing God's work', cried one unhappy Vicar to a Crusade curate, 'but why, oh why, did he send you to me?'[150] It was only where exceptional circumstances made a prolonged stay possible that the Crusader's mission could be fully expressed. Among those who achieved this were St John Groser in Stepney, Jim Wilson in Burslem, Jack Bucknall in Delabole, Cornwall, and Etienne Watts at All Saints', Manchester.

The Catholic Crusade asked a good deal from its members, who, though never numbering more than three hundred,[151] made themselves heard with great effect on numerous occasions and in several places. It eventually broke up on the Trotsky-Stalin issue[152] at a Chapter held at Burslem in 1936. However, the stalwarts of the anti-Stalin camp (Conrad Noel, Harold Mason, Jim Wilson, Jack Bucknall, and others) quickly formed a new group which they called The Order of the Church Militant.[153]

(f) The Order of the Church Militant

No time was lost in bringing together a consultation of members of the old committee of the Crusade. One of their first decisions was to found a new periodical. In this, *The Church Militant*, it was explained that for some years 'a cleavage both in temper and policy'[154] had been growing deeper within the Crusade so that the feeling grew that it was no longer able to speak to the world with a united voice. This came to a head in 1936 when it was clear that the majority were insistent on 'a severe criticism of Marxist philosophy and Russian action'[155] and were also anxious to return to what they understood as the original principles of the Crusade. It was agreed that it would be unfair for either of the differing parties to retain the label 'Catholic Crusade', and the new group under Noel started to look for a new title.

There was already a youth movement which called itself 'The Mili-

[149] *Ibid.*, p. 6.
[150] *Ibid.*
[151] *Ibid.*, p. 2.
[152] Evans, *op. cit.*, p. 27.
[153] Groves, *Crusade*, p. 23.
[154] *The Church Militant*, No. 1., November 1936, p. 2.
[155] *Ibid.*

tant Catholics' and was happy to merge with any new groupings, and after 'The Good Companions',[156] 'The Order of Divine Justice' and 'The Society of the Redemption' had been discarded as possible titles, 'The Order of the Church Militant' was adopted as the name for the new society. The aims of the Order were stated as being:

To revive the whole Catholic Faith, especially remembering such Articles of it as have been neglected.

To proclaim the Blessed Trinity as the Source, Sustenance and Goal of Life: striving to re-shape the World after the pattern of this Social God.

To accept Jesus as Redeemer of all nations, believing that His Church is to be the organ of a new World Order, in which none should be afore or after, none greater or less than another, yet a world not of dull uniformity but of variety in unity.

To create groups of people so filled with the Spirit, that they should be a fore-taste and inthrust of Christ's International Commonwealth.

TO THIS END

We would encourage the rising of the people in the might of the Risen Christ and the Saints, using persuasion and every ordered method to establish His Kingdom, leaving it to our opponents to resort to sedition and violence, if such must be their method, and only then ourselves resorting to arms in defence of righteous law.

To demand such proportion of common with personal ownership, as shall encourage our self-expression as free people in the fellowship.

To defend the individuality of the person, the family, the nation, and all natural groupings, within the fellowship of God's Commonwealth.

To obey all the rules of the Catholic Religion: not as ends in themselves but as means by which we train ourselves as eager and alert servants of the Redemption.

To require, therefore, in ourselves and in others, confession of sins to God and to man, and reformation of personal life, not for soul-saving but for service.

To revive all the Sacraments, especially in their forgotten social significance, and including the much neglected Sacrament of Unction and Healing.

To proclaim God's Eternal Standards amidst the changes and compromises of this shifting world.

The Order's periodical boldly proclaimed the political stance the organization was taking.[157] Although there was no Red Flag emblem on the front page there was the quotation:

His blood-red banner streams afar;

[156] *The Good Companions*, a novel by J. B. Priestley, was published in 1929.
[157] *The Church Militant*, No. 1, November 1936, p. 2.

Who follows in His train?[158]

It was equally strident in its attitude towards the way in which the Russian Communist state had developed:

We should be disloyal to the truth if we did not criticise freely, when occasion demands, any wrong tendency to Russia. We view with disquiet a government that appears to be hardening into a bureaucracy. The mass trials do not carry conviction. Pacts with capitalist governments weaken revolutionary fervour. We can admire what has been done—we have supported as far as we could Russia's wonderful achievements, but as true friends we cannot condone what seems to us wrong. Indiscriminate praise is the kind of praise which is valueless.[159]

The Order was officially committed to the Trotsky cause[160] and praised 'his wonderful achievements' and deplored 'the falsification of the records of the revolution in order to blot out his memory'.[161] However, this matter of Trotsky was once again to prove to be a subject of controversy and division among Christian Socialists (as among Socialists in general) when the Second World War broke out, and in the course of events the USSR entered the War on the side of the Allies, having disavowed the pre-war pact with fascist Germany which had disheartened so many of their former admirers in Western Europe.[162] With some difficulty an uneasy peace was maintained within The Order of the Church Militant during the lifetime of their main inspiration and leader, Conrad Noel.

Noel died on 22 July 1942 aged seventy-three, having been Vicar of Thaxted for just over thirty-two years.[163] He had been blind, because of diabetes, since 1935 but had continued his writing, being 'the same gay, courageous rebel he had always been'.[164] His obituarist was accurate in claiming that Noel was 'in the direct line of those who have striven to awaken England and the English Church, Maurice and Kingsley, Stewart Headlam and Charles Marson'.[165]

For Conrad Noel, the social and individual aspects of Christian life were bound up with one another and were quite inseparable. This, I am con-

---

[158] *Ibid.*, No. 1, p. 1, *seq.*

[159] *Ibid.*, No. 4, February 1937, p. 1.

[160] A belief in 'permanent revolution', Palmer, *op. cit.*, p. 368.

[161] *The Church Militant*, No. 44, September 1940, p. 2.

[162] Palmer, *op. cit.*, p. 275.

[163] Gordon Hewitt, *A History of the Diocese of Chelmsford. A History of the first seventy years of the Anglican Diocese of Chelmsford, from 1914–1984 and including an account of earlier Christianity in Essex and East London*, 1984, p. 134.

[164] Groves, *Noel*, p. 324.

[165] *The Church Militant*, No. 63, September–October 1941, p. 3. (For Marson see Reg Groves, *To the Edge of Triumph, A Study of Charles Marson*, 1985.)

vinced, is the true view, and our religion suffers very greatly from a tendency to isolate the individual life from its social context and to attend only to such influences upon individual character as can be exercised irrespective of those of the community itself. But the community is the greatest educator that exists, and the principles embodied in its structure are impressed upon the growing mind by a process of unceasing suggestion more potent than any exhortation or instruction. Consequently the right ordering of the community is an indispensable means to the right development of individual character. This is the truth which Conrad Noel grasped so surely, and he found a full and rich insistence upon it through the Bible and conspicuously in the New Testament.[166]

At Conrad Noel's Requiem at Thaxted a poem of William Morris was adapted and sung as a hymn; it contained the words:

Hear a word, a word in season,
    for the day is drawing nigh,
When the Cause shall call upon us,
    some to live and some to die.[167]

It was the specific details of what the 'Cause' should be which could not be agreed by members of the Order. Early in 1943 the two camps (pro- and anti-Stalin) were asked by the Order's Central Committee to set out in *The Church Militant*[168] their opinions on a series of subjects. Jack Bucknall and Hugh Benson gave one set of answers, while Jim Wilson provided another. They were clearly divided: for instance, on the subject of Russia, Wilson, although agreeing that there was much to criticize in that country, did not want criticism to undermine the Russian social order. In contrast Bucknall and Benson were anxious to denounce 'the essentially dictatorial nature of Stalin's regime',[169] and to expose atheistic communism and reveal its dangers. However, there was a more fundamental difference of opinion which struck at the very *raison d'être* of the Order, as Wilson understood it:

Although some of the clergy including a few Bishops now preach social righteousness they do not generally relate their social ideas to the faith, nor do they see the social significance of the Mass and the political action which naturally derives from it. Until this vital matter has been accepted I do not think we should stress in the paper matters which are calculated to put the people off from those important issues which have always been the driving force of The Catholic Crusade and The Order of the Church Militant.[170]

[166] *Ibid.*
[167] *Ibid.*, insert.
[168] *Ibid.*, No. 68, June 1943, pp. 2–3.
[169] *Ibid.*
[170] *Ibid.*

Sneyd, Burslem was once again the venue for a crucial Christian Socialist conference when the Order's Chapter met there on 13 and 14 November 1943. At this meeting it became clear what were the matters that Wilson believed were 'calculated to put people off from the important issues'. The Chapter adopted this resolution about its future programme:

> In view of the present situation the emphasis of the Order shall be on—
> A Christian Social Order which will be three-fold as elucidated by Rudolf Steiner.
> The exposure of the false socialism of Russia.
> The clear strategy of Revolution which may entail violence.
> The promulgation of spiritual service as the exposure of the false materialism of science today.[171]

The influence of some non-mainstream Christian theology can be detected in this resolution, particularly the influence of Rudolf Steiner.[172] In contrast those who now separated from the Order were clearly strictly orthodox and wished to promote those principles which they understood as belonging to the tradition of the Catholic Church. *The Church Militant* gave space for them to state their conviction that the immediate need of the Church was

> the rebuilding of its community life by forming groups, inspired with the social purpose of Christ which will challenge the false values of the world and become active in building Christ's Kingdom on earth.[173]

Thus, with Conrad Noel barely fifteen months in his grave, the Order of the Church Militant had divided asunder with Jack Bucknall and his friends going off to follow the ideas of 'that queer Genius'[174] Rudolf Steiner (and Bucknall himself eventually returning to the even more eccentric Rosicrucian ideas of his youth),[175] while Wilson and his colleagues[176] gave their mind to calling a conference for those interested in forming a federation of groups. It was this conference which led to the commencement of the publication called *The Leap*,

[171] *Ibid.*, No. 70, November–December, 1943, p. 8.

[172] *Rudolf Steiner, A Sketch of his life and work*, n.d., *passim*; 'German Spirituality', in Gordon S. Wakefield, ed., *A Dictionary of Christian Spirituality*, 1983, p. 171.

[173] *The Church Militant*, No. 70, November–December 1943, p. 8.

[174] V. A. Demant, *Theology of Society: More Essays in Christian Polity*, 1947, p. 178.

[175] *The Church Militant*, August 1954, not numbered, on the death of Bucknall.

[176] Nancy Price, H. O. Daniels, Fr Geoffrey Keable, Doris Pulford are listed as resigning: *ibid.*, No. 70, November–December, 1943, p. 8.

which was to have an important part to play in the history of the Parish Communion Movement.[177]

3   The Eucharistic Principles and Practices of the Christian Socialists

We now turn to look at the *liturgical* aspirations of those leaders of Christian Socialism whose political policies have already been described.

The association between high church sacramental theology and practice on the one hand and a sensitivity about social conciousness on the other, became increasingly explicit in the pastoral thrust of the work of those whom Athelstan Riley categorized as 'The Sub-Tractarians'. That is, those who built upon the teachings of the original Tractarians after 1845 and were the first Anglo-Catholic priests to believe that their vocation lay in ministering to those who were forced to live in the festering slums of the new industrial towns and cities of England.[178] The extent to which these priests needed to start from scratch in working out a Tractarian theology of social action to justify their ministry is a matter of debate.

Fifty years ago W. G. Peck argued that there were social implications to be derived, at least implicitly, from the teaching of the Tractarians[179] but more recently A. M. Allchin has stated that he finds such an opinion hard to sustain,[180] and in this he is supported by Peter Jones.[181] Dieter Voll finds evidence in the work of the Socialist slum-priests to sustain his thesis that there existed an underlying relationship between the Evangelical Revival and the Oxford Movement which comes together in a synthesis which he entitles 'Catholic Evangelicalism'.[182] The fact is, of course, that the clergy now had available both the writings of the Tractarians and of Maurice, and it was the implications of this particular combination, after it had passed through the hands of, first of all, Stewart Headlam and later Henry Scott Holland, rather than any other which gave these socialist Sub-Tractarians their *modus operandi*. However, Anselm Hughes, in his racy style, does not agree:

[177] See p. 141, *infra*.
[178] Marcus Donovan, *After the Tractarians*, 1933, p. 17. On Peck see James A. Pike, ed., *Modern Canterbury Pilgrims*, 1956, pp. 101 ff.
[179] W. G. Peck, *Social Implications of the Oxford Movement*, 1933, *passim*.
[180] A. M. Allchin, *The Silent Revolution—Anglican Communities, 1845–1900*, 1958, p. 218.
[181] Jones, *op. cit.*, p. 91, n. 9.
[182] Dieter Voll (trans. Veronica Ruffer), *Catholic Evangelicalism. The acceptance of Evangelical Traditions by the Oxford Movement during the second half of the Nineteenth Century. A contribution towards the understanding of recent Anglicanism*, 1963, p. 89 and *passim*.

Now men such as F. D. Maurice, Charles Kingsley, and Stewart Headlam are always referred to by subsequent writers and workers in the sociological field as the sources of their inspiration. But the slum priests, if they had even heard of these prophets or had read their writings, would most certainly have denied with vigour any suggestion that the source of their inspiration could be found elsewhere than in the four Gospels: and many of them, if catechized upon the intellectual basis of their practical efforts, would have replied shortly to the effect that they had neither spare cash to buy the books nor spare time to read them.[183]

Dom Anselm's personal (if not idiosyncratic) account of the Catholic Movement is to be read for its occasional good anecdote rather than as a reliable assessment of historical value. Instead, we shall examine carefully the influence of both the earlier and the later Christian Socialists on the worshipping life of the Church of England.

It is a demonstrable fact that the Christian Socialists of each succeeding phase looked upon John Frederick Denison Maurice as both the founding father and prophet of their Movement. In 1853 Charles Kingsley addressed him as 'dearest master';[184] Headlam listened to Pusey and found him 'awfully dull', whereas of a walk with Maurice in the early 1870s his biographer F. G. Bettany could say, 'the young man's heart burned within him as he moved beside the man who had given him inspiration and hope';[185] Henry Scott Holland speaks in 1897 of Maurice as 'a teacher of teachers above all' and declares that he believed that the Teacher's work had borne fruit to such an extent that 'it has even been said, "we are all socialists now"'.[186] Conrad Noel, in his autobiography, recorded that in the 1930s he had written that he was proud to claim membership of the Church of England because it was 'the Church of Maurice and Kingsley, of Scott Holland and Stewart Headlam', and that this was still his boast in the last years of his life.[187]

(a) The Sacramental Teaching of F. D. Maurice

Maurice's writings were prophetic and prolific; in his lifetime he produced nearly forty volumes which contained an average of 400 or 500

---

[183] Dom Anselm Hughes, *The Rivers of the Flood, A Personal Account of the Catholic Movement in the Twentieth Century*, 2nd ed., 1963, p. 118.

[184] Kingsley, *op. cit.*, I, 375 (cf. p. 373 'my dear master').

[185] Bettany, *op. cit.*, p. 22. Brenda Colloms, *op. cit.*, p. 256 mistakenly says 'He (Headlam) never met Maurice but he was profoundly influenced by the whole Maurician attitude to Church and Society'.

[186] *The Commonwealth*, vol. ii, No. 7, July 1897, p. 203.

[187] Dark, *op. cit.*, pp. 90–91.

pages apiece. Most of his writings were dictated, and they bear evidence of that, often repeating themselves and often being extraordinarily tangled and obscure. One of his early biographers, C. F. G. Masterman, testified to his obscurity,[188] and more recently A. M. Ramsey has spoken of Maurice as a bad writer, excusing him this fault only on the grounds that 'those for whom writing and talking and poking the fire were dangerously mixed up' are likely to find themselves in this position. Yet Ramsey believes that 'sometimes in his obscurity he could be telling the truth which clearer words might utterly fail to tell'.[189]

It is inevitable that we approach Maurice's writings with a certain expectation. As A. R. Vidler has said, from what we know of Maurice's theology we expect that his eucharistic teaching would draw out its social character and its universal witness. 'We shall not expect him to talk about "making my communion"' says Vidler.[190] We are not disappointed, for we find that it was this universal witness which Maurice was anxious to emphasize:

Do you think that any ordinance of Christ can have reference merely to the advantage or enjoyment of those who submit to it? If this feast does not show forth or declare something to the world, if we only seek in it for some benefit to ourselves, it cannot be a communion in the body, or in the mind of Jesus Christ.[191]

Individualism and self-serving piety have no part in such a concept of the Holy Communion or of the Church, Maurice taught. His thinking is dominated by an ardent desire for unity and fellowship for that which is universal and common to all and which can unite all men irrespective of rank or worth. Christensen in his study of Maurice's theology, to which he gives the title *The Divine Order*, says:

Maurice was the sworn enemy of individualism. Where he saw it loom large in the Church and in society, where he saw its fruits in the shape of barriers and dividing-lines between men, where he perceived particularism and exclusiveness, it aroused his passionate anger and called forth his sternest criticism.[192]

Writing to a correspondent who asks him about the Holy Commu-

[188] C. F. G. Masterman, *Frederick Denison Maurice*, Leaders of the Church 1800–1900 series, 1907, p. 219.

[189] A. M. Ramsey, 'The message of F. D. Maurice', in *Canterbury Pilgrim*, 1974, p. 41.

[190] Alec R. Vidler, *F. D. Maurice and Company: Nineteenth Century Studies*, 1966, p. 121.

[191] F. D. Maurice, *Sermons Preached in Lincoln's Inn Chapel*, IV, 1892, p. 100.

[192] Torben Christensen, *The Divine Order: A Study in F. D. Maurice's Theology*, Acta Theologica Danica, vol. xi, 1972, p. 245.

nion, Maurice urges her not to hesitate to frequent the Communion
Table, assuring her that no thoughts about our own feelings or qualifications, the amount of our faith, the consistency of our lives or the
sincerity of our repentance ought to keep us away from the Holy
Communion. We go to Communion, Maurice tells her, to ask that
God will give us what we have need of out of His fullness. Then he
goes on to make a more important point, to emphasize to her the
social significance of the Sacrament. 'But above all,' Maurice writes,

we want the witness and pledge of a common salvation, of a God who cares
for all in Christ as much as for us. [193]

Maurice acknowledges that there are problems about understanding
the nature of the eucharistic sacrifice and teaches that the Eucharist is
a feast celebrating the completed Sacrifice of Christ. [194] But when we
come to the Eucharist recollecting that perfect Sacrifice, Maurice
maintains, we are also asking that we might have a Spirit of Sacrifice
ourselves. We are, in effect, asking that

the Spirit, who is within us convincing us of righteousness, of judgement, may
dwell in us and quicken us to all the good works which God has prepared for
us to walk in. [195]

Torment about 'the meaning and extent and necessity of Christ's Sacrifice' [196] will not easily disappear, Maurice tells his correspondent,
but the more that the concept of Christ's Sacrifice is connected with
Communion,

the more you interpret its meaning, its extent, its necessity, by the fellowship
it establishes between you and God, between you and your brother ... the
more you will overcome these difficulties practically if not theoretically, and
the practical conquest of this is what we need, the other will come so far as we
require it. [197]

The 'practical' outcome of frequenting the Communion Table is thus
explained; it is for the good not only of ourselves but of our brothers
whom we are called to serve in 'the Spirit of Sacrifice'. 'Brotherhood'
and 'fellowship', as has been seen, are crucial words for Maurice.
Writing to Ludlow he further explained:

Socialism—or the acknowledgement of brotherhood in heart and fellowship

[193] *Maurice: Life*, II, p. 394.
[194] *Ibid.*, p. 365.
[195] *Ibid.*
[196] *Ibid.*
[197] *Ibid.*

in work seemed to me the thing which you were aiming at, the special craving of this time; the necessary fulfilment of the principle of the Gospel.[198]

It follows then that if 'brotherhood' and 'fellowship' are part of what is involved in Holy Communion, it is a further emphasizing of what Maurice believed, that the principles of Christianity cannot be expounded fully or satisfactorily except in terms of the Sacrament of the Holy Communion. Vidler says that for Maurice the Holy Communion expressed those principles 'in a deep, practical and universal way—in a way that dogmas cannot do, not even the Bible'.[199] Maurice himself asks where else he could find 'a Christianity of acts, not words, a Christianity of power and life . . . so exhibited as I find in this Sacrament?'[200]

It was Maurice's hope that the Church and churchmen would stop expending their energies on rivalry and argument over true doctrine and practice in relation to the Church, and instead use their precious resources in a more practical rivalry over what is the Church's true doctrine and practice in relation to society. Richard Heaton has carefully and thoroughly examined the inter-relationship of sacramental and ethical concerns in Maurice and has come to the conclusion that it was inevitable that the social movement in the Church of England, as it began with Maurice as the leader, should focus on what had given the Church its unique public role, namely its worship.

It was apparent by 1859, as the efforts of Maurice and his colleagues began to achieve some notoriety for Christian Socialism, that the worship of the Church could provide the best rallying point for reform in the Church and for the relating of the Church to social reform.[201]

Maurice would have perhaps been somewhat embarrassed by the more extravagant liturgical practices of many of the later Christian Socialists who nevertheless claimed him as their prophet. But these priests were convinced that they could have explained to him that their Sacramental Socialism was all a matter of natural progression. Indeed, Headlam was quite confident that he could have completely convinced his hero that a continuity existed between his more flam-

[198] *Ibid.*, II, p. 128.

[199] Vidler, *op. cit.*, p. 126.

[200] Maurice, *Kingdom*, p. 287.

[201] Richard L. Heaton, *The Inter-Relation of Sacramental and Ethical Concerns in the thought of Frederick D. Maurice, Henry S. Holland, Charles Gore and William Temple*, unpublished Edinburgh Ph.D. thesis, 1968, p. 58.

boyant liturgical style and Maurice's more austere and strictly Prayer Book observances, which had no additions or subtractions and no interest in ecclesiastical millinery, because both were based on a common teaching.

Headlam wrote:

> In certain directions I may have gone—have gone—further than Maurice went in his day—thus in my devotion to the service of the Sacrament of the Altar though not further, perhaps, than he would have gone had he been alive today.[202]

Or, as it has been said, the bulk of Maurice's 'honey' passed into the 'Ritualistic hive'.[203]

(b) The Sacramental Teaching of the Guild of St Matthew

It had already been shown how Liverpool-born Stewart Duckworth Headlam spearheaded, with the founding of his Guild of St Matthew in 1877, the second stage of the Christian Socialist Movement in the Church of England.[204] The Guild came on to the scene at a time which was reminiscent of the political and social situation that had faced Maurice and his followers earlier in the century. After twenty years of prosperity in the 1850s and 1860s the nation was now on the edge of the great depression. The old confident industrial prominence was now being challenged and optimism was beginning to fade. In addition there had been a series of agricultural disasters in the early 1870s which proved to be more serious and long-lasting in their results than any of the set-backs which industry or commerce had already suffered.[205] How the Guild of St Matthew saw its role and the role of Sacramental Socialists at a time when all around there were 'signs of the pressures and strains in a community undergoing the process of growth and change'[206] can best be seen through the pages of its journal *The Church Reformer*.

The Church Reformer appeared monthly from January 1882 and said from the beginning that it proposed to fill a gap, because none of the

---

[202] Bettany, *op. cit.*, p. 21.

[203] Masterman, *op. cit.*, p. 5; Hugh Martin, ed., *Christian Social Reformers of the Nineteenth Century*, 1927, p. 220.

[204] See pp. 89 ff, *supra*.

[205] G. Kitson Clark, *The Making of Victorian Britain. The Ford Lectures 1960*, 1962, p. 57.

[206] *Ibid.*, p. 64.

existing organs of church opinion were devoted exclusively, or even mainly, 'to momentous issues involved in the readaptation of the ecclesiastical machinery to the wants of the age, and to supply this need'. The new journal stated that it believed that it was beyond controversy that the work of the Church was being seriously impeded by the existing state of affairs. *The Church Reformer* acknowledged that although that generation was not responsible for the situation, it was none the less for them to prepare for the not too distant time when 'the National Church must stand for judgement at the bar of public opinion'. *The Church Reformer* called its readers to redeem the past and at the same time prepare for the future.[207]

'It goes without saying that *The Church Reformer* will not please everybody', its first editorial admitted, and for many months it concentrated in its pages on the plight of the unbeneficed clergy, the need for readjustment of clerical revenues, and 'the infamous trade in souls which is the shame of every son of the Church' by which was meant the sale of advowsons.[208] But from the first issue it had said it would 'plead for a fuller recognition of the rights of the poor to worship without let or hindrance in their parish churches',[209] and this 'Socialistic Christian Radical' paper[210] increasingly took up a positive approach to the subject of worship. In June 1882 it stated that it believed that a revision of the Book of Common Prayer was overdue for the good of the people.

The Prayer Book remains much as it was when first compiled; to the hurt of the English people, to the disgust of some, to the contempt of others, and to the, too just, support of the popular taunt that the Church of England is a rusty and old-fashioned machine which is sadly behind the times.[211]

In addition to advocating the removal of obsolete words and phrases, the excision of material now no longer useful and the simplification of rubrics, it spoke out against the grouping together of services, that is, against the combining of Matins and the Holy Communion, and perhaps the Litany as well, in one service. This custom, *The Church Reformer* was of the opinion, had proved to be completely unedifying to the ordinary folk of the industrial towns, and it condemned it roundly:

[207] *The Church Reformer*, vol. i, No. 1, January 1882, p. 1.
[208] *Ibid.* 'Advowson': The right of appointing a clergyman to a parish (*ODCC* (ed. 2), p. 20).
[209] *The Church Reformer*, ibid.
[210] Headlam, Letter, *ibid.*, p. 12.
[211] *Ibid.*, vol. i, No. 6, June 1882, p. 11.

What wonder if, instead of brightness and joy to dreary enough lives, such a service became but one more element of bitterness.[212]

Any Prayer Book reform which might be achieved, the journal suggests, was not to be regarded as final, but only as an adaptation to the needs of that present time. With commendable foresight, it lays down the principle that any new forms of worship,

will again need to be changed as the years roll on, in order that as long as the Church of England lasts it may preach Jesus Christ the same yesterday, today, and for ever, to living men and living women and living children in living homes.[213]

The first extended expression of 'Sacramental Socialism' comes in 1883. In the leader of the July issue the clergy are asked how far they have pondered the significance of the fact that they are called upon, by the Book of Common Prayer, to address all worshippers, rich and poor alike as 'dearly beloved brethren'. The clergy are reminded that they declare, 'by the most solemn sacramental rites' that all have been made members of Christ and that all are knit together in one mystical body. If they have grasped the significance of this, then the clergy are challenged by the leader writer to consider how far they are helping their poorer brethren to perceive in the Liturgy an expression of their social yearnings, or conversely, how far they are helping their richer brethren to 'set in the Christian faith the solution of the democratic problems'.[214] The anonymous leader writer then takes up one of F. D. Maurice's favourite themes by declaring that it will not be until all those who attend the celebrations of the Holy Communion are encouraged to think of their attendance as being 'for a larger purpose than their own personal salvation' that congregations will begin to understand them as expressing 'the inexpressible yet irrepressible instincts of humanity'.[215]

The Guild of St Matthew had as one of its three objectives the promotion of 'frequent and reverent worship in the Holy Communion',[216] and *The Church Reformer* was naturally anxious through its pages to promote this worthy objective. The Guild realized that, if it was going to be possible for church-people to worship at the Holy Communion with greater frequency, the first necessity was that 'the Holy Eucharist must be restored to its true position', and secondly

[212] *Ibid.*, vol. i, No. 7, July 1882, p. 11.
[213] *Ibid.*
[214] *Ibid.*, vol. ii, No. 7, 16 July, 1883, p. 1.
[215] *Ibid.*, p. 2.
[216] Bettany, *op. cit.*, p. 80.

that efforts must be made 'by every possible means to get rid of the notion that The Holy Communion is only for the select few'. Next, revealing its High-Church prejudices, *The Church Reformer* states that it is of the opinion that the service should be 'surrounded with all dignity and beauty of ritual and symbolism'. Finally in this programme of eucharistic renewal for the ordinary church people, not the privileged few, the journal advocates that the celebration of the Communion must be

at the best time in the day, not only early in the morning—certainly not after a long ornate Matins—but be made really the central act of worship. Having then assisted at the Divine Service, and from time to time made his communion, the Catholic Churchman will be free in conscience and in mind to enjoy the Lord's Day to the top of his bent.[217]

Here we have the advocacy of a fully worked-out programme of eucharistic worship for a parish in which the Holy Communion is to be at the centre of Sunday worship; where that service is celebrated at an hour at which it is possible for all to attend and where the parishioners, having been present at this service, are not placed under any pressure to attend further services, their duty having been done. This pattern suggested by the Christian Socialists in 1883 is as near perfect a prototype of what was later known as the Parish Communion as is discoverable until the experiment in 1890 of Frere, whose 'socialistic bent' has already been noted. The scheme has, unfortunately, one major flaw discernible in the phrase, 'from time to time made his communion'. It would seem that, as yet, there is no idea of a general communion of all the faithful in this revolutionary pattern. That ingredient had still to be added.

From the beginning of 1884 *The Church Reformer* decided to give less space to the abuses of patronage, the unequal distribution of clerical incomes, and the conditions under which the unbeneficed clergy worked, in order to concentrate more on getting people to understand that Baptism conferred a franchise, that the Church is a real society, and that each person admitted to that society has rights and duties to perform. That 'Church work' which was the responsibility of all members of the Body could, they believed, be 'briefly described as secular and socialistic'. To this end *The Church Reformer* says:

Every measure, whether social or political, which tends to bring about a better distribution of wealth and leisure will be supported by us. Because we are earnest loyal churchmen, we shall endeavour to be thorough Socialists.[218]

In the first edition in its new style, the Guild's journal emphasized once again its policy to promote frequent and regular communion,[219] and then at the end of that year indicated why Christian Socialists believed the Eucharist was so important:

Restore the Mass to its true position as the one, common, necessary service and you preach a gospel which infidelity and plutocracy must give way to. We would urge upon our readers that there is no point in church reform of more importance than this of restoring the Mass to its proper central place.[220]

It is interesting to note that this is the first time that the Eucharist is referred to as 'The Mass', a term which was to become the continuing custom for many Christian Socialists in succeeding years. We can be confident that this article was written by Headlam (he was named as Editor of *The Church Reformer* from January 1884). One of the original members of the Guild, the Rev'd W. H. C. Malton,[221] commenting on the fact that Headlam always refused to join the Anglo-Catholic English Church Union, said:

It is a fact, however, that the phrase 'It is the Mass that matters' was on his lips frequently long before it was in common use. Headlam used the word 'Mass' when to employ it was to be counted among the extremists. But it was part of his practice of giving things always their right names. He used the words he meant; he refused to hide or camouflage his meaning; there were no euphemisms or shams in his vocabulary.[222]

There were equally no euphemisms in further articles which appeared under Headlam's editorship (although we cannot be sure whether or not they derive from his authorship). In these articles the readers were challenged about the current Anglo-Catholic campaign for the restoration of the Eucharist to a central place in the Church's life and asked to consider if, now that so much was being made of the altar, it was also being made clear that the Mass was not for the select few but for all the people? Only in this way, would the Church be

exalting the revolutionary Carpenter, the great Emancipator and He himself

[218] *Ibid.*, vol. ii, No. 12, 15 December 1882, p. 1.
[219] *Ibid.*, vol. iii, No. 1, 15 January 1884, p. 18.
[220] *Ibid.*, vol. iii, No. 12, 15 December 1884, p. 269.
[221] Bettany, *op. cit.*, p. 82.
[222] *Ibid.*, p. 211.

will, with the fire of his presence, make it clear what He wants ... and many ... will be drawn by Him to work for the people's cause.[223]

In addition to the articles in *The Church Reformer* the sermons and lectures of Guild members give a clear indication of their teaching about the social significance of the Eucharist. In a sermon entitled 'What the church might do for London' in a course on social subjects, Headlam said that the most important thing that the Church could do was to make much more of the Holy Communion, because it told men that they were brothers not merely at church and in religion but in politics, labour, and life in general. He then deals with the three titles for the service: the Lord's Supper, the Eucharist, the Mass.[224] This is a subject he returned to when he published a series of lectures in which each of the Eucharistic titles were given a full lecture apiece. In the lecture on the Lord's Supper he employs a phrase which becomes popular with Christian Socialists and which we have already seen *The Church Reformer* using, Jesus as 'Emancipator'. In this sermon he speaks of the Lord's Supper as 'the Feast of National Emancipation'[225] and reminds his hearers that

At every administration of the Lord's Supper you should not be content to plead only your own personal needs, but should bring before the Saviour and Emancipator of mankind the needs of your nation.[226]

In the lecture on 'The Holy Communion' Headlam reminisced about the development of the past seventy years and remarked on the release from the restricting ideas of personal religion,

But Christ knew that Society was necessary, so that we might help each other, and hold together. And so during the past seventy years we have made much of the Holy Communion, the service that tells of brotherhood, solidarity, co-operation. Social religion has become as necessary as personal religion.[227]

Headlam, perhaps to the audience's surprise, spoke in his lecture of the early Christians as 'Communists', but he could have claimed Maurice's support for such an assertion.[228]

If the Church celebrates 'the Eucharist' with a spirit of thanksgiving the result can be infectious, Headlam asserted in his lecture on

---

[223] *Ibid.*, vol. iv, No. 12, December 1887, p. 286.
[224] Stewart Headlam, *A Lent in London, A Course of Sermons on Social Subjects*, 1895, p. 128.
[225] Stewart D. Headlam, *The Meaning of the Mass, Five Lectures with other sermons and addresses*, 1905, p. 18 (*cit.* Headlam, *Meaning of the Mass*).
[226] *Ibid.*, p. 23.
[227] *Ibid.*, p. 29.
[228] Maurice: *Life*, II, pp. 8–9.

that subject. He was of the opinion that the service should be performed in such a way that anyone casually coming into the church,
knowing little about theology or even religion, might be convinced
that the worshippers were really in earnest, that priest and people
alike were giving of their best.

Believe me, a church full of people here every Sunday at 10 o'clock, all
hearty, intelligent worshippers, would be more powerful for the Gospel in the
neighbourhood than years of eloquent sermons.[229]

The hour at which this exemplary service is taking place is note-
worthy—ten o'clock.

In the final lecture, on 'The Mass' Headlam justifies its use as holding up an ideal of international brotherhood and providing an antidote to 'our insolent, insular isolation'.[230]

'Brotherhood' is always an element which is focussed upon in the
eucharistic teaching of the Guild of St Matthew. Preaching at the
12th Annual Festival the Rev'd F. M. Garrett recalled the work that
had been done by Catholics for the restoration of the Eucharist to its
rightful place in the life of the church. But now that first battle had
been won, it was for the Guild to carry abroad the witness of the fact
that the Eucharist was not just for the strengthening of the individual.
In his sermon Garrett asserted:

If the unity of Humanity is shown at the altar to be a truth, it must influence
business, society, politics. The class divisions into which Society is split up are
no longer tolerable when they are seen to contradict that unity which is the
ground of all real Communion in Christ. Socialism ... is founded on the very
truth the Holy Communion has borne witness to through eighteen centuries—however deaf we have been to its message. Socialism asks us to deal,
not with isolated individuals, but with a community.[231]

Although *The Church Reformer* ceased to appear in 1895,[232] and the influence of the Guild of St Matthew faded as that of the Christian
Social Union grew, Stewart Headlam continued to speak out boldly

---

[229] Headlam, *Meaning of the Mass*, p. 42.

[230] *Ibid.*, p. 44.

[231] 'The Witness of the Eucharist to the True Social Life', Sermon preached in the
Church of St Mary the Virgin, Soho, at the 12th Annual Festival of the Guild of St
Matthew by the Rev'd F. M. Garrett. *The Church Reformer*, vol. viii, No. 11, November
1889, p. 252.

[232] *Ibid.*, vol. xiv, No. 10, October 1895, p. 222.

and persuasively for the cause of Christian Socialism and its more profound expression in the Holy Eucharist. He reserved some of his most barbed criticism for those who shared his enthusiasm for the Mass but had failed to see the vision of the socialist brotherhood gathered around the altar serving the deprived and poor, those who were more concerned about the niceties of rubrics and ritual:

Let them postpone the question as to the exact spot by the Altar at which the Gospel should be said until each one of their dearly beloved brethren has a comfortable home, and their children a clean bed, and good fresh air to sleep in, and a moderate amount of healthy food. These are the real questions of church order and discipline.[233]

These are vintage words from a Sacramental Socialist and pioneer.

(c) The Eucharistic Teaching of the Christian Social Union

The Christian Social Union, as has been observed,[234] was less exclusively Anglo-Catholic than the Guild of St Matthew. Robert Woodifield has said of them:

They were neither flamboyant Ritualists nor extreme Socialists of the type of Stewart Headlam, but they were Christian Socialists, deeply influenced by the teaching of Westcott and Maurice and thoroughly alive to the social and political no less than to the intellectual needs of the age.[235]

Their magazine was entitled The Commonwealth and was edited by Henry Scott Holland. In an introductory article Holland said 'the entire Commonwealth is touched if there be that in the social body which is diseased',[236] hence the name of the magazine.

Those who had been members of the Guild carried over into the Christian Social Union their understanding of the social implications of the Eucharist, although Llewelyn Davies[237] was not as militant in his advocacy of this isuse as perhaps Headlam might have been when

---

[233] The Optimist, vol. xi, No. 1, 15 April 1916, p. 49.

[234] See pp. 91 ff, supra.

[235] Robert Woodifield, Catholicism: Humanist and Democratic, Theology for Modern Men, iv, 1954, p. 96.

[236] The Commonwealth, a Social Magazine (cit, Commonwealth) vol. 1, No. 1, January 1896, p. 10; Paget op. cit., p. 206.

[237] A tangible link with F. D. Maurice. He was sent for to give Maurice his last Communion on Easter Day 1872, Maurice, Life, II, p. 641.

he gave a paper to the 1897 Church Congress at Nottingham on the Christian Social Union. In it he said:

We have vindicated the right to freedom of worship, and we are learning more and more of its due beauty and reverence. We have now to justify all we have gained by showing how it directly ministers to the moral elevation of mankind. It was in view of these social responsibilities which are common to all Christians alike that the Christian Social Union was founded.[238]

But there was no bitter rivalry between the Guild and the Union. In his address to the Annual General Meeting of the Guild at Sion College on 23 September 1889 Headlam generously said, 'We are, it is said, to be honoured by being imitated. A Christian Social Union is to be started . . . Good luck to them and more power to their elbow'.[239]

There is altogether a more intellectual air about *The Commonwealth* and it is far less likely to use the tub-thumping phrases of *The Church Reformer*. Yet it is, none the less, firmly committed to the same concepts about the Eucharist, as can be seen from this extract which does indeed use 'militant' phrases like 'fortress' and 'conquest':

Many of us have been led to sympathy with socialist ideals by the very pressure of sacramentalism. The sacramentalists taught us to ask for a transformation of Humanity here and now, by the possessing efficacy of the Divine Power tabernacling among men. Sacramentalism has not led us to exclude the secular earth, but to prophesy its entire inclusion within the working of that spirit which holds the sacraments as fortresses by which it can push forward to conquest.[240]

In *The Commonwealth* Holland used the Eucharist to make an important point about competition. He was convinced that competition was not 'the main original formative force' of the social order and that the church contained within itself an alternative model which ought to be used for the reordering and reconstruction of society. For Holland that more perfect way was shown to the world by the brotherhood and fellowship which is created, experienced, and sustained quite explicitly by the Christian Eucharist.[241]

It can be seen, then, that the Christian Social Union continued to teach through *The Commonwealth*, in Charles Gore's words, 'the essen-

---

[238] *Commonwealth*, vol. 2, No. 11, Nov. 1897, p. 336.
[239] *The Church Reformer*, vol. viii, No. 10, October 1889, p. 221.
[240] *Commonwealth*, vol. 5, No. 2, February 1900, p. 32.
[241] *Commonwealth*, vol. 2, No. 1, January 1897, p. 4.

tially social character of the sacraments'.[242] The same insights can be seen in the writings and speeches of those who were prominent in the Union.

Brooke Foss Westcott, Bishop of Durham,[243] was for many years the President of the Christian Social Union. His son said, 'No year in my father's later life would have been complete without some work done for the C.S.U'.[244] In 1890 he had fluttered 'the ecclesiastical dovecots' at the Church Congress with an address on Socialism,[245] and he used his practical sympathies to help settle the 1892 Durham Miners' Strike.[246]

Westcott was more in touch with the general public than the other important Cambridge scholars with whom he must be grouped: Lightfoot and Hort.[247] All three came under the influence of F. D. Maurice; none of them aimed at popular appeal; and Bernard Reardon says of Westcott that he had 'more than a little of the Maurician obscurity'.[248] Nevertheless Westcott was able to exercise a wide influence, not least through his preaching which communicated his clear concern about the social and industrial problems of the day. But even then his uttered words were not the actual means by which his influence was exercised. Even Scott Holland had to admit that:

There was a famous address, at the founding of the Christian Social Union, delivered to us in Sion College, which none who were present can ever forget. Yet none of us can ever recall, in the least, what was said. No one knows. Only we know that we were lifted, kindled, transformed. We pledged ourselves; we committed ourselves; we were ready to die for the Cause; but if you asked us why, and for what, we could not tell you. There he was; there he spoke; the prophetic fire was breaking from him; the martyr-spirit glowed through him. We too, were caught up. But words had become only symbols. There was nothing verbal to report or to repeat. We could remember nothing, except the spirit which was in the words; and that was enough.[249]

Like his inspiration Maurice, Westcott understood in the gospel

[242] Ibid., vol. 8, No. 3, March 1903, p. 70.

[243] 1890–1901, DECH 3rd ed. 1948, p. 192.

[244] Arthur Westcott, Life and Letters of Brooke Foss Westcott DD, DCL. Sometime Bishop of Durham, 1903, II, p. 281.

[245] Ibid., p. 111. Text of address in Brooke Foss Westcott, The Incarnation and Common Life, 1893, pp. 223 ff.

[246] Geoffrey Best, Bishop Westcott and the Miners, The Bishop Westcott Memorial Lecture 1966, 1967, passim.

[247] Bernard M. G. Reardon, From Coleridge to Gore: A Century of Religious Thought in Britain, 1971, pp. 346–359.

[248] Ibid., p. 346.

[249] Henry Scott Holland, Personal Studies, 1905, pp. 131–132.

proclamation of man's unity a necessary consequence of social obligation. This brought him to a socialism which was always ethical rather
than political, a socialism which was antidote to the principle of self-
interest and individualism. As he expressed it in that address to the
Church Congress in Hull in 1890:

The aim of Socialism differs from Individualism both in method and in aim.
The method of Socialism is co-operation, the method of Individualism is competition. The one regards man as working with man for a common end, the
other regards man as working against man for private gain. The aim of
Socialism is the fulfilment of service, the aim of Individualism is the attain-
ment of some personal advantage, riches, or place, or fame. Socialism seeks
such an organisation of life as shall secure for every one the most complete development of his powers; Individualism seeks primarily the satisfaction of the
particular wants of each one in the hope that the pursuit of private interest
will in the end secure public welfare.[250]

For Westcott this work would be done by bringing 'the doctrine of the
incarnation to bear upon the dealings of man with man and of nation
with nation'.[251] This 'incarnationalist' theology, as it has been called,
provided the ultimate rationale of his Christian socialism, a conviction which was equally true of Charles Gore, one of those who in the
next generation of theologians brought together both their theology
and their social consciousness.[252]

  In the Christian Socialist pantheon no one in the period from the
last quarter of the nineteenth century through to the end of the First
World War shines more brightly, or attracts more adherents, than
Henry Scott Holland. Like Headlam he was an Etonian, having had
the same tutor, and was himself a disciple of Maurice.[253] Like Headlam he quickly recognized the need for the church to move out from
'dreamy old agricultural pastoral sleepiness'[254] and to tackle such
areas as the London slums.

It is the one thing set before us to do in this age, and it has all to be done—a
new temper lies hid there, a new religious want; and the Church has done
nothing yet to fit itself on to the new force. One feels so certain that if this
generation of ours cannot manage it, it will never be done.[255]

[250] Westcott, *The Incarnation and Common Life*, op..cit., p. 226.
  [251] *Ibid.*, pp. 233–234.
  [252] Westcott had no liturgical interests, although one of his biographers says that he
was 'always anxious for a weekly communion to be instituted'. Joseph Clayton, *Bishop
Westcott*, Leaders of the Church 1800–1900 Series, 1906, p. 147.
  [253] Reckitt, *Maurice to Temple*, p. 136.
  [254] Paget, *op. cit.*, p. 61.
  [255] *Ibid.*

Holland would not be unaware of the outstanding examples of such heroic attempts as those of Mackonochie, Lowder, Prynne, or Dolling, 'the pioneers in the parish', to make sacramental worship the centre of the church's ministry in areas of urban deprivation.[256] Dolling had connections with the Guild of St Matthew and gave a Quiet Day for its members at St Frideswide's, Poplar in 1891 at which he praised the example of F. D. Maurice and also told members that they should 'prove the sufferings of the poor by suffering with them'.[257] Despite this, Holland and his friends felt that there was at that time no society which continued the spirit of Maurice. Of the Guild they said:

There was the Guild of St Matthew: but while we felt grateful for it, it did not in some ways suit our purposes. So the movement agreed to find its own organ in a new Society, and the Christian Social Union was the result.[258]

The new society was 'to awaken the Church ... to the social duties which, if it wished to claim the names of Christian and Catholic, it could not ignore'.[259] This the Christian Social Union did by a more theological approach than that which the Guild had employed. Holland was a theologian, a claim that Headlam would never have made for himself. Maurice Reckitt contrasted them in this way: Headlam 'strove to vindicate the outcasts and defy their oppressors', he not only stood for the people's cause, he was also at home among them. Whereas Holland, spontaneous and unconventional as he was, was always 'a don among dons'. His interests were primarily academic and he sought to win men to his own understanding of what that interpretation required.[260]

Charles Gore could say of Holland that he never fell into the ways of those enthusiastic preachers of the social gospel who had sat very loosely to orthodoxy of belief and therefore had caused people to identify the social message with lax theology. This kind of accusation could never be made of Holland, Gore asserted, because he derived the motives for his crusade not only from the doctrine of the Incarnation but also from the doctrine of the Holy Trinity, which doctrine, Gore writes,

bids us see in God's eternal being a fellowship of persons, a fellowship of love,

---

[256] Geoffrey Rowell, *The Vision Glorious: Themes and Personalities of the Catholic Revival in Anglicanism*, 1983, pp. 116–140.

[257] *The Church Reformer*, vol. xi, No. 1, January 1892, p. 17.

[258] Charles Gore 'Holland and the Christian Social Union', in Paget, *op. cit.*, p. 242.

[259] *Ibid.*, pp. 242–243.

[260] Reckitt, *Maurice to Temple, op. cit.*, p. 137.

which must be reproduced in every society of men, made in the divine image, if they would be true to their origin and purpose.[261]

And when this doctrine of the Trinity is taken together with the understanding of the Church and the sacraments as 'the extension of the incarnation',[262] it gave Holland the warrant for the type of ministry he advocated. For he saw

the doctrine of the Church and the sacraments, as the continuous expression of the incarnation which at every point teaches us that our union with God is not otherwise to be realized than in fellowship of men with one another.[263]

Gore saw the roots of Holland's being running deep into Catholic theology, and although he believed that he would have liked to widen the Tractarian outlook, he never showed signs of deserting it. 'Social enthusiasm, for him, flowed inevitably from that fountain and that fountain alone'.[264]

Some indication of the way in which Holland might have liked to 'widen the Tractarian outlook' can be seen in one of his last published books. It appeared during the 1914–18 war and in it he reflected upon the then current controversies regarding Reservation of the Blessed Sacrament.[265] Holland is impatient:

It would be a strange and cruel bit of irony if, at such an hour, just when the worst and blackest moment of the war has been reached, the Church should select this occasion for showing itself incapable of self-control and of keeping of the peace. It would be all the more disastrous if this open strife broke out over matters that belong to the spirit.[266]

It has been seen how the National Mission received a mixed reception from Christian Socialists,[267] but Holland does not hesitate to derive lessons from its experience. He said that the Mission had revealed how individualistic and self-preoccupied worship was in the Church of England; it had not generated any power for good:

We have crowded our beautiful churches with devout worshippers, who have

---

[261] Gore in Paget, op. cit., p. 246.

[262] The phrase was applied by Jeremy Taylor (1613–1667) to the Eucharist in *The Worthy Communicant*, chap. 1:2, quoted in A. M. Ramsey, *From Gore to Temple: The Development of Anglican Theology between Lux Mundi and the Second World War 1889–1939. The Hale Memorial Lectures of Seabury-Western Theological Seminary 1959*, 1960, p. 115.

[263] Gore in Paget, op. cit., p. 246.

[264] *Ibid.*

[265] See p. 35, *supra.*

[266] Henry Scott Holland, *Sacramental Values*, n.d. (1917) (cit., Holland, *Sacramental*) p. 2.

[267] Cf. pp. 96 ff and pp. 99 ff, *supra.*

fed their souls on Holy Food from the Altar, Sunday after Sunday, year after year; and yet how much power had gone abroad to shake the tyrannies of wrong and to carry forward the Kingdom. Round many such churches the thick darkness of evil has hung unrepelled.[268]

Holland condemns this type of Anglo-Catholicism which 'leaves the slums to reek with shame and misery'. They are 'no better than the stuffiest Anglicanism', he says, having failed to realize that sacramental belief in the sanctity of the Body demands much more. The worshippers pour in 'to take of the food, to feed on the glory, to yield their souls to the Hush and the Holy', and meanwhile nothing changes in the grim environment around them,

and if you want to know why, you have only to look into the little books of holy devotion in their hands which were so wholly taken up with personal and individual details of self-examination, so pre-occupied with self-direction, self-practices, self-oblation, self-correction, that all memory of corporate and social responsibility had vanished away.[269]

Holland grants that there have been notable exceptions and he specifically mentions Fr Stanton and Fr Dolling 'who gave their hearers no rest, they drove them to public service'.[270] On these grounds he expressed himself very unhappy at the increasing cultus surrounding the Reservation of the Blessed Sacrament. Holland feared that it would hold the worshippers 'entranced within the shrine' and leave no place in their thoughts and imaginations for

the energetic life of the Kingdom of God with its war against wickedness in high places, its prophetic aggression, its sweeping advances, its worldwide demands.[271]

There is no sign in this of any kind of timidity in proclaiming the message of sacramental socialism. Perhaps it was because Holland saw God's judgement in the affairs of the age. Speaking on 'The Coming of Christ' in Liverpool at about the same time, he warned the congregation in the Church of Our Lady and St Nicholas that in that 'Coming' the significance of all the past would be summed up in a moment and then be revealed.

[268] Holland, *Sacramental*, pp. 12–13.
[269] *Ibid.*, p. 13.
[270] *Ibid.*, pp. 13–14.
[271] *Ibid.*, p. 14.

The hidden secret which has always been true, that even in the act by which we work out our salvation it is God that worketh in us, will be made manifest when God openly and overpoweringly enters on the scene to fill it with Himself. So the Eucharist, the typical expression of that slow inward movement by which the Spirit lays hold on the earth, here loses its sense of the pressure of that final Appearing. Grace rests on the Coming.[272]

Contemporary with Holland, and like him a follower of Maurice and a member of CSU, as well as a member of the Holy Party was Charles Gore.[273] He preached that:

We deny the verity of the Incarnation in its principle if we deny the Christian spirit the privilege, aye, and the obligation, to concern itself with everything that interests and touches human life.[274]

He too, saw great significance in the word 'brotherhood', speaking of it as 'the heart and soul of churchmanship'.[275] This brotherhood would be strengthened and sealed by the Holy Communion received in the Eucharist. For Gore the separation of Communion from the Eucharist, the idea of a high celebration at which only the priest received communion, was an abomination. Headlam's implied idea that Communion would only be received occasionally represented for Gore a defective theology. He expounded this in his book *The Body of Christ* which influenced many who were not taking the Anglo-Catholic line, which was frankly imitative of current Roman practice. Gore pointed to the directions of the Book of Common Prayer which he said

were deliberately calculated to make the communion of the people, or of sufficient number of their representatives, an indispensable element in a celebration of the Eucharist; so much so that, when communicants were not forthcoming, the celebration was not to take place.[276]

He also advocated a 'parochial communion', an idea which will be examined later.[277] He too, like Holland, was unhappy about the extra-liturgical cultus of the Reserved Sacrament, being of the opinion that

---

[272] H. Scott Holland, *The Real Problem of Eschatology, Liverpool Lecture 1916, delivered in St. Nicholas Church, Liverpool on 19 June 1916.* Liverpool Diocesan Board of Divinity Publication No. xiv, 1916, p. 12.

[273] Prestige, *op. cit.*, p. 97. The degree to which Gore was influenced by Maurice has been more recently questioned, cf. James Carpenter, *Gore: A Study in Liberal Catholic Thought*, 1960, pp. 244–245.

[274] Quoted Carpenter, *op. cit.*, p. 244.

[275] *Ibid.*, p. 252.

[276] Gore, *Body of Christ*, p. 274.

[277] See p. 166, *infra.*

'the eucharistic presence is controlled by the purpose for which the sacrament was instituted'.[278]

Gore became the President of the Christian Social Union in 1901 on the death of Westcott.[279] But on its reorganization in 1910 he resigned, 'saying that he thought that it would be better if it were now to be wound up and a new organization formed in order to "liberate forces into another channel"'.[280] This proved to be the Industrial Christian Fellowship.[281] Gore had already tried to give up the Presidency in 1906, feeling at that time that it would be better to leave the Christian Social Union to go its own academic way and let the Socialists make a fresh start. He himself had already 'turned from mere enquiry into social problems to active advocacy of particular reforms'.[282] In the event he did not join the Church Socialist League and carried on, somewhat half-heartedly, with the Christian Social Union. It is to the sacramental ideas of those who were following what Gore acknowledged[283] as a more distinctly socialist line that attention must now be given.

(d) The Sacramental Teaching of the Church Socialist League

In 1906 the Rev'd Samuel Proudfoot founded, a review which he called The Optimist. It was the result of an idea born at the annual reunion of the Manchester Scholae Episcopi on 18 July 1905. He discerned at that meeting 'a questioning spirit ... which could not be satisfied with the present organisation of society ... In a word it was tacitly admitted that there was a Social Problem'.[284] Having come to this conclusion Proudfoot decided he could help best by founding a review. In the first issue Proudfoot said that, at a time 'when Social questions were so urgent', he wished that the books of Maurice might be 'more frequently found on the shelves of rich and poor alike'.[285] The first few issues took an interest in the local meetings of the Christian Social Union[286] but the fourth issue contained an article with the heading 'A Notable Gathering'. This article described the meeting at

---

[278] Gore, Body of Christ, p. 276.

[279] Prestige, op. cit., p. 241.

[280] Ibid., p. 282.

[281] Studdert-Kennedy, Dog-Collar Democracy, p. 4.

[282] Prestige, op. cit., p. 274.

[283] Studdert-Kennedy says Gore was 'nudging Socialists at Mirfield ... towards the "Church Socialist League"' (Studdert-Kennedy, Dog-Collar Democracy, p. 15).

[284] Optimist, vol 1, No. 1, January 1906, p. 3.

[285] Ibid., p. 47.

[286] Ibid., p. 7.

Morecambe on 13 June 1906 at which the Church Socialist League was formed.[287] At the Scarborough Conference of the new League held a year later, on 2 June 1907, it was decided to vote *The Optimist* £4 per quarter from League funds,[288] and the following year it was announced that '*The Optimist* is now the exclusive property of the Church Socialist League'.[289] As a consequence of this from the beginning of 1909 it was known as *The Church Socialist Quarterly or Optimist*[290] until 1913 when it reverted to being again simply *The Optimist*. After this the editor of *The Optimist* tried to work in association with the University Settlement Movement. F. J. Marquis of the Liverpool University Settlement was made an associate editor.[291] But this arrangement proved unworkable, and publication came to an end in 1916.[292]

In January 1912 the Propaganda Committee of the London branch of the League published the first edition of *The Church Socialist* as an attempt to provide a monthly magazine which would not only have interest for the members of the London branch but might also be a link between the various branches and the scattered members of the League. It was also hoped that it might be 'a means of propagating our views among the general public'. In 1912 responsibility for *The Church Socialist* was assumed by a central Literature Committee of the League.[293]

In order to discover the Sacramental teaching of the Church Socialist League *The Optimist*, *The Church Socialist Quarterly*, and *The Church Socialist* will all be examined.

In 1906 *The Optimist* gave a most enthusiastic, if brief, review to a book by W. H. Abraham, *The Position of the Eucharist in Sunday Worship*.[294] In this book Abraham argued for a 9 a.m. Eucharist. Would it not be possible, the anonymous reviewer asked, for many more parishes to have a Sung Eucharist at 9 a.m. with a short sermon? From what experience Abraham was writing cannot be gauged, but, he says, 'where such a service has been provided, excellent results have followed'.[295]

---

[287] *Ibid.*, vol 1, No. 4, October 1906, pp. 63–65.

[288] *Ibid.*, vol. 2, No. 3, July 1907, p. 130.

[289] *Ibid.*, vol. 3, no. 4, October 1908, p. 250.

[290] *The Church Socialist Quarterly or Optimist (cit. CSQ)*, vol. 4, No. 1, January 1909. *Ibid.*, vol. 3, No. 4, October 1908, p. 250.

[291] *Optimist*, vol. 8, No. 3, July 1913.

[292] *Ibid.*, vol. 11, No. 4, October 1916.

[293] *The Church Socialist*, vol. i, No. 1, January 1912, p. 1.

[294] W. H. Abraham DD, *The Position of the Eucharist in Sunday Worship*, 1904.

[295] *Optimist*, vol. 1, No. 4, October 1906, p. 67.

The following year G. W. E. Russell contributed an article to *The Optimist* in which he wrote of the Eucharist 'as the central Mystery of the Catholic faith', and that round this the ideal church would arrange her worship 'with a generous latitude in details and incidents and with an elastic richness'. Russell saw this richness as resembling 'the pliant growths and many-coloured raiment of the natural world'.[296] This kind of language prefigures the more 'Bohemian' approach to the Sacraments which developed as Conrad Noel emerged as a leader of one section of the Christian Socialists.

There is a good deal of confidence and self-congratulation among members of the League in the wake of the 1906 Liberal Victory with its high proportion of Labour MPs returned. They say,

it is common knowledge that those who are called Sacerdotalists in the Church of England are in the van of all progressive movements. Hundreds have given their unflagging support to the Labour Movement and Socialist clergy within the Church are a very large and increasing body.[297]

'But who are the Sacerdotalists?', *The Optimist* asks. Replying to its own question the magazine expresses the hope that every priest in the Church of England would rejoice in the name, because it expresses 'all that is best in Catholic teaching and practice'.[298] It then visualizes the priest standing in the midst of his people

celebrating common bread and common wine with common rites at a common table and it would be strange indeed if he did not learn therefore that he was compelled to be in every way a 'Holy Communist'.[299]

When the ninth edition of Percy Dearmer's *The Parson's Handbook* was published in 1907 there appeared an important review. *The Optimist* reviewer, J. H. Hastings, said that in the first place perhaps the most important lesson to be learnt from the book was the imperative need to reinstate the Holy Communion in its right and proper place as the chief service of each Sunday. He said,

This should be the aim of every earnest person, whether he uses much or little ritual.[300]

[296] *Optimist*, vol. 2, No. 1, January 1907, p. 13.
[297] *Ibid.*, vol. 2, No. 3, July 1907, pp. 126–127.
[298] *Ibid.*, p. 127.
[299] *Ibid.*
[300] *Ibid.*, p. 211.

Hastings then goes on to pick up a crucial suggestion that Dearmer makes in this new edition. Instead of Matins being the climax of morning worship, Dearmer suggests that it should precede the Sung Eucharist at 9.00 a.m. or 9.30 a.m.[301] Hastings, in his review, says that 'the hour of eleven' is not sacred as the service time and that in many places it would be found advantageous

to revert to the old canonical hour of nine for the principal Eucharist of the Sunday. *The Parson's Handbook* will give much help to those who desire to return to the real mind of the church on this point, which is also the mind of the Primitive Church, to which we appeal so often in other matters, but to which, strangely enough, we so seldom hear this appeal as to the position of the Holy Communion.[302]

Here we have one Christian Socialist firmly supporting the proposals of another for a more enlightened pattern of worship which would make the Eucharist available to all, because that service, *par excellence*, speaks of the mission of the church to every part of life, a point which is emphasized in an article by Paul Stacey in the very same issue of *The Optimist*. The Lord's Service, says Stacey, shows how the sacramental system is bound up with our daily life and if it is the Lord's service it is also the People's Service in which 'the great Liberator' speaks to all of 'Divine Socialism, of which all partial socialisms are but the faintest image'.[303]

The first mention of a feature in the Eucharist which became one of the rallying-points in the forthcoming Parish Communion movement comes in 1908. In an article entitled 'An Internal Policy for Socialist Churchman'[304] Stephen Liberty, the Sub-warden of St Deiniol's Library, Hawarden, in urging the restoration of the Eucharist 'on social grounds', made an appeal that care should be taken:

to make the oblations of the elements understood to be a real offering of the product of the people's labour.[305]

No ceremonial suggestions are made, there is no mention of an 'Offertory Procession', there is merely the theological point briefly made.

---

[301] Percy Dearmer, *The Parson's Handbook*, 7th ed., 1909, p. 209.

[302] *Optimist*, vol. 2, No. 3, July 1907, p. 211 (for derivation of the phrase 'canonical hour' see p. 165, *infra*).

[303] *Ibid.*, p. 212.

[304] *Ibid.*, vol. 3, No. 3, July 1908, pp. 198 ff.

[305] *Ibid.*, p. 205. This dating contradicts Buchanan's contention that the Offertory Procession has its origins in an imitation of Roman Catholic usage at Klosterneuburg and confirms its Anglican—and Sacramental Socialist *provenance*. Cf. Colin Buchanan, *The End of the Offertory: An Anglican Study*, Grove Liturgical Study No. 14, 1978, p. 29.

The theme of offering is always a theme for the Sacramental Socialists. They see the inevitable connection between the Eucharistic Sacrifice and the sacrifice of service to which worshippers are called. G. C. Binyon wrote in another article[306] that all are the guests of God at the Holy Table where there can be 'no fellowship without service, no unity without bearing and forebearing, no communion without sacrifice'. So the Holy Table is also the Altar of Sacrifice and the service in church is a rehearsal for our service out in the world. That is why we offer to God

in intelligent, disinterested and active service our sacrifice on behalf of our fellow men.

The result is that the communicant leaves the church strengthened and renewed by the fellowship of Christ and his Saints, seeing a brother in everyone he meets,

and as His Master's Body was broken and Blood shed in the cause of the Kingdom of God, so, willingly, joyfully, he accepts pain and sacrifice, spends himself, goes on undismayed by disappointment or failure, if so be that haply he may set forward God's Kingdom, which is for the world's atonement and the unveiling of Christ.[307]

The Church and the Sacraments as the extension of the Incarnation is a commonly repeated idea in the pages of the League's journals. Hewlett Johnson, who had become Vicar of St Margaret's, Altrincham in 1908,[308] took this theme a stage further when he wrote of the communicant fed by the Body of Christ being the Body of Christ in the world. He used an idea which has been popularized in a prayer said to derive from St Teresa of Avila. Hewlett Johnson wrote:

You it is who are henceforth to be my Body. You are My eyes, feet, hands, lips: you are the Body with which henceforth I live on earth and work My Father's will.[309]

During the War the divisions in the ranks of the Church Socialist League became increasingly apparent, and at the cessation of hostilities The Catholic Crusade and The League of the Kingdom of God,

---

[306] *CSQ*, vol. 4, No. 4, October 1909, pp. 334 ff.
[307] *Ibid.*, p. 338.
[308] Hewlett Johnson, *Searching for Light, an Autobiography*, 1968, p. 40.
[309] *CSQ*, vol. 6, No. 1, January 1911, p. 18.

as has been said, went their separate ways. Their sacramental attitudes will be considered separately, taking first those of the League and its brainchild the Summer School of Sociology.

(e) The Sacramental Principles of the League of the Kingdom of God

The newly formed League drew up a list of six objects:

1. The insistence on the prophetic Office of the Church, and the Kingdom of God as the regulative principle of theology.
2. The awakening of Churchmen to the lost social traditions of Christendom and the re-creation of a Christian sociology consonant with the needs of the age.
3. The restoration of the Eucharist as the central act of Christian worship—the Sacrament of fraternity and the embodiment of Christian values.
4. The recognition and enforcement of the Church's social discipline over her own members.
5. The winning of those indifferent or hostile to the Catholic Faith while standing for justice in the common life, and those within the Church who resist the Christian ordering of society.
6. Co-operation with other bodies, religious or secular, on occasions when fundamental issues of social righteousness are at stake.[310]

In the third object the League made it clear, at the outset, the basis of its Eucharistic policy and it used its journal *L.K.G. Quarterly* to propagate its viewpoint. Under the initial editorship of Dudley Symon, then the Headmaster of Woodbridge School and later to be one of the 'founder members' of the Church of England Liturgical Commission,[311] and then later under the editorship of W. G. Peck, a Manchester incumbent, it vigorously applied itself to the task. 'All English Catholics are desperately anxious to see the Blessed Sacrament is accorded the rightful place in the life and worship of the Church', an editorial said.[312]

During the 1928 debate on the Prayer Book the League argued that the only people who could pacify the fears of Englishmen concerning Sacramental religion were the Anglo-Catholics themselves. In this operation they believed that Sacramental Socialists had an important part to play, because they could help both to clarify doctrine and also to state forcefully the practical implications of a Eucharistic emphasis. The League made it clear why they thought they should do this rather than leaving it to other Anglo-Catholics, by saying that

[310] *L.K.G. Quarterly: The Organ of the League of The Kingdom of God* (cit. *LKGQ*). No. 1, January 1926, p. 2
[311] *Prayer Book Revision in the Church of England, op. cit.*, p. viii.
[312] *LKGQ*, No. 11, July 1928, p. 86.

some of the sacramental teaching 'makes it easier to understand why Modernists and Evangelicals regard the Catholic Movement with suspicion'.[313] The League wanted to emphasize first of all why Sacramentalism is native to Christian faith and practice and then insist that Sacramental religion provides the most definite sanctions for Christian ethics, sociology, and politics. The *LKG Quarterly* goes on:

The League of the Kingdom of God ... views the Blessed Sacrament not merely as the soul's way to heaven but as Society's way to the Kingdom of God. It finds in it the mystical bond whereby an incarnate society discovers the true ground and principle of its association. It sees the Mass saturated with ethical meaning and capable of regulating all economics and politics.[314]

The League intended to remind the Church of the constructive social meaning of the sacraments for that present time because it was only by this means, it believed, that the Anglo-Catholic movement could convince the Christian mind of England.

We call ourselves the League of the Kingdom of God and we believe that the Holy Eucharist sets forth our Lord in his divine Kingship over the whole of life. Let us make it plain why we believe that, and we shall make all that is honest and vigorous in English life Catholic once more. And when that is done, there will be a speedy end of this civilisation of brass and jazz.[315]

Percy Widdrington and other members of the League of the Kingdom of God were among the driving forces behind the establishment of the Summer School of Sociology in 1925.[316] At the first Summer School Francis Underhill pointed out that although Anglo-Catholicism had from the start 'cared for men's bodies almost as ardently as for their souls',[317] these efforts had been no more than charitable palliatives and it was not until towards the end of the nineteenth century that a large section of the Oxford Movement had been 'permeated by Christian Socialism, sometimes vaguely conceived'. Meanwhile others only found in their religion support for 'a romantic loyalty to the memory of a more Christian past', or were so immersed in the ecclesiastical difficulties of the time that they neglected the obligations of citizenship or, he said,

indolently accept the opinions and prejudices of their own class and circle

---

[313] *Ibid.*, p. 87.
[314] *Ibid.*
[315] *Ibid.*, p. 88.
[316] Reckitt, *Widdrington*, pp. 97–98.
[317] *Towards a Catholic Standard of Life. Being a Short Report of the First Summer School of Sociology under the auspices of the Anglo-Catholic Congress held at Keble College Oxford in July 1925*, 1926, p. 11.

without troubling to investigate their ethical validity or attempting to correlate them with religion.[318]

Underhill thought that now that many external difficulties of the Anglo-Catholics were much less acute and their internal confusions more manageable, the time was ripe for a similar consolidation of thought and action on 'some of the larger questions of social ethics', because there was danger in the fact that much Christian Social enthusiasm was now being shown by Liberal Protestants and in that there was 'the danger of doing more harm than good for lack of a sound dogmatic basis'.[319]

The following year the School reassembled to work out this 'sound dogmatic basis' on the subject of 'The Social Teaching of the Sacraments'. Before the members of the School arrived in Oxford they were sent a syllabus of study and a questionnaire. One of the questions was very significant:

Is it true that the idea of the Eucharist as a family feast of the people of God is often unemployed and often forgotten? If so, what changes in current teaching and practice are needed to restore the balance?[320]

The report of the Conference tells how the discussion circle which dealt with this question were agreed that this aspect of the Eucharist was 'lamentably neglected' and made two practical suggestions. They thought that there ought to be an earlier hour for the Parish Mass so that it might be followed by a common meal and also that only one wafer should be used at the celebration in order to preserve the symbolism of the one loaf.[321]

These Summer Schools were one of the sources from which The Christendom Group grew. This group gathered together both the followers of Percy Widdrington and also those who were involved in the Conference on Politics, Economics and Citizenship (COPEC) which William Temple organized in Birmingham in 1924.[322] The journal of this grouping was *Christendom* which commenced publication in March 1931 and was edited by Maurice Reckitt. It was to the Chris-

[318] *Ibid.*

[319] *Ibid.*, p. 12.

[320] Maurice B. Reckitt, ed., *The Social Teaching of the Sacraments. Being the Report of the Second Anglo-Catholic Summer School of Sociology held at Keble College, Oxford, July 1926*, p. 20.

[321] *Ibid.*, p. 133.

[322] Lloyd, *op. cit.*, p. 306.

tendom Group that Archbishop Temple entrusted the preparation of the programme of his second great conference which assembled at Malvern in the early days of the Second World War and which will be considered later.[323]

(f) The Sacramental Principles of The Catholic Crusade

From the start The Catholic Crusade was dominated by the character of Conrad Noel, 'the son of a poet and the grandson of a peer', who had 'all the incalculable elements of the eccentric aristocrat; the sort of eccentric aristocrat who so often figures as a particularly destructive democrat.'[324] Noel applied his liturgical principles during his long ministry as Vicar of Thaxted in Essex. On arrival at Thaxted in 1910 Noel instituted a 9 a.m. Sung Eucharist[325] and made it the centre of parish life. He reordered the church, clearing out years of clutter, white-washed the walls, introduced colourful vestments and ceremonial, taught the people plainsong and generally made it what the patron Lady Warwick had hoped he would, 'a centre and a "Mecca" for Socialists'.[326] Many of Noel's liturgical ideas had developed during the time that he had been a part-time curate to Percy Dearmer at St Mary's, Primrose Hill.[327] Dearmer, an active Socialist from his membership of the Guild of St Matthew at Oxford in 1889, had always understood Socialism as more than an instrument for change; it meant for him the opening of the appreciation of art and beauty for all.[328] Noel like Dearmer loved beauty, but it must be shared; if it was not, it was cold and dead.[329]

For Noel, worship, as one visitor to Thaxted put it, 'looked forward to a new social order inspired by Catholicism of which the Holy Sacrament of the Altar was its symbol and life'.[330] Noel himself spoke of the Mass as Christ's 'special trysting place with men until the kingdom come'.[331] He likened the Church to an army left to fight for a new world in which nourishment and pleasure commonly shared are the expression of the God-centred life. As a sign of that He gives them

[323] Ibid., p. 310 and p. 213 infra.
[324] G. K. Chesterton, Autobiography, 1937, p. 159. 'A champion of democracy who behaved like an aristocrat on occasions', Groves Noel, p. 183.
[325] Dark, op. cit., p. 89.
[326] Groves, Noel, pp. 61–63.
[327] Nan Dearmer, op. cit., p. 162.
[328] Percy Dearmer, Art and Religion, 1924, p. 17.
[329] Nan Dearmer, op. cit. pp. 35–36.
[330] Groves, Noel, p. 190.
[331] Ibid., p. 195.

bread and wine, which taken in fellowship, is the means by which they are nourished 'as a stirrup cup to battle'.[332] In this worship everything that appealed to the senses and the imagination by drama, colour, and expression through symbol and ceremony could be used to demonstrate truths which could not always satisfactorily be explained comprehensively to the human reason. Yet one truth was 'plain as a pikestaff', that the Holy Eucharist must be at the centre of all church life, and it was this principle which activated the life of the Catholic Crusade, a principle for practice, not theory. As Noel put it:

The corporate worship of God in the Mass appealed to the early Christians and to modern Catholic Socialists alike, as the highest form of adoration. It is of no use arguing overmuch about it. You must experience it habitually, and you will discover for yourself the truth of this.[333]

The Crusade issued a series of booklets which were intended to popularize their approach. In the booklet called *The Sacraments*[334] Noel makes clear the communal aspect of the Eucharist of this pre-eminently social feast with its material symbols and the fellowship of 'the common table'.[335]

So dominant was the communal aspect of the Eucharist in the early ages, that the "This is My Body" is sometimes interpreted as meaning the people gathered together into a compact brotherhood, for Christ is to be found in the body of men, and fellowship is heaven and the lack of fellowship is hell (the mediaeval motto). St Paul reproves the Corinthians for their individualistic selfishness, "their avarice which is idolatry", their separateness, turning the sacrament instituted as sign of fellowship to "their own damnation", "not discerning the Lord's Body"; for the bread, he reminds them, is the "fellowship of His Body, the cup the fellowship of His Blood". "For one loaf, one body, we the many are; for all of us partake of the one loaf."[336]

All this type of teaching was taken by Noel, Wilson, Bucknall, and others into the Order of the Church Militant, so that the eucharistic ideas of the two bodies will be seen to be all of a piece.

(g) *The Sacramental Principles of the Order of the Church Militant*

The editor of the Order's magazine *The Church Militant* was Harold

---

[332] *Ibid.*

[333] Conrad Noel, *Jesus the Heretic*, Religious Book Club Edition 1940, p. 49.

[334] Conrad Noel, Priest, Servant of the Catholic Crusade, *The Sacraments*, n.d. (He speaks of Headlam in the present tense on p. 12 'Mr. Headlam says ...', so before Headlam's death in 1924? Cf. Paget, *op. cit.*, p. 239).

[335] *Ibid.*, p. 15.

[336] *Ibid.*

Mason. He had worked as a layman at Thaxted before ordination,[337] had been present at the inaugural meeting of the Catholic Crusade in 1918,[338] and had now succeeded Wilson as Vicar of Sneyd, Burslem.[339] In an article in the third issue called 'Christ's Mass' Mason contributed a spirited defence of the Christian Socialist anti-individualistic approach to the Eucharist.

How often at the Parish Mass have pietists turned the Sacrament of Fellowship into a Sacrament of Selfishness. Mass is the meal of fellowship, the worship of the Church, the Body of Christ. All, therefore, should follow the liturgy, the Mass is not the moment for private prayers.[340]

During the life-time of *The Church Militant* there was a very discernible increase of Parish Communion-type services, and when the book of essays which Fr Gabriel Hebert edited, *The Parish Communion*,[341] was published in 1937, it was reviewed at great length by Jim Wilson. In his review Wilson says that there is a growing dissatisfaction being felt by Church people with the widely prevailing custom of 'making one's communion' at an early service and then worshipping at a later sung service with only the priest communicating. The Mass can never be just something done by the clergy for the people. Of Hebert's book, Wilson says that it shows

an awareness and something of a revolt against this clericalism, and against the individualism of present-day worship. It sees the collective nature of the Mass and the value of the parish communion at or about nine o'clock when the whole Church in the parish can act together as a body in Worship.[342]

But all is not praise; the book, he said, was in some ways disappointing. Wilson criticises its failure to see the purpose of the Kingdom behind and in the Mass and the impact that it can make upon the world. He admits that it is true that there are in the book signs of a consciousness that something more is needed but he regrets that he detects no passion for 'the regeneration of life and of all material things outside the life of the parochial group'. He fears that

The revolt against individualism and clericalism will end in collective pietism and a certain degree of comradeship, unless the Church recovers more than this and becomes fired with the Vision of a God of Righteousness as the Creator of the Universe who is ever working redemptively to express His Spirit in

[337] Groves, *Noel*, p. 144.
[338] *Ibid.*, p. 202.
[339] *Ibid.*, p. 320.
[340] *The Church Militant* (*cit. Militant*) No. 3, January 1937, p. 6.
[341] See pp. 204 ff, *infra.*
[342] *Militant*, No. 11, September 1937, p. 4.

and through His whole Creation—unless it sees worship as man's conscious co-operative activity in this purpose.[343]

Fr Wilson grants that it is an important book but warns that

The Parish Mass will still fail to be what Christ meant it to be unless this purpose of world and life redemption becomes the conscious purpose and passion in the hearts and lives of those who worship. This is only dimly seen in Fr Hebert's book which has in it so much that is valuable.[344]

In the following issue there is a description of what is called 'The People's Mass' in the parish of which Wilson was the Vicar for many years, Sneyd near Burslem, where Mason was now the incumbent. 'G.M.K.'[345] described the service in detail, firmly putting the church in its industrial setting:

Outside, the smoke banners of the pot-banks; inside the whitewashed church, the gay flags and ensigns of a different world. Just to step into Sneyd church, therefore, is to face a challenge, for the two pictures do not seem to belong to the same order.[346]

The service was at 9 a.m. and the correspondent outlines the contents of it, which were not entirely those of the *Book of Common Prayer*:

So past the mutual confession by priests and people, and the Kyrie to the first announcement of the angel's message *Gloria in Excelsis*. A word on the music at this point; it was grounded in traditional plainsong, evidently much enjoyed and lustily sung by the entire congregation, and only ornamented by the choir at the more dramatic moments by a richer polyphony, and by a judicious and imaginative organ accompaniment. Then in swift succession the rest of the dynamic ritual of the foreshadowing of the Kingdom, the Gospel, Creed, people's offerings of alms and oblations, the *Sanctus* and Canon up to the Consecration, the invocation of the Holy Spirit, the kiss of peace, and the Communion of priests and people. The service ended with the people's saying of the *Angelus*.[347]

It was not the order of service that impressed the visitor, it was something more than that:

In the Sneyd Mass, there were many things which no doubt I, along with others, missed, but certain impressions one could not miss. One could not miss

[343] *Ibid.*

[344] *Ibid.*, pp. 4–5.

[345] ?Geoffrey Keable. For a description of the work of Geoffrey and Gladys Keable see Michael and Mollie Hardwick, *Alfred Deller: A singularity of voice*, 1980, pp. 58–64 and pp. 67–74.

[346] *Militant*, No. 14, December 1937, p. 3.

[347] *Ibid.*, p. 4.

the outstanding impression of having taken part, not in a "church service", but as fellow guests of one host at a very lovely party; and all the many stories of Jesus about the feasts of the Kingdom were naturally in one's mind. Moreover, had the prodigal son arrived in the middle, there cannot be the least doubt that he would have been welcomed, and the fatted calf produced on the spot; an impression which is unhappily wanting in many Christian congregations. One recognised here the exalting of the Christian principles of friendliness, co-operation and sharing; and as we saw old and young, learned and simple, each taking his share, one felt the attempt to realise the condition of true equality. There was a rich family, owners of the world and its fulness; with no distinction of master and servant, man and woman, not even of teachers and taught, except the natural distinctions of character and leadership.[348]

In the description of this service the spirit of Conrad Noel can be very much felt, a freedom and lightness of touch. Perhaps Wilson was being unfair to Hebert in not detecting among his contributors the same 'love of life and excitement in believing that at each mass potentially the world is being changed'. Some were comparative newcomers to the conception of the Lord's own people around the Lord's Table, whereas it had been part of the stock-in-trade of militant Christian Socialists for many years. For them the Mass was a foretaste of the Kingdom:

The Mass is not merely "a service" which has been drawn up and arranged for man's convenience; it is a real part of the offering of Christ, it is the memorial of His whole life and purpose, of His redemptive work, of what He has done and is doing now. It is a part of His offering; for that includes the whole human race and the whole material creation, which is being made by Him to be a Sacrament: that is, something which will express and respond to the Father. All human relationships can be redeemed when men learn to act together in Christ, making their whole life and activity and use of things an offering of worship to God. In this way the Mass declares the whole purpose of God in creation and is in itself a foretaste of the Kingdom of God.[349]

This is real eucharistic militancy altogether worthy of 'The Order of the Church Militant'. Despite criticism, however, we shall see that Wilson and some of his colleagues did make an important contribution to the next stage of the evolution of the Parish Communion.

(h) The Leap

At the 'dividing of the ways', when the members of the Order of the

[348] Ibid.
[349] Militant, No. 17, January 1939, p. 5.

Church Militant split into two camps, it was noted that one of these decided to give their energies to the encouragement of 'groups'.[350] The idea of these 'groups' echoed a subject which had been occupying space in *The Church Militant* during the previous two years, and had been particularly stressed in an article by Alan Ecclestone (thinly disguised as 'A.E.') in the April issue of 1941 in which he described how they operated. Deploring the parochialism of much of the Church's work, Ecclestone stated that it was essential that these divisions should be broken down if any vision of a world-wide church was to be built up.

How was it to be done? The occasions for extra-parochial and inter-parochial work have been few and spasmodic. There has been little to encourage the steady growth of the sense of parishes co-operating. But a start must be made somewhere and these notes simply indicate what has happened on a small scale.

The foundation is that group life which The Order of the Church Militant takes for granted as essential in the living church, and which the Order and the Catholic Crusade have done much to develop. In that life, with its common worship, prayer, study and other activities we have the active agent for the wider work.[351]

In his 1941 article, which he calls 'Over the Wall', Ecclestone says that he can already see the building up of an outlook which is wider than the parish and yet intensely rooted in appreciation of the work of the parish, and it is to the strengthening of that work that Jim Wilson and his group of ex-members of the Order now give their support and interest.

The first issue of a new magazine appeared in July 1944. Its title shows that it follows the theme of Ecclestone's article in *The Church Militant* by being called *The Leap*, and Psalm 18.31 is quoted under the title: 'with the help of my God I shall leap over the Wall'. The first article declares that:

The Leap is an attempt to jump over parish boundaries and to join forces in our Christian struggle. Inside each parish there are people who constitute the nucleus of an active militant Church in that place ... It is to link up such groups that this bulletin is produced.[352]

Jim Wilson makes the aims of the magazine even clearer in his article in the first issue. It was obvious, he believed, that the Church

[350] See p. 108, *supra*.
[351] *Militant*, no. 50, April 1941, pp. 5–6.
[352] *The Leap*, July 1944, p. 1.

had largely lost its purpose. Instead of training a band of people to function as his Body, to be fellow workers with him in the redemption of the world order and in the building of the Kingdom, most parishes, Wilson observed, were spending all their energies in providing 'services' and spiritual privileges for the members of the Church and in training their souls for heaven. 'Most parishes fail to set any standard of Christian living which definitely challenges the world's way of living', he says. The sadness is that, although

the teaching of the Church and the services of worship provided do stir people's sense of the holiness of God and their personal devotion to him is true, ... in many cases this devotion has little relationship to his moral character and purpose as it is seen in Christ's intense love for the poor and the oppressed, in the spirit of justice, in his indignation with injustice and the denial of human rights.[353]

By February 1945 Fr Wilson is speaking of the possibility of a Federation and of calling together a conference[354] but that does not take place for another two years. But later that year the front page of the magazine included for the first time a statement about its purpose which it continued to print on most issues until the last. It said:

THE LEAP
is a link between Parishes which are trying to recover THE NATURE OF THE CHURCH as the Body of Christ.
THE LEAP
advocates no new theology, no new society, but stands for the fullest use of the Parish Communion, the Parish Meeting, Action inspired by Worship and discussion in fellowship.
THE LEAP
jumps across parish boundaries and age-long divisions—to the end that the Common Life of the Body of Christ may be more perfectly realised.[355]

The circulation of *The Leap* had grown to 550 by 1946[356] and its policy had become more precise with its twin advocacy of the Parish Communion and the Parish Meeting. By this means Wilson, Ecclestone, and a growing number of supporters believed that each parish could have a core 'not Pharisaically apart from the rest, but more determined than the general loose aggregates called congregations; more informed and deliberate in purpose because of the weekly meeting'. And they were equally convinced that it was necessary to link up

[353] *Ibid.*, pp. 10–11.
[354] *Ibid.*, February 1944, p. 3.
[355] *Ibid.*, No. 8, October 1945, p. 1.
[356] *Ibid.*, No. 10, February 1946, p. 12.

those groups 'over the walls' of parochial and diocesan boundaries so that a new consciousness of membership of the Church might be born and new possibilities of action grasped.[357] Each issue of *The Leap* (it appeared six times a year in February, April, June, September, October and December) contained a feature 'News from Parish Meetings' giving details of activities and also providing an indication of the spread of the principles of what was still only a loosely-knit fellowship. There were many growing pains. One Vicar, Robert Nelson of St Matthew's, Barrow-in-Furness, admitted that his Parish Meeting was 'too much like an "Adult Religious Education" Class' but further admitted that it was his fault that it had developed in this way and he was trying to make it 'less academic and more organic'.[358]

In order to help parishes two leaflets were issued in April 1946[359] and others contributed articles in *The Leap* which were intended to widen its appeal. For example E. R. Wickham, who said he wrote 'as Industrial Chaplain to the Bishop, without parochial charge, a free lance', and had the opportunity of making many experiments in contact with men and women in the sphere of employment, appealed to parish meetings that they should consider forming a wider group in the parish which could meet either on or off church premises and to which their nominal Christian fellows could be invited. But Wickham emphasizes that this wider-based meeting should not replace the meeting together of the Christian Family in each parish.[360]

The long-awaited conference took place in April 1947 at Holy Trinity, Darnell, Sheffield. Speakers included Gabriel Hebert, Jim Wilson, Ted Wickham, and Ernest Southcott. At the conference the object always in mind was 'the transformation of the local Church life so that it becomes steadily nearer to being serviceable to, and expressive of, the Common Life in the Body of Christ'.[361] To this end a further conference was planned for the August of the same year at St Wilfred's, Halton, at which eighteen parishes were represented.[362] The laity present at the Halton Conference grew confident in their role:

The clergy are not in possession of all the answers, for the answers to a multitude of questions are not yet given. A living Church in the power of the Spirit

[357] *Ibid.*, No. 11, April 1946, p. 1.
[358] *Ibid.*, p. 8.
[359] *The Leap Leaflets*: No. 1, 'The Parish Meeting'; No. 2, 'Over the Wall' n.d. Alan Ecclestone is named as the author of No. 1 but there is no name given on No. 2.
[360] *The Leap*, No. 13, p. 5.
[361] *Ibid.*, No. 17, June 1947, pp. 2–3.
[362] *Ibid.*, No. 19, October, p. 1.

is set to lay hold of these truths, and the Parish Meeting is the place and the occasion for the seeking of them.[363]

The meeting was sufficiently a success for a further conference to be planned at Darnell, Sheffield in 1948. At this point Robert Nelson wrote to *The Leap* saying that although, in his opinion, a new organization was not at that time necessary, it was important that these Conferences should become a regular feature of the Church's life.[364] But other plans were being hatched in other places and at Queen's College, Birmingham in January 1948 a Conference was called together by Kenneth Packard and Henry de Candole for those concerned with the Parish Communion, the Parish Breakfast, the Parish Meeting, and other such initiatives. Michael Stancliffe reported to readers of *The Leap* that the Birmingham Conference asked itself this question:

Has the time come to attempt some co-ordination of these 'initiatives', these new endeavours towards living 'the common life in the Body of Christ?' Would not these initiatives, if co-ordinated and reinforcing each other, have a very powerful effect on the life of the whole Church of England, especially now that there is such a powerful support from the theologians? And is there not beginning to be more general understanding among both clergy and laity of the Church as the beloved community, the People of God?[365]

The Conference answered the question in the affirmative and set up a new organization, giving it the name 'Parish and People'.[366]

(i) Parish and People

The new organization commenced its own journal *Parish and People*, but it said it was 'incorporating "*The Leap*"'.[367] In the first issue of the new journal Jim Wilson wrote an article, 'This Further Leap', in which he said:

For five years that little paper tried to catch the eye and the ear of those who would think about the nature of the Church.

[363] *Ibid.*, p. 3.
[364] *Ibid.*, pp. 3–5.
[365] *Ibid.*, No. 24, March 1949, p. 3; Peter J. Jagger, *A History of the Parish and People Movement (cit.* Jagger, *History)* 1978, pp. 20–23.
[366] *Ibid.*
[367] *Parish and People incorporating 'The Leap' (cit. P. & P.)* vol. 1, No. 1, June 1950.

The Leap was concerned with 'being the Church', with rescuing the Church from its "going to church" mentality. Those of us who started it resolutely refused to let it be organised into "a Society"; it was to be a paper in which those who were trying to restore the lost sense of community in the Church would be able to find, and share in, the experience of others of a like mind.

The Leap had its day. Those who had contributed to its columns became absorbed in "leaping". It no longer drew contributions, and now *Parish and People*, a larger movement which has so largely adopted *The Leap* ideas and widened them, has taken its place. It will help greatly to make this further leap a useful and successful one if those who read and paid for *The Leap* will continue their support of this new venture.[368]

Michael Stancliffe in an editorial in the same issue is complimentary about the work of *The Leap*.

Some of our readers will already be familiar with *The Leap*, a paper with a significance that was out of all proportion to its size. *The Leap* acted as 'a link between parishes which were trying to recover the true nature of the Church as the Body of Christ'.

... with the full consent of Alan Ecclestone (Editor) and Jim Wilson, who were together responsible for *The Leap*, we are now taking it over and incorporating it with *Parish and People*, and we ask the support and interest of all who formerly read it.[369]

The movement for the promotion of the Parish Communion had now moved from the narrow confines of Anglo-Catholicism and was beginning to make its claims upon the Church of England as a whole. The new journal stated clearly that *Parish and People* refused to be ticketed with any of the traditional party labels, believing that it would be a great mistake to suppose that the Liturgical Movement in the Church of England is only the concern of one section.[370] Gordon Hewitt, contributing an article 'Evangelism and the Liturgical Movement',[371] admitted that although as yet the Parish Communion was still rare in Evangelical parishes he detected an increasing willingness among 'alert Evangelical clergy' to experiment and learn from other traditions, ways which can contribute to

overcoming the passivity and individualism of worshippers, and in avoiding the 'clericalization' of the Eucharist: and a realization that these ends cannot be achieved merely by austerity in ceremonial.[372]

[368] *Ibid.*, pp. 5–6.
[369] *Ibid.*, p. 2.
[370] *Ibid.*, p. 1.
[371] *Ibid.*, pp. 6–10.
[372] *Ibid.*, p. 10.

Over the ensuing years this attitude grew among Evangelicals to the great benefit of the Church of England as a whole and reached a high point at the National Evangelical Anglican Conference held at Keele University in 1967,[373] which admitted:

We have failed to do justice in our practice to the twin truths that the Lord's Supper is the main service of the people of God, and that the local church, as such, is the unit within which it is properly administered. This is not to undervalue in any way attendance at other services of the day, but to admit that we have let the sacrament be pushed to the outer fringes of church life, and the ministry of the Word be divorced from it. Small communion services have been held seemingly at random, often more than one a Sunday and the whole local church seldom or never comes together at the Lord's Table. As individuals we have lacked both a concern that the local church should amend its ways, and also a personal discipline of attendance.[374]

As a consequence 'rather to its own surprise'[375] the Conference recommended that

We determine to work towards the practice of a weekly celebration of the sacrament as the central corporate service of the church, and some of us would recommend the use of 'one loaf' (1 Corinthians 10.17) as biblical and symbolic of that corporate unity.[376]

It might be speculated whether the increasing social awareness of many Anglican Evangelicals in recent years has made this liturgical decision easier. In 1946 Max Warren was deploring Evangelicals' poor record since the days of Wilberforce and Shaftesbury in the field of social righteousness and suggesting that it was due to their failure to proclaim the Gospel by both Word and Sacrament.[377] Perhaps the acceptance of the Parish Communion by some Evangelicals is a portent of a willingness to re-establish the twin proclamation.

No one would be foolish enough to think that the mere decision to adopt the Parish Communion automatically guarantees that a full appreciation of all the liturgical and theological implications has also been accepted by either priest or people in a parish. Consequently it needs to be asked of both the Catholic and the Evangelical parties in the Church of England whether the close connection between the

---

[373] Paul A. Welsby, *A History of the Church of England 1945–1980*, 1984, pp. 214–215.

[374] *The Report of the Keele Conference 1967*, 5, ii, 76, p. 35.

[375] Colin Buchanan, *Evangelical Anglicans and Liturgy*, Grove Worship Series No. 90, 1984, p. 15.

[376] *The Report of the Keele Conference 1967*, ibid.

[377] Max Warren, *Strange Victory: A Study of the Holy Communion Service*, 1946 (*cit.* Warren, *Strange Victory*), pp. 115–116.

Eucharist and Social Witness argued in this book as the underlying feature in the evolution of the Parish Communion survived the wide spread adoption of that service in the parishes. Some indication of the relative importance given to social over against liturgical concerns (or *vice versa*) can be gained from the nature of the topics dealt with in the Parish and People Movement's journal *Parish and People*. The Movement itself had declared at the outset that it was to be an association for the study and dissemination of the principles underlying the Church's corporate worship and for the application of those principles in the life of the parish and the world.[378]

Although many of the articles in the early issues were not completely church-bound, none the less, they tended to deal mainly with liturgical matters, and it was not until the ninth issue that there was an article which quite definitely challenged the reader about the relationship between worship and the Church's witness in the world.[379] Significantly it was an article on the teaching of Bishop John Wordsworth of Salisbury, who will be later acknowledged as one of the forerunners of the movement.[380] In the article S. B. Calver described Wordsworth as one of those who held the teaching of F. D. Maurice in some esteem. He was also of the opinion that Parish and People ought to remember Wordsworth with gratitude as one who had 'first sowed the seed that is at last beginning to bear fruit'.[381]

In the following four issues there appeared 'Communion and Community',[382] Max Warren on 'The Scandal of Worship' in which the challenge of commitment to the world in Word and Sacrament was fairly and squarely put,[383] an account of a Church Trade Union Group,[384] and also an article which was a positive link with *The Leap*, advocating the values of the Parish Meeting.[385] In 1957 Robert Nelson was writing about that part of the liturgical action which started at 10.30 a.m. on Sundays and ended at 9.30 a.m. the next Sunday 'and which is lived out not in symbols but in the real world'.[386] All these discussions went alongside 'liturgical' articles on

---

[378] *P. & P.* vol. i, No. 1, June 1950, p. 1.

[379] S. B. Calver, 'Bishop John Wordsworth and his teaching', *P. & P.*, vol. iii, No. 3, pp. 9–14.

[380] See pp. 163 ff, *infra*.

[381] Calver, *op. cit.*, p. 9.

[382] *P. & P.*, vol. lv, No. 1, July 1953, pp. 10–11.

[383] *Ibid.*, vol. iv, No. 2, October 1953, pp. 2–12.

[384] *Ibid.*, vol. iv, No. 3, February 1954, pp. 25–26.

[385] *Ibid.*, vol. v, No. 2, November 1954, pp. 6–7.

[386] *Ibid.*, No. 20, September 1957, p. 5.

the significance of the Offertory and the possibility of Old Testament readings at the Parish Communion, and accounts of the activities of the Roman Catholic Liturgical Movement.

Parish and People was subject throughout its life to constant self-examination and re-appraisal, as Peter Jagger's book, *A History of the Parish and People Movement*,[387] which draws heavily on the papers of Henry de Candole, makes very clear. However, its leaders were constantly aware of the continuing danger of the Movement becoming completely pre-occupied with the way things were done in church with a resulting forgetfulness about the totality of the Church's mission.[388] In 1962 a liaison was commenced with a radical church reform group which called itself the Keble Conference Group after the Oxford College where its first meetings were held. In 1963 the two groups merged but it 'was no easy marriage because the Keble Group was more radical and political than the generality of the members of Parish and People'.[389] It is very true that the average Parish and People member was not an out-and-out radical in either his church or national politics, yet the fact was that the organization which he had joined had its origins in such an approach, and if Parish and People had failed to sell its emphasis on socio-political concerns to the majority of its members, this was a measure of its overall failure.

Parish and People certainly gave an impetus to the popularization of the Parish Communion in the 1950s and 1960s, and many mistakingly thought that this was the total purpose of the Movement. An examination of its journal shows that throughout its life it was diligent in keeping the larger issue of the social significance of the Eucharist in front of its membership, but this was not what was generally required by many of the membership. Equally a growing frustration with those who had a narrow vision of the Eucharist tempted those whose political concerns were more rampant into the merger with the Keble Group while still keeping the name 'Parish and People'. For many this seemed like the end of the Parish and People Movement as they knew it whereas, in fact as this work shows it was actually returning to its roots. Unfortunately many in the resulting radical movement failed to appreciate the necessity for preserving the centrality of the Eucharist in their plan for action in Church and State.

[387] Jagger, *History, passim.*
[388] *Ibid.*, p. 61.
[389] Welsby, *op. cit.*, p. 136.

PART THREE

THE EMERGENCE OF THE PARISH COMMUNION

1 Early Experiments

Claims to be the first parish to have had a 'Parish Communion' in England are not easy to substantiate. The validity of any such claim will depend upon the definition of what constitutes a 'Parish Communion'.

If the simple definition is accepted: 'a eucharist which is intended to be the main, but not necessarily the only, service of the day for that parish, at which all communicants are encouraged to communicate', then there are a number of early examples which must be examined. It was only at a later stage of development that other elements came to be considered as the hallmarks of a Parish Communion, for example the offertory procession and congregational participation in some of the prayers hitherto reserved for the priest.

Where then can the parochial roots of the Parish Communion be discovered? In 1962 the Parish and People Conference chose as its theme 'The Parish Communion Today'. In an opening address, to which he gave the title 'The Parish Communion after 25 years', the Chairman of the Council of Parish and People, the Rt Rev'd Henry de Candole, Bishop of Knaresborough, explained that originally he had intended to speak about '35' and not '25' years. The Bishop said that in December 1927 he had assisted in the transformation of a 10 a.m. Children's Eucharist at St John's, Newcastle.[1] But he was quick to admit that St John's was far from being the first exponent of the Parish Communion, even in the north-east of England; and he spoke about the pit villages where a 9 a.m. celebration of the Holy Communion was commenced so that they could conveniently be served at such an hour by a single-handed priest who needed to be at the parish church for the sacred hours of 8.00 a.m. and 11.00 a.m. It may have been an accident that started it, Bishop de Candole said, but such districts did, in fact, have the Holy Communion as their one morning service, whatever it might be called, and whatever theological principles may or may not have been attached to it.[2]

Even so, the origins of the Parish Communion, that is, a service which corresponds to the simple definition above, have to be found elsewhere. In the nineteenth century some Anglo-Catholic parishes held a fully choral Eucharist at an early hour on a Sunday, but they

---

[1] David M. Paton, ed., *The Parish Communion Today. The Report of the 1962 Conference of Parish and People*, 1962, p. 1; c.f. Peter J. Jagger, *Bishop Henry de Candole: His Life and Times 1895 to 1971*, 1975 (*cit.* Jagger, *de Candole*), p. 1.

[2] *Ibid.*, p. 2.

were part of a Sunday package of services which included either a
later non-communicating Sung Eucharist or Choral Matins. For instance there is the example of W. J. E. Bennett's weekly 'High Celebration' at 8 a.m. which he introduced at Frome, Somerset, perhaps
as early as 1855.[3] At first this service consisted of rather simple but
dignified Tractarian worship and only later did it attract to itself the
ritualistic features of later Anglo-Catholic tradition; but it had no sermon, and there were other celebrations of the Communion during the
day and a fully Choral Matins. Nevertheless it has been claimed for
Bennett that he:

holds a place in the history of the Parish Communion Movement something
like that which Wycliffe holds in the history of the English Reformation. Like
Wycliffe, Bennett was the forerunner of the restoration or revival of a truth or
an ideal before that truth or ideal had any groups of people actively promoting its acceptance. Bennett anticipated and put into practice much which the
Parish Communion strove to introduce over half a century later ... In the
same way as Wycliffe to a certain extent influenced the Reformation Movement which began after his death, so also Bennett, through the example he set
at Frome, influenced after his death the Parish Communion Movement; and
so, in the same way as Wycliffe has been described as the 'Morning Star of the
Reformation', Bennett may be described as the 'Morning Star of the Parish
Communion Movement'.[4]

In 1958 R. H. Martin of Queen's College, Birmingham, tried to
discover the earliest examples of a Parish Communion-type of service
in England. Martin wrote to the Church press and asked readers to
give him details of 'a Parish Communion or any equivalent such as a
Sung Eucharist with a general communion before 1918'.[5] There was
a good response consisting of seventy-six replies, although the letters
were of varying usefulness.[6] Bishop de Candole made reference to the
evidence that Martin had accumulated at the 1962 Conference of
Parish and People,[7] and Peter Jagger refers to it in his *A History of The
Parish and People Movement.*[8]

The correspondence drew attention to some of the earliest

---

[3] Bennett, *op. cit.*, pp. 200 ff.

[4] Robin H. Martin, *The Act of the Brethren, A History of the Parish Communion movement.*
Unpublished BD thesis, University of Birmingham, 1961, pp. 87–88.

[5] *Church Times*, 21 February 1958.

[6] The MS letters are in the possession of the Rev'd R. H. Martin of Lumb-in-Rossen-
dale. He very kindly loaned them to me, and I have made this assessment of the evidence they contain (*cit. Martin Correspondence*).

[7] Paton, *op. cit.*, pp. 2–5.

[8] Jagger, *History*, pp. 10–14.

examples of what might conceivably be considered as services which prefigured later developments, such as Bennett's 'High Celebration' which has already been noted and W. J. Butler's early morning Choral celebration at Wantage. This latter service, unlike that established at Frome, was not held weekly, but monthly and at festivals.[9] Writing in his journal of his decision to hold an early morning sung service in 1848, Butler expressed himself as being conscious of making an important decision. He wrote:

I am not sure whether this will answer or do harm. It is a very serious step, more serious than perhaps at first sight appears. It seems like the beginning of a great work.[10]

It was indeed 'a great work' and probably predates Bennett by some seven years, and therefore to a certain extent challenges Bennett's claim to the title of 'Morning Star'. However, it must be admitted that the non-weekly basis of Butler's arrangements greatly weakens that challenge.

The correspondence makes great claims for the work of Fr Naters at St Columba's, Seaton Burn, Newcastle-upon-Tyne. He was Vicar of the parish for thirty-five years, and one of his successors, F. H. Mountney, was of the opinion that Naters had introduced an 8 a.m. Sung Eucharist in 1870. Unfortunately there are no parish records for this period beyond baptismal registers.

There is also evidence amongst the *Martin Correspondence* of two isolated attempts to establish something similar. Both are in Wiltshire, at Easterton[11] and at Wilperton, but it would seem that the attempt to sustain a sung service at 9 a.m. in these parishes did not survive for very long. These west-country parishes are *not* the root from which the Parish Communion sprang. Two names emerge as the pioneers of a type of service from which the present-day Parish Communion can be seen to have direct descent; they are those of Walter Frere and John Burn.

It was Frere's brief work as curate-in-charge of St Faith's, Stepney and Burn's long ministry at All Saints', Middlesbrough which are the liturgical corner stones upon which others would eventually build.

---

[9] *Life and Letters of William John Butler*, 1897, p. 58.

[10] *Ibid.*, footnote quotation from Butler's Parish Journal for 7 May 1848 in 'Early Communion'.

[11] An unsubstantiated footnote in Brother Edward, Priest-Evangelist, ed., *Sunday Morning: The New Way, Papers on the Parish Communion* (cit. *Sunday Morning*) 1938, p. vii, gives the date 1874 for the start of the service at Easterton.

But there is another factor of great significance about the work of Frere and Burn: both were to some degree Christian Socialists. Frere wrote to his friend the Rev'd Dr Hugh F. Stewart soon after leaving Stepney to work at Pusey House, Oxford, telling him that he was 'preaching rank socialism to the fashionable congregation of Oxford in compressed doses of twenty minutes'.[12] Stewart himself bears witness to Frere's socialism.

Before he left Cambridge he was drawn to Socialism and this increased when he came to Pusey House and the influence of John Carter.[13]

C. S. Phillips, the editor of the Memoir of Bishop Frere, says that Socialism was a 'bent' (sic) that Frere retained to the end of his life.

It was the Christian Socialism of the early nineties, idealistic and religious to the core, rooted in compassion for the misfortunate and less a comfortable vision of a planned society than a call to self-sacrifice.[14]

Even in his days as Bishop of Truro[15] this 'bent' was obvious,[16] and occasionally too obvious for some: it is recalled that Cornish squires thundered from time to time, 'The Bishop is nothing but a damned Socialist'.[17]

The squires' opinion would doubtless have been confirmed by such incidents as Frere's championing of Jack Bucknall, a Catholic Crusader who was threatened with dismissal by his Vicar because of his political activities.[18] The campaign against Bucknall reached the Truro Diocesan Conference and at the meeting two Admirals of the Fleet led the attack against Bucknall whom they described as 'this disloyal agitator'. Frere would have none of it:

Only a courageous defence of Bucknall, and to some extent of the ideas that he represented by Bishop Walter Frere thwarted the Admirals and their supporters. 'Mr. Bucknall is to stay, and I take full responsibility for his remaining', Frere told the Conference at the end of an angry debate.[19]

The Christian Socialists expressed their appreciation of the Bishop's stand. The journal of the League of the Kingdom of God suggested to its members:

[12] C. S. Phillips and others, *Walter Howard Frere, A Memoir*, 1947, p. 34.
[13] *Ibid.*, p. 28. For Carter see Jones, *op. cit.*, pp. 126 and 189 ff.
[14] *Ibid.*, p. 34.
[15] 1923–1935. *DECH*, p. 617.
[16] A. L. Rowse, *A Cornish Childhood, Autobiography of a Cornishman*, 1942, p. 136.
[17] C. S. Phillips, *et al.*, *op. cit.*, p. 35.
[18] Rowse, *op. cit.*, pp. 160–162.
[19] Groves, *Noel*, p. 312.

Let us thank God for the brave utterance and action of the Bishop of Truro in defending a Priest in his freedom against reactionary Christians.[20]

The Community of the Resurrection, of which Frere was a founder and also Superior from 1902 to 1913 and again from 1916 to 1922, was very much involved in both the Christian Social Union and the Church Socialist League.[21] From the outset CR was determined not to let their essential monastic function of regular and constant worship

overshadow their deep concern for the quality of British social life or to turn them into a purely contemplative order, remote from the needs and necessities of the outside world. Throughout its history CR has revealed an abiding commitment to human liberty and a willingness to become deeply involved in the moral struggles of the everyday world; its tradition now stretches from the British working-class movement of the 1890's to the battle against apartheid in South Africa in the 1950's and 1960's, from the Christian socialist Father Paul Bull to the anti-racist stalwart Father Trevor Huddleston.[22]

E. K. Talbot, who was also a Superior of the Community (1922–40),[23] wrote in the Frere memoir that the Bishop's sympathy was with the Labour Movement and that he had a strong impulse to identify himself with the underdog and dispossessed.[24] It is as well that these memories of his brethren are recorded, for Bishop Frere's papers, deposited by the Community of the Resurrection with the University of York, contain nothing that would betray this side of his character; they are almost entirely concerned with historical and academic liturgical matters.[25]

---

[20] *L.K.G. Quarterly*, No. 4, October 1926, p. 31.

[21] Peter F. Anson, *The Call of the Cloister*, 2nd ed., 1964, pp. 124–125; Donald O. Wagner, *The Church of England and Social Reform since 1854*, 1930, pp. 227–228. Wagner claims that Frere was a member of CSL.

[22] Jones, *op. cit.*, p. 228. No official history of the Community of the Resurrection has yet been written; the only work available is *CR 1892–1952*, 1952, the Diamond Jubilee Book. The Community has now commissioned the writing of one which will be ready for their Centenary in 1992 (private information).

[23] G. P. H. Dawson, ed., *Edward Keble Talbot. His Community and His Friends*, 1954.

[24] C. S. Phillips, *et al.*, *op. cit.*, p. 58.

[25] *Mirfield Deposit. Frere Papers*, Borthwick Institute of Historical Research, University of York. A recently discovered 'lost' journal of Frere adds no real light on this subject, although it does bear witness to Frere's anxiety that the new Community should be 'a stricter and poorer house' and that they should look for 'an opening for real parish work among the poor'. Martin Jarrett-Kerr CR, 'A Lost Journal of Walter Frere CR', *C.R., Quarterly Review of the Community of the Resurrection*, No. 325, St John Baptist 1984, p. 17.

John Burn's 'socialism' can be traced back to the days of his curacy in Scarborough. It was a time in which he had the opportunity to read the works of F. D. Maurice.[26] The book which most influenced Burn was *The Kingdom of Christ*,[27] and no doubt it was passages like the following that inspired him in his future 'championship of the poor and denunciations of the rich, sometimes perhaps too scathing and unqualified'.[28] Maurice had written:

Men feel that they are not merely lost creatures; they look up to heaven above them and ask whether it can be true that this is the whole account of their condition; that their sense of right and wrong, their cravings for fellowship, their consciousness of being creatures having powers which no other creatures possess, are all nothing ... If religion will give us no explanation of these feelings, if it can only tell us about a fall for the whole race and an escape for a few individuals of it, then our wants must be satisfied without religion. Then begins Chartism and Socialism and whatever schemes make rich men tremble.[29]

Burn told his curates at All Saints', Middlesbrough that *The Kingdom of God* brought him to a fuller understanding of the nature of the Catholic Church, its ministry and sacraments, at a time when he was still sorting out his theological position.[30] Burn's biographer, Thomas G. Fullerton, says that during the last twenty-five years of his life,[31] Burn was 'commonly regarded as a Socialist, and in fact called himself one'.[32] There was an active branch of the Christian Social Union in his parish at Middlesbrough which evolved a system of feeding and caring for the unemployed and distressed during the 1907–1908 industrial disputes and trade depression. To preserve the dignity of the recipients they were known as 'CSU guests'.[33] Many of these 'CSU guests' came along to the 9.00 a.m. Parish Mass with mixed results, but Burn was as always charitable. He was

full of a loving faith in human nature, and he had no fear that they came because of the loaves and fishes. Many were confirmed that year and the next;

---

[26] T. G. Fullerton, *Father Burn of Middlesbrough*, 1927, p. 66.
[27] F. D. Maurice, *The Kingdom of Christ*, Everyman Edition, 1938 (*cit.* Maurice, *Kingdom*).
[28] Fullerton, *op. cit.*, p. 79.
[29] Maurice, *Kingdom*, p. 321.
[30] Fullerton, *op. cit.*, p. 67.
[31] *i.e.* 1900–1925.
[32] *Ibid.*, p. 199.
[33] *Ibid.*, pp. 203–204.

a good number fell away, but not a few remained faithful, and still do remain; God bless them.[34]

Having explored the political motivations of these two pioneers of the Parish Communion (interestingly, one working at the time in the Northern Province of the Church of England and the other in the Southern), it is now time to examine the other side of the coin.

From the scanty evidence which is now available it would seem possible to suggest that the first weekly celebration of a service which is recognizably a direct link with what becomes known as the Parish Communion is the service which W. H. Frere introduced when he became priest-in-charge of St Faith's, a daughter church of Stepney Parish Church, in 1890.[35] We are not able to ascertain the exact date for the introduction of this service as the church was badly damaged during the 1939–45 War and all records were lost, but as Frere left the parish on 18 January 1892[36] it would be between 1890 and 1892. More than forty years later a correspondent to *The Church Times* remembered:

The mission church of St Faith was about to be built, and it was Frere who had charge of mapping out the future of the daughter church. He suggested the then unknown hour of 9.30 for the Parish Communion, thus, as he said, giving a chance to the family of worshipping together and going home to prepare the Sunday lunch.[37]

Frere never wavered in his advocacy of the necessity for the centrality of such a service in parochial life. In a book which he hoped would make a contribution towards the revision of the Book of Common Prayer, he wrote twenty years later that he favoured a celebration on a Sunday morning at 9.00 a.m. or 9.30 a.m.[38]

In 1884 John Stote Lotherington Burn became Vicar of All Saints'

[34] *Ibid.*, p. 204.
[35] C. S. Phillips, *et al.*, *op. cit.*, p. 33.
[36] Jarrett-Kerr, 'A Lost Journal of Walter Frere CR', *op. cit.*, p. 13.
[37] *The Church Times*, 8 April 1938.
[38] W. H. Frere, *Some Principles of Liturgical Reform. A Contribution towards the Revision of the Book of Common Prayer* (cit. Frere, *Principles*) 1911, p. 160. In 1925 Frere appointed G. W. Hockley as his Diocesan Missioner and Archdeacon of Cornwall in the Diocese of Truro. In Advent 1917 Hockley, as Rector of Liverpool had introduced a 10 a.m. Holy Communion 'sung to simple music with a short sermon ... to give the Holy Communion its proper place of dignity in our Sunday observance' and to assist those who wished to make the Holy Communion their chief act of worship on a Sunday, *Liverpool Parish Magazine*, November 1917, p. 104.

Middlesbrough. Although he had been brought up as an Evangelical, and served a curacy at Scarborough Parish Church which was of that ilk, by the time Burn became Vicar of All Saints', he was turning to a more catholic frame of mind. At Middlesbrough he inherited the commonest Victorian pattern of worship, that is, Holy Communion at 7.30 a.m., Matins, Litany, and Sermon at 10.30 a.m., and Evensong. On the major festivals two earlier celebrations of the Holy Communion were added, and on festivals there was a choral celebration after Matins.[39] Burn did not make any changes in the service times straightaway. In fact, he waited until 1893, after he had been in the parish some nine years, before he made any alteration. During these nine years he had not been idle in liturgical matters, and already many of the external signs of catholic worship had appeared at All Saints': candles, vestments, and a daily Mass.

It might have been imagined that when he came to change the pattern of services Burn would be anxious to replace the 10.30 a.m. Matins with a Sung Eucharist after the practice of the majority of Anglo-Catholic parishes, but instead he chose to add a simple Sung Mass at 9 o'clock to the list.[40] When originally introduced, the service was intended to be primarily for children, but from the outset he discovered that there was a small congregation of adults. Burn taught the children to sing the service to the music of Merbecke, and there were hymns and always a sermon. At this stage this service does not conform to the criteria already laid down of the definition of a 'Parish Communion', because Matins at 10.30 a.m. 'remained for the choir and many others the main service'.[41] Also it was not uncommon for Anglo-Catholic parishes at this time (and for many years later) to have a Children's Mass at around 9 o'clock in the morning, while the adults were still expected to communicate at an early celebration and to attend as non-communicants at the Sung Mass at 11 o'clock. In the typical Anglo-Catholic parish communicants were neither expected nor encouraged at the Children's Mass. Where Father Burn's policy developed and differed was in that he was glad to have adult communicants at the 9 o'clock Sung Eucharist, even if that had not been his original intention. Burn was noted for refusing to take 'the Party line', and in this matter he was being typically individualistic and only incidentally pioneering.

The effect of this attitude towards the 9 o'clock service was that the

[39] Fullerton, *op. cit.*, p. 82.
[40] Fullerton, *op. cit.*, p. 107.
[41] *Ibid.*, p. 107.

number attending Choral Matins at All Saints' started to decline while the numbers at the 9 a.m. Eucharist began to increase, with the effect that this service was becoming 'in all respects the principal service of Sunday mornings'.[42] Fullerton wrote of the Vicar's intentions in developing this policy for the parish:

Father Burn was convinced that the true ideal for Sunday morning worship is a Sung Mass at an hour early enough for people to make their Communion fasting, and for women to be able to cook dinner afterwards. The truth of this belief was abundantly proved through many years. Nearly a hundred people usually received Holy Communion at the Sung Mass, and working mothers, sometimes with babies in arms, were to be found at All Saints' in great numbers.[43]

Burn was also pioneering in his attitude towards music in the service. He was anxious that the whole of the congregation should join in the singing, and taught them the Merbecke setting for this purpose. It was no part of his plan to have them as a passive audience while the choir sang. This, in a time of much choral activity in churches of all persuasions, was very unusual. He was not anti-music, for besides the church organ there was a stringed orchestra to add to the music of the service, but rather that he wished to encourage the fullest possible congregational participation. Burn's parochial policy falls short of the full ideal of the Parish Communion in that it was not the only celebration of the Eucharist on any Sunday but it was intended to be the principal and primary service, at which he hoped that all committed church people would be present each Sunday.

Middlesbrough was blazing a trail that eventually many others in the northern Province would follow. In the *Martin Correspondence* claim is made that at Chollerton, Hexham, under the incumbency of Wilfrid Bird Hornby (later Bishop), the main service of the day was a 9 a.m. celebration of the Holy Communion. Hornby was Vicar from 1897–1903.

There is one further interesting series of letters dealing with the period before 1900. They are about the parish of St Anne, Limehouse. In 1894 Francis Gurdon became the Vicar of the parish, and by 1898 the parish magazine advertised the time of 9.30 a.m. for 'Holy Communion (sung)'. The service was the third of the day, the earlier ones being at 7 a.m. and 8 a.m., but a correspondent wrote to Martin tell-

[42] *Ibid.*, p. 107.
[43] *Ibid.*, p. 108.

ing him from personal memory that it was a fully choral service with a choir and that the congregation made their communion. This example makes an interesting link with the previous evidence which has been examined for not only was Francis Gurdon a cousin of Frere, but he had also assisted Frere at St Faith's, Stepney.

Martin is able to summarize the position at the end of the nineteenth century:

We find that a few churches, at least, have started on the road leading to what later came to be called the Parish Communion though even the mere idea, let alone the practice, of the early Sung Eucharist remained comparatively unknown. To the vast majority of Churchmen the great questions of the day were those concerning non-communicating attendance, fasting Communion, ritualism, and Sunday observance. To them the idea of cutting straight across the two former questions by having the high celebration at an hour early enough for people to receive fasting seemed both impracticable and too idealistic—any other time than eleven or thereabouts for THE service of the Sunday was for most unthinkable. The occasional suggestion that the Eucharist as the principal service could be held earlier was brushed aside on the assumption that churchgoers simply would not come any earlier—at least to a sung service with a sermon.[44]

In the opening years of the new century there is a multiplication of the number of examples of parishes where the doubters were proved wrong. From the letters contained in the *Martin Correspondence* it is possible to find examples of a number of parishes which during these years made the experiment. Claims are made for:

1901 St Peter, Wimbledon.
1902 St Saviour, Poplar.[45]
1902 St James, Stavely, Kendal.
1903 St Andrew, Whitburn, Cumberland.

---

[44] Martin, *op. cit.*, p. 127.

[45] This is the only example for which there is evidence other than that in *Martin Correspondence*. Mark Trollope returned from Korea and served as Vicar at St Saviour's for a brief period before returning overseas as Bishop. His biographer wrote that in 1902 there was an opportunity to make some alterations in the services. 'The experiment was so successful that 8 a.m. became the hour of the Parish Mass and from the first attendance was better than the 8 a.m. and 11 a.m. combined.' There was no sermon, but the service was fully sung. The Book of Common Prayer was used. Constance Trollope, *Mark Napier Trollope, Bishop in Korea 1911–1930*, 1936, pp. 31–32. It is also described by an ex-choir boy in *Father Joe: The Autobiography of Joseph Williamson of Poplar and Stepney*, 1963, pp. 47–49. See also p. 199, *infra*.

1904 St Edward King and Martyr, Holbeck, Leeds.
   St Jude, South Shields.
1905 St John, Princes End, Tipton, Lichfield.

It needs to be noted that both St Peter, Wimbledon, and St Andrew, Whitburn were at that time daughter churches and that St Edward, Holbeck did not gain full legal independence until 1921. It would seem that the need for experimentation in new housing areas was sometimes the catalyst for such liturgical ventures. The correspondence contains 26 further examples of this type of service established before the commencement of the First World War. Out of these, together with the 7 examples already given, 22 (or two-thirds) were in parishes situated within the Province of York.

These facts set in context Brother Edward's remark in 1938 that, 'Some of us look to Temple Balsall as the Jerusalem of this movement'. The service at Temple Balsall was established as a result of a mission in that parish conducted by Fr Seyzinger CR in 1913,[46] but as we have seen there were earlier examples. However, Temple Balsall does seem to have been widely influential,[47] and the result of the experience on Brother Edward's subsequent ministry makes the exaggeration understandable.[48]

2   Bishops, Convocations, and Writers

After its rejection Lord Hugh Cecil[49] said of the 1928 Prayer Book:

It lacks the authority of a Parliament and the authority of the Pope, but it has the real and full authority of the Church of England expressed in the synods and by the episcopate.[50]

It might be suggested that for many years the Parish Communion

---

[46] *Sunday Morning*, p. vii.

[47] Hebert, *Parish Communion*, pp. 261–268.

[48] Kenneth Packard, *Brother Edward, Priest and Evangelist* (*cit.* Packard, *Brother Edward*) 1955, *passim*.

[49] Hugh Richard Heathcote Gascoyne-Cecil, Baron Quickswood, 1869–1956, *DNB, 1951–1960*, 1971, pp. 201–203.

[50] Quoted by the Dean of Chichester at the Annual Meeting of the Alcuin Club, December 1934. A. S. Duncan-Jones, *Why Change the Communion Service?*, Alcuin Club Papers, 1934, p. 8.

enjoyed something like a similar status within the life of the Church of England. For although, as has been seen when dealing with the programme of official liturgical revision which resulted in the 1928 débâcle, the Convocations did not have the establishment of anything like the Parish Communion among their objectives, yet at other times the Convocations were capable of recognizing the need to encourage this development. Equally, some Bishops, and notably for the main part those who had some kind of connection with the various Christian Socialist organizations, when distracted long enough from the necessity to provide the answers to the Royal Letters of Business, did put their weight behind a parochial liturgical policy which centred on a Parish Communion. In fact, it is a member of the episcopate, Bishop J. A. Kempthorne of Lichfield, who first uses this particular title (with two capital letters), as far as can be discovered.

Thus it becomes necessary to investigate, first of all, those rare Convocation debates during which the Liturgy is discussed from a parochial and pastoral point of view rather than as part of the long-winded Prayer Book revision process. Then next to take a look at the writings of those individual Bishops who had the necessary vision to see the strategic opportunities for the work and witness of the Church that the adoption of such a kind of service could afford.

There is one other avenue for exploration, and that is the emergence of references to this type of service in the theological journals and other writings. This comes to an important juncture with the work which Fr Gabriel Hebert of the Society of the Sacred Mission at Kelham commenced in the years immediately after the First World War.[51]

It is to John Wordsworth who was Bishop of Salisbury from 1885 to 1911[52] that attention must first be given. This erudite scholar-bishop made his first suggestion which he hoped would accommodate the principle of fasting communion while still retaining what he liked to call the 'festal character' of Sunday, to the tenth Synod of the Diocese of Salisbury in April 1899. Wordsworth told the Synod:

There is, however, one point which I wish to bring to the notice of both clergy and laity who wish to restore the discipline of fasting reception of Holy Communion. It is this, that there is a very strong tradition of the Universal Church against the practice of turning Sunday into a fast day, a practice which was stigmatised by St Augustine (Ep. 71) as 'heretical' and as a 'great scandal'. Those who press fasting reception, and yet have Sunday celebrations late in the day, are, it seems to me, either breaking this tradition or

[51] P. See pp. 195 ff, *infra*.
[52] *DNB, 1901–11*, 1912, pp. 705–707.

acting contrary to the law and spirit of the Church of England, which makes every Eucharist an open Communion.[53]

To this end the Bishop announced that he was going to give a positive lead in this matter:

In order therefore to set an example, which I hope that others may follow, I have determined to hold my ordinations in future at nine o'clock, so that those who desire to receive the Communion fasting (as many do) may do so without injury to the festal character of the Lord's Day. I hope also to be able to arrange generally for consecrations of churches at the same hour.[54]

Bishop Wordsworth returned to the matter two years later when writing in the *Salisbury Diocesan Gazette*. In this article he expressed the hope that consideration should be given to a celebration of the Holy Communion at 9 o'clock on a Sunday morning. The Bishop said that he was of the opinion that it would be worthwhile to

try a nine o'clock Matins with Holy Communion, wherever the morning service is really badly attended. This would give rest to the weary old limbs, and yet be over soon enough to enable the young people to get their bicycle rides without a sense of Sabbath breaking. I always now intend to have the ordination services at 9 a.m. A parochial service might be over by 10.30 or 10.45, which would give time for cooking the mid-day dinner, and admit of Sunday School for an hour before the parson had his. I do not recommend this where the present order is successful, unless it were asked for by the people.[55]

The Bishop of Salisbury appears, at first sight, not to be advocating this change from any theological or liturgical principle but from a straightforwardly practical argument which is concerned with filling the church pews. However, the Bishop's attitude may not have been as blatantly pragmatic as it might seem at first sight. In his book *The Ministry of Grace*, published the following year, he argues in favour of nine o'clock as the correct time to hold the Holy Communion Service.

As regards the hour of communion in our own country and elsewhere in the

[53] *Salisbury and Winchester Journal*, Supplement, Saturday 15 April 1899 and *Guardian*, No. 2785, 19 April 1899, p. 519.
[54] *Ibid.*
[55] *Salisbury Diocesan Gazette*, quoted in *The Guardian*, No. 2847, 27 June 1900, p. 932. The original copies of the *Salisbury Diocesan Gazette* for 1900 are not extant: information from the Diocesan Office, Diocese of Salisbury, and the County Record Office, Trowbridge.

west, there is a good deal of evidence in favour of 9 a.m. on Sundays as the 'Canonical Hour', Matins having been said previously. There is also, I venture to think, not a little to be said for returning to it.[56]

As will be noted, Wordsworth puts his emphasis on this unusual phrase the 'Canonical Hour'. For this idea he derives his evidence from Scudamore's *Notitia Eucharistica*,[57] in which authorities are quoted to support the theory that the usual time for the service of Holy Communion is nine o'clock in the morning. One of the principal authorities for Scudamore's contention was the work of Anthony Sparrow, the seventeenth-century Bishop of Exeter (and later of Norwich),[58] who was in his time an author of a 'new species of literature, the Prayer Book commentary'.[59] Bishop Sparrow in his *Rationale* had said:

The usual hour for the solemnity of this service was anciently, and so should be, Nine of the clock, Morning. This is the Canonical hour. Thence probably called, the holy hour, in case of necessity it might be said earlier or later but this was the usual and canonical hour for it. One reason which is given for it is, because at this hour began our Saviour's Passion, the Jews crying out crucify etc. At this hour therefore is the Communion Service (part of which is a commemoration of Christ's Passion) performed. Another reason given is, because this hour the Holy Ghost descended upon the Apostles. Lastly because it is the most convenient hour for all to meet, and dispatch this with other offices before Noon. For, till the service was ended men were persuaded to be fasting; and therefore it was thought fit to end all services before Noon, that people might be free to eat.[60]

In the same year that Bishop Wordsworth was recommending nine o'clock as the hour for the Holy Communion Service on the grounds of antiquity, as well as pastoral convenience, a man who was to become in twelve months' time the Bishop of Worcester[61] came to the subject from another angle. Charles Gore, like Wordsworth, was a high churchman and supporter of Christian Socialist causes, and, as

[56] John Wordsworth, *The Ministry of Grace: Studies in Early Christian History with reference to Present Problems*, 1901, pp. 318–319. *Cf.* Calver, *op. cit.*, pp. 9–14.

[57] W. E. Scudamore, *Notitia Eucharistica: A Commentary, Explanatory, Doctrinal and Historical on the Order for the Administration of the Lord's Supper or Holy Communion according to the use of the Church of England*, ed. 2, 1876, p. 157.

[58] *ODCC*, (ed. 2) p. 1297.

[59] Cuming, *History*, p. 112.

[60] Anthony Sparrow, Lord Bishop of Exon, *A Rationale upon the Book of Common Prayer of the Church of England with a caution to his Diocese against false doctrines*, 1684 (1st ed. 1655) p. 211 (spellings modernized throughout).

[61] Prestige, *op. cit.*, p. 227.

has been seen, both he and Wordsworth were unhappy about the strict line that many of their colleagues were taking on the subject of non-communicating attendance at the Eucharist.[62] Gore was determined to show the un-catholicity of their arguments and did so in his book, already referred to, *The Body of Christ*. In it he affirmed his unwavering support for the Catholic party's campaign to restore the Eucharist to its central place 'as the chief, if not the most largely attended act of Sunday worship'. He stated that he would not be content with anything short of this, but was equally seized of the necessity that such a service must include the communion of the people.

It cannot be said too strongly that any practice which divorces communion, or which rests content on a 'high service' with the communion of the priest alone, really represents a seriously defective theology.[63]

In *The Body of Christ* Gore then went on to advocate what he called 'the parochial communion'.[64] He recognized the difficulties of establishing such a service with 'our modern habits of late rising on Sunday', but believed that the advantages of the outcome gave every justification to a careful search for the solution to the problems surrounding the issue of fasting communion, which, as has already been noted, Gore recognized as 'a very ancient and venerable custom'.[65]

The first occasion on which either of the Convocations discussed the possibility of encouraging a 'Parish Communion-type' service came as a result of a brave attempt made by Canon H. Bell in May 1902 to get the Convocation of York to consider the provision of a 'shorter and more reasonable form of morning service'.[66]

Bell moved the following motion in the Convocation:

That in view of the anomalies and practical inconvenience involved in the present arrangement of Sunday morning service—including, as it does, Matins, Litany, and Holy Communion—it is desirable that the question should be carefully considered, and that the Liturgical Committee be invited to consider it and make a report upon it at an early debate.[67]

Unfortunately, there was only a short debate in a thin house before

[62] For the Bishop of Salisbury's views on fasting communion see: John Wordsworth, *The Holy Communion, Four Visitation Addresses AD 1891*, 1893, *passim*.
[63] Gore, *Body of Christ*, p. 276.
[64] *Ibid*.
[65] *Ibid. Cf.* p. 20, *supra*.
[66] *Guardian*, no. 3021, 18 October 1903, p. 1644.
[67] *York Journal of Convocation*, vol. 11 for session 3 and 4 May and 4 July 1902, p. 106 and *Guardian*, no. 2944, 7 May 1902, p. 686.

the matter was committed to the Convocation's Liturgical Committee. This committee produced their report later the same month and in it they stated that they were of the opinion that it was

not desirable at the present time to make changes ... Where it is necessary to shorten Morning Service it is better effected by separation of Services than by making structural changes.[68]

Canon Bell was not willing to leave the matter there and the next year wrote a strong letter to the *Guardian* newspaper stating that he was in favour of just the one service for a Sunday morning, 'well thought out'.[69] His letter provoked a long correspondence[70] about the virtues and problems of the existing system, but the main issue got sidetracked onto the issue of fasting communion. In an editorial article, at the close of the correspondence, the *Guardian* expressed disappointment that this had happened, and then referred to 'the canonical hour of 9 a.m.', saying that there was 'a good deal to be said for the plan and we should like to see it fully tried'.[71] But the matter was allowed to rest there by both the newspaper and its readers.

The next event which gave support and encouragement to the idea of a celebration of the Eucharist on a Sunday morning which gathered together the various elements of parish life, was the series of lectures in Pastoral Theology given by Cosmo Gordon Lang, then Bishop of Stepney, at Cambridge University in 1904. In these lectures Lang expressed doubt about whether the Church of England had yet succeeded in finding an ideal plan for Sunday worship in town parishes. Such a plan, maintained Lang, should be both suited to the social conditions of the people and also faithful to the principles of Christian worship. Bishop Lang thought that he detected among all sections of church people a growing desire to give the Holy Commu-

[68] *York Journal of Convocation*, vol. 11, Appendix V: Report of Liturgical Committee.
[69] *Guardian*, no. 3021, 18 October 1903, p. 1644.
[70] Among those who took part in the correspondence was Wilson Carlile, the founder of the Church Army (Sidney Dark, *Wilson Carlile, the Laughing Cavalier of Christ*, 1944). On 20 January 1904 he pleaded the cause of the working man who was, he believed, non-communicant 'not because of the Prayer Book but because of the services', and commended his own *Congregational Communion: Music without Choir. Lasting thirty minutes apart from the administration*. The Archivist of the Church Army states that this publication is referred to in a report for 1896 as 'our now popular Congregational Communion', and that it may date back to 1894 (private correspondence from Sister Joan Wilbourne CA) See also Kenneth Storey, *Wilson Carlile and the Church Army: A Study of his Life and Teaching*. Unpublished Manchester University Ph.D. thesis, 1984, pp. 688 ff.
[71] *Guardian*, no. 3037, 17 February 1904, p. 277.

nion 'the place on the Lord's Day which it never ought and was never meant to have lost'.[72] The restoration of such a place would not be achieved, Lang thought, until there was

one great parish communion every Sunday in which the aspect of the fellowship of the Body can be realized—the common sacrificial Meal, if one may with reverence so describe it, of the Household of God.[73]

Lang next dealt with the recurring problem of the appropriate time for the type of service he was advocating. He realized that it could not be so early in the morning as to result in 'a real loss of that rest which our working people sorely need on the rest day'[74] and yet it ought not to be so late in the day that very few could communicate. Lang's High Church inclinations would not allow for any relaxation of what he believed ought to be the Church's rule on fasting communion. With these factors in mind he makes a firm proposal:

I cannot but think that if a real effort were made to have the parish communion at, say 9 o'clock or even 9.30, these difficulties might be largely overcome.[75]

There was to be music at the service. Lang said that the service would be accompanied by 'any assistance which simple reverent congregational music can give', and so would be 'the great gathering of the Christian body'.[76] It was in this direction, the Bishop ventured to suggest, that

a truer conception of worship, a readier recognition of the missionary duty of the Church in large towns, and the altered habits of life among the people all seem to point.[77]

The liturgical policy which Lang described in his lectures was certainly the earliest fully worked-out policy statement on a parish communion[78] that was made in the Church of England. There is not, however, any evidence that Lang maintained the same level of enthusiasm for this pattern of worship during his subsequent episcopal ministry, culminating as it did with the Primacy at Canterbury.[79] If

[72] C. G. Lang, *The Opportunity of the Church of England: Lectures delivered in the Divinity School of the University of Cambridge in 1904*, 1905, p. 185.

[73] *Ibid.*

[74] *Ibid.*

[75] *Ibid.*

[76] *Ibid.*

[77] *Ibid.*

[78] Capital letters are not employed in the printed text, *ibid.*, pp. 185 and 186.

[79] Lockhart, *op. cit.*, p. 147 ff.

it had, perhaps the wide-spread adoption of this type of service might have been achieved much earlier. Providentially, the torch was taken up by others and the momentum thus maintained.

Lang's lectures were given greater circulation when the text was published in 1905. It can be assumed that this book was widely read because the Bishop of Colchester[80] referred to it the following year in an important speech to the Canterbury Convocation.

It was at the May 1906 meeting of the Convocation of Canterbury that the subject of the parish communion was first raised, hiding coyly behind a title 'Sunday Services—Choral Celebrations' in the *Chronicle of Convocation*.[81] The debate was initiated by the Bishop of Colchester who moved a resolution which stated:

That, in the opinion of this House, the Holy Eucharist might with much spiritual advantage, particularly in town parishes, be more frequently cele-brated chorally as the one essential act of Divine worship on Sundays at 9 a.m. or 9.30 a.m., an hour late enough for a longer morning rest, and yet early enough to meet the habits of the very large and increasing number of Churchmen who observe the ancient and pious custom of Fasting Commu-nion—Matins and sermon being fixed for such an hour as parochial circum-stances may render suitable.[82]

Although the resolution 'was his own child', the Bishop of Colches-ter admitted that he had received much encouragement from the Bishop of Stepney's book, *The Opportunity of the Church of England*, which was the title given on publication to Lang's Cambridge lec-tures. Bishop Whitcombe said that he had hoped to have prefaced his resolution with a preamble which would have set his resolution in the correct context. That preamble would have spoken of the need to reassert the value of the Holy Communion, not only as an individual act of communion, but as 'a corporate act of communion with our Lord, and with one another in this holy fellowship'.[83] He rehearsed in his speech the need to provide extra hours of rest for workers on a Sunday, but put most emphasis on the need to make the Holy Com-munion 'the one essential act of Divine Worship on the Sunday'. This service would be choral with general communion.

The Bishop was not speaking as some young man with a bright new

[80] Robert Henry Whitcombe, Bishop of Colchester 1909–1922, *Crockford's Clerical Directory 1975–76*, 86th issue, 1976, p. 1465.

[81] *Chronicle of Convocation of the Convocation of Canterbury (cit. Chronicle)* NS vol. xxiii, 1906, p. 135.

[82] *Ibid.*

[83] *Ibid.*, p. 136.

idea, but from the experience of forty-eight years of ministry. When he commenced his ministry, early celebrations were not common; now he rejoiced that they were possible in almost every parish. His proposal, he explained to the Convocation, was not intended to get rid of these early celebrations, rather was his intention to encourage a service at which those who needed rest on a Sunday could have both their communion and an act of worship without the strain of fasting 'till one o'clock or so'.[84]

In the subsequent debate there were three favourable and five critical speeches and two which equivocated. There was one reference to Bennett's 8 a.m. Choral Celebration at Frome,[85] but eventually the procedural device of 'the previous question' was moved, and the debate came to an end, yet not before the Bishop of Colchester was able to observe, with some satisfaction, that he and his friends had desired the discussion of the subject, and that had been secured. In that positive spirit he pronounced the Benediction, and the House was prorogued.[86] So it was that the first synodical debate on the idea of the parish communion came to an abrupt close with no guidance on the subject having been given to the Church as a whole. The Convocation did not return to the subject until ten years later.[87]

The subject next surfaced in the Diocese of Worcester. In 1908 the Worcester Diocesan Conference appointed a committee 'to consider how best the administration of the Lord's Supper or Holy Communion can be made the principal service of the Lord's Day'. In the event two reports were received by Gore's successor as Bishop of Worcester,[88] which were bound together and published as *The Report on the Place of Holy Communion in the Service of the Lord's Day* and duly presented by the Bishop to the Diocesan Conference in 1910.[89]

In the debate at the Conference it was said that, although there were two reports, the second was not to be considered as a minority report. The two committees had worked independently and produced separate reports,[90] but it was clear what was the issue which had separated the two Committees, and that was the idea of a 'Parochial Eucharist'. Speaking in support of the second report, of which he was one of the authors, Canon Streatfeild said that his committee 'dis-

[84] *Ibid.*
[85] *Ibid.*, Canon Tetley, p. 139. *Cf.* p. 153, *supra.*
[86] *Ibid.*
[87] *Chronicle, op. cit.*, NS xxxiii, 1916, p. 185.
[88] Huyshe Wolcott Yeatman-Biggs, Bishop of Worcester 1906–1918. *DECH*, p. 677.
[89] *Worcester Diocesan Magazine*, vol. xvii, No. 7, July 1910, pp. 204–205.
[90] *Ibid.*, p. 208.

tinctly and strongly disapproved of the "Parochial Eucharist"'. The real objective of such a service, he told the Conference, was that there should be 'non-communicating attendance on the largest possible scale'.[91]

Replying on behalf of the members of the committee responsible for the first report, Canon Wylde tried to take the heat out of the debate by saying that there seemed to be a mistaken idea about what was being advocated in the report. What they wanted to see was all the communicants of a parish joining together in a service in which some made their communion and others did not, but nevertheless were all present at the one Eucharist. This is certainly an unusual way of perceiving what would come to be known in later years as 'the Parish Communion principle'. Incidentally, in his speech Canon Wylde referred to the service as the 'Parish Eucharist' rather than by the title which had been used earlier in the debate, the 'Parochial Eucharist'.[92]

The Worcester Report cannot be heralded as an early advocacy of the principles on which the Parish Communion came into being. The members of the first committee are of the opinion that an early morning Sung Eucharist is not practical in the majority of parishes. They refer to the 'Canonical Hour', this time calling it the 'Mediaeval Rule', and say

The suggestion that the principal service of the day should be a sung Eucharist at 9 o'clock or 9.30, in accordance with Mediaeval Rule, does not commend itelf to your Committee. First, because the habits of people have changed. Men rise at least two hours later than in the Middle Ages, and in consequence 9 o'clock in the Middle Ages corresponds to 11 o'clock today. Nine o'clock is too late for those who come before breakfast, and too early for those who would come afterwards. It is not a convenient hour for anyone.[93]

The Conference spent the whole day discussing the Report. At one stage there was a suggestion that the debate might have to be continued in private because of the wide divergence of views, but the

[91] *Ibid.*

[92] Streatfeild in the early speech, said that the 'Parochial Eucharist' was being advocated in the correspondence columns of *The Guardian*. The letters to which he referred appeared from March to June 1909. The phrase had been used by the Rev'd Douglas Macleane in an article 'Morning Service' in *The Guardian*, 3 March 1909, No. 3300, p. 351, which provoked the correspondence to which Streatfeild referred in his speech. In the article Macleane asked whether the introducton of the Early Celebration was, after all, a mistake. He questioned whether the Sunday forenoon 'Parochial Mass' ought to be celebrated before half the parish is out of bed.

[93] *The Report on the Place of Holy Communion in the Service of the Lord's Day*, 1910, p. 35.

Bishop did not accept the suggestion, and the Diocesan Magazine records that he told the Conference that

if the speeches were made in the same admirable spirit as they were in the morning, and if the reports were published fairly, fully, and not merely the spicy bits selected, and the arguments rejected as too heavy for the general public, he did not think there was any necessity for the debate to be conducted in private.[94]

The debate continued in public with the advocates of the Parochial Communion defending their position against a determined opposition. At the end of proceedings a resolution was moved that any statement issuing from the Conference should consist simply of a statement that there ought to be a celebration of Holy Communion in every parish each Sunday;[95] but the members were anxious to give a clearer lead, and passed a resolution proposed by the Bishop which stated:

This Conference, having received from the Lord Bishop two reports from the Committee appointed by the Conference 'to consider how best the administration of the Lord's Supper or Holy Communion may be made the principal service on the Lord's Day', advises that the service of the Lord's own institution should find a principal place in all churches on the Lord's Day.[96]

Thus ended a debate which at times seemed capable of producing a more exciting result; however it did result in providing a clear signpost for one diocese at least.

Chronologically, the next two significant contributions to the growing awareness that the Parish Communion could perhaps be capable of providing the best expression of the eucharistic life of the Church in the early twentieth century are in books which have already been noted. It has been seen that in the seventh edition of his continuingly popular book *The Parson's Handbook*, published in 1909, Percy Dearmer advocated a Sung Eucharist at 9 a.m. or 9.30 a.m.[97] In the fourth edition of the book in 1903 Dearmer had written approvingly of Bishop John Wordsworth of Salisbury's stand on non-communicating attendance at the Holy Communion.[98]

The second book was W. H. Frere's *Some Principles of Liturgical*

---

[94] *Worcester Diocesan Magazine, op. cit.*, p. 211.
[95] *Ibid.*, p. 218.
[96] *Ibid.*, p. 215.
[97] Percy Dearmer, *The Parson's Handbook*, 7th ed., p. 209. *Cf.* pp. 131–2, *supra*.
[98] *Ibid.*, 4th ed., 1903, p. 179.

Reform which first appeared in 1911 and was reprinted twice in that same year, a sign of both wide circulation and interest. Frere introduced the book as being only concerned with 'the large issues which are of general concern'. It can be assumed, therefore, that he considered that the matter of a communicating Eucharist as the main ingredient of Sunday morning worship was one of the 'large issues', from the fact of its inclusion.[99]

There are, Frere suggests, two possible alternative forms of Sunday morning worship, which in their different ways conflict with the ideal. One is the late Choral Eucharist, which, he says, is not in any real degree a Communion and the other is the late Choral Matins. Writing about this latter service Frere is blisteringly critical. He says it has

ousted the service of our Lord's appointment and worked havoc deeper even than the inversion of the relative value of services, for to it is due much of the disastrous alienation of the old-fashioned instructed Churchman from communion altogether.[100]

What Frere advocated was a compression of the services of Matins, Litany, and Holy Communion, with the omission of various items, especially those that repeated features included in another service, to form a complete service of reasonable length.[101] Believing that there was a growing revolt against 10.30 a.m. or 11 a.m., Frere suggested that this compressed service might be held at 'an earlier hour, such as eight, nine, or half-past nine'.[102] Frere does not tackle the problem of the eucharistic fast, stating that the suggested 'compressed service' will be after breakfast for some, and before breakfast 'for the communicant who does not prefer (or has not available to him) an earlier celebration'.[103] From this it can be seen that his assumption is that Holy Communion would be received fasting.

Another bishop to advocate the type of service which is under investigation was Edward Stuart Talbot. He was the first Warden of Keble College, Oxford, and was Bishop of Rochester from 1895–1905, the first Bishop of Southwark from 1905–1911, and finally from 1911 to 1924 Bishop of Winchester.[104] Talbot was theologically of the *Lux Mundi* school, to which he contributed the essay on 'The Preparation in History for Christ',[105] and he was supportive of the work of the

[99] Frere, *Principles*, p. x.
[100] *Ibid.*, p. 159.
[101] *Ibid.*, pp. 154–158 and pp. 195–196.
[102] *Ibid.*, p. 160.
[103] *Ibid.*
[104] *ODCC* (ed. 2) p. 1337.
[105] Gore, ed., *Lux Mundi*, pp. 129–178.

Christian Social Union.[106] Writing to one of his Southwark clergy in 1906, Talbot shows that he is aware of the problems of the working man and recommends a policy to accommodate his needs:

There are many upon whom labour presses heavily during the week and late on Saturday, who might properly take late rest on a Sunday and begin the day with the High Celebration. But if these prove insufficient there is the method of moving the celebration to the time which was I believe the usual one in earlier days in England, about 9 a.m.[107]

Talbot had presumably read the writings of his fellow Bishop, John Wordsworth of Salisbury, on 'the Canonical hour' and had accepted his findings. To a clerical correspondent Talbot writes that it had been a great wish 'on his part to see this arrangement tried, I have felt it would suit with the late hours of labour to which I have referred'.[108] In Bishop Talbot's mind the pastoral needs of parishoners seemed to predominate, although as a friend and colleague of Charles Gore his appreciation of the 'teaching about the incarnation with its consecration of humanity and about the Church as the inspired body'[109] would not allow the necessity that the Holy Eucharist should be available to all members of the Church of God to be perceived at only one level.

Talbot's sons continued their father's emphasis in their own ministries. Edward Keble Talbot was an early member of the Community of the Resurrection[110] with its left-wing interests; Neville Stuart Talbot was an energetic army Chaplain in the 1914–1918 war,[111] who made strong recommendations, which have earlier been considered,[112] about how worship should be shaped after the war was over. A third son who was killed in that same war gave his name to Toc H.[113]

In 1916 the Canterbury Convocation, at its February meeting, considered a motion of Canon Heygate of Lincoln in which he suggested

---

[106] Gwendolen Stephenson, *Edward Stuart Talbot 1844–1934*, 1936, p. 83.

[107] *Ibid.*, p. 163.

[108] *Ibid.*, pp. 163–164.

[109] *Ibid.*, p. 50.

[110] *CR 1892–1952*, p. 30.

[111] Brabant, *op. cit.*, pp. 57–72.

[112] See pp. 43 ff and p. 49, *supra*.

[113] Brabant, *op. cit.*, pp. 63–65; Tresham Lever, *Clayton of Toc H*, 1971, p. 43.

that a Committee of the House be appointed to consider without delay how the Church may best be prepared to meet the spiritual needs of sailors and soldiers of the King returning to their homes and civil occupations when the present War is over, especially with respect to worship, public and private.[114]

Canon Heygate, in his supporting speech, said that although some would return from the War little affected by their experiences, there would be others who had been 'deeply stirred'. Of these, many had not been in close contact with any form of organized religion before the War, but, since joining the Army, they had come into contact with the Church in many different ways. When these men returned to their homes and parishes, Heygate asked, would they find what their souls desired in the ordinary Matins and Evensong? He was afraid that they would not. To the confirmed 'the Holy Communion would be the great central act of worship and would supply their souls' spiritual needs'. But even they, he believed, would want 'something in addition in the shape of a service of a very different character'.[115] In his speech Canon Heygate compared the problems of following the services of the Prayer Book with the clarity of *A Simple Book of Prayers for Soldiers* which was supplied by the Roman Catholic Church for their men. He felt strongly that the Church ought to show to the soldiers and sailors that it was deeply interested in their spiritual welfare and was longing to do all that lay in its power to meet their needs when they returned. Heygate perceptively observed that the process of Prayer Book Revision in which the Convocation was involved, did not engage any of the issues that concerned those who were involved in the horrors of the War. He said he didn't know whether to laugh or cry when he read some words in a letter written by a soldier at the front, who said:

You would have roared to hear the round of laughter that rose up at our Mess this morning when I opened the paper and read out that the Lower House of Convocation was spending its time upon the question as to whether King Charles should be canonised or not.[116]

Heygate thought that in the light of such an attitude, the forces were entitled to think:

Here are we at the front shedding our blood for our country, and there are they at home spending their best intellectual efforts on such a subject.[117]

[114] *Chronicle, op. cit.*, NS vol. xxxii, 1916, p. 172.
[115] *Ibid.*, p. 173.
[116] *Ibid.*, p. 174.
[117] *Ibid.*

Among the suggestions made in the subsequent debate were for a Lay Folk's Mass Book and for the provision of a running commentary on the Communion Service as it went on,[118] but the most substantial contribution came towards the end of the discussion from H. K. Southwell, the Archdeacon of Lewes. Speaking bluntly, he said that quite frankly the services of the Church of England had not attracted the men. The Service which started at eleven o'clock and ended at a quarter or twenty minutes past one was 'no use to them at all'. The report of the debate says that the Archdeacon was of the opinion that

it never had attracted them, and it never would attract them. In the revision of the Prayer Book the clergy had been thinking very much of their own wishes and likes and dislikes, and perhaps, sometimes, they had been rather anxious too that another party should not get any advantage in the matter.[119]

Southwell asked the Convocation if they had ever asked themselves the question, 'Is the book as it stands a book which is likely to win souls?'[120] He was quite sure that the men would not be helped or reached by what people were at that time accustomed to. Speaking for himself, the Archdeacon said that he had a firm belief

that a simple Service of Holy Communion, with music if desired, at some such hour such as eight or nine o'clock, as the principal Service of the morning would, if the men were taught, both bring and hold them.[121]

He did not think that there was much in 'the sacred hour of eleven'.[122]

The outcome of that debate on 18 February was that a Committee was quickly set up, of which the Archdeacon of Surrey (the Ven. A. G. Robinson) was Chairman, and both Canon Heygate and Archdeacon Southwell were members, and by 13 April its report was ready, thus providing an example of speed which present-day ecclesiastical legislators would find quite amazing.[123]

The Report states from the beginning that, although it might have emerged from an unusual situation, it is concerned with those for whom the church at home has had, and will have, a responsibility.

The men with whose spiritual welfare this Report deals are essentially

[118] *Ibid.*, p. 175.
[119] *Ibid.*, p. 184.
[120] *Ibid.*, pp. 184–185.
[121] *Ibid.*, p. 185.
[122] *Ibid.*
[123] *Report of the Committee on the Spiritual Needs of Sailors and Soldiers after the War*, Convocation of Canterbury Lower House, No. 496, 1916. (*cit. Report on Spiritual Needs*).

civilians, though they are at present serving in the King's Forces. Whatever failures in the religious life and training of these men have been brought to light are due to some failure in ordinary parochial Church life and work. The efforts of the naval and military chaplains may prepare the ground, but it will be in the parishes that the real work of renewal and rebuilding will have to be done.[124]

At the front religion has been much talked about and services have been eagerly attended. In particular, 'Celebrations of the Holy Communion have been held near the fighting line which will never be forgotten'.[125] With this in mind the Committee made a number of suggestions. They urged a vast improvement of the Church's work of teaching,[126] a building up of the sense of fellowship in the Church,[127] a consideration of the form of public worship,[128] and for encouragement to be given to simpler and freer services, such as prayer meetings.[129]

On the subject of Christian fellowship the Committee said that ordinary people believed in brotherhood and might be shown that

the Christian Church too believed intensely in brotherhood; but it takes, or should take, a much wider view of what brotherhood means. It deals with the whole of man's nature, his bodily and spiritual needs alike. It knows no class or racial distinctions, but is Catholic, all embracing.[130]

Yet the Committee admitted that things could be improved:

Even in the more directly spiritual side of the Church's work, the sense of fellowship is strangely weak. Men and women join in the Service of Holy Fellowship, but outside the church the fellowship often has but little meaning. A man may be for years a Church member without ever getting the feeling that he is one of a band of brothers.[131]

When the Committee turned to consider Public Worship it quoted with approval some words which the Archbishop of York[132] had addressed to his clergy on what he had called 'The Service of Holy Fellowship',

I am sure that just in so far as the anxieties, sorrows, and awful issues of this time of war open in the hearts of men a sense of the need of God, so, in the

[124] *Ibid.*, p. 2.
[125] *Ibid.*
[126] *Ibid.*, pp. 3-5.
[127] *Ibid.*, pp. 5-7.
[128] *Ibid.*, pp. 7-9.
[129] *Ibid.*, pp. 9-10.
[130] *Ibid.*, p. 5.
[131] *Ibid.*
[132] Cosmo Gordon Lang, *DECH*, p. 690.

worship of our churches they will yearn for something that speaks of a God, Who, while He draws their hearts upwards to Him, comes Himself down to meet them. Is not this just to say that in the Eucharist the spirit of worship is most fully alike aroused and satisfied? We must try everywhere, patiently, gently, hopefully, to restore that holy service to its rightful place as the central act of the Church's worship.[133]

Lang had told them that if the Eucharist could be lifted out of the region of doctrinal or ritual controversy and celebrated everywhere with awe and reverence, it could not fail to appeal, 'as no other service can, to hearts of men and women yearning in the stress of this anxious time for communion with a living and personal God'.[134] The Archbishop continued:

It has a *converting*[135] power which is all its own, and expresses far more completely than Matins or Evensong the joy of worship and of fellowship.[136]

This note of 'fellowship' is strongly emphasized by the Committee and is echoed later by the advocates of the Parish Communion.

The Report was well received by the Lower House on 3 May and four resolutions were eagerly agreed to:

1. That in the judgment of this House there is a serious need for more careful and definite religious teaching, more especially in regard to the privileges and responsibilities which belong to membership in the Body of Christ; and that their Lordships of the Upper House be asked to consider the desirability of issuing a manual of instruction which would give guidance to those who desire it.

2. That it is of urgent importance that efforts should be made to quicken the

---

[133] *Report on Spiritual Needs*, pp. 7–8.

[134] *Ibid.*, p. 8.

[135] *Cf. Wesley's Journal*, vol. 2, pp. 360–362, 27 June 1740 'In the ancient church, every one who was baptised communicated daily. So in Acts we read, they 'all continued daily in the breaking of bread, and in prayer'. But in latter times many have affirmed that the Lord's Supper is not a converting, but a confirming ordinance. And among us it has been diligently taught that none but those who are converted, who have received the Holy Ghost, who are believers in the full sense, ought to communicate.

But experience shows the gross falsehood of that assertion that the Lord's Supper is not a converting ordinance. Ye are the witnesses. For many now present know, the very beginning of your conversion to God (perhaps, in some, the first deep conviction) was wrought at the Lord's Supper. Now one single instance of this kind overthrows the whole assertion.'

[136] *Report on Spiritual Needs*, p. 8.

sense of Christian fellowship among our communicants and in our congregations.

3. That no arrangements for worship should be regarded as satisfactory which do not provide for a Celebration of the Holy Communion as the principal Sunday service, at an hour when the greatest number can be expected to communicate.

4. That, in addition to the regular services, there should be simpler and freer services, at which our lay people should be encouraged to take their part in speaking and in praying.[137]

However, their Lordships of the Upper House were not similarly seized of the urgency of the situation, and the Prolocutor had the unhappy task the following day of reporting to the Lower House that:

The Bishops of the Upper House recognise the urgent importance of some of the matters referred to in the Resolutions appended to the *Report of the Committee of the Lower House (no. 496) on the Spiritual Needs of Sailors and Soldiers after the War*, especially with regard to worship public and private. The Bishops are giving to the questions thus raised their anxious and careful consideration, and they desire to assure the Lower House that they will collectively or in their several dioceses take such steps as may seem to be desirable and practicable for meeting the difficulties and using the opportunities which are likely to arise when the men who are now serving return to their homes, and to which attention is directed in the Report of the Lower House.[138]

Once again, as in 1906, the Convocation of Canterbury had come so near to giving a positive lead in the matter of restoring the Eucharist to the principal place in the Sunday worship of the Church of England. This time it was the House of Bishops, despite the personal opinions of some of their number, who proved to be half-hearted and not inclined to give the proposals their undivided support. However, even this episcopal cold water was unable to kill off the enthusiasm which was building up in many places.

It has already been noted that as a result of the National Mission of Repentance and Hope a report was produced in 1918 entitled *The Worship of the Church*. The contents of that report were examined at an earlier stage in order to assess the contribution made by the Army Chaplains.[139] As the Mission was in process of preparation, a number of background documents were produced for those involved in its planning. The Mission had set itself the task of preparing the Church

and as a part of this preparation it must set itself to ascertain by what faults

---

[137] *Ibid.*, p. 11.
[138] *Chronicle, op. cit.*, NS vol. xxiii, 1916, p. 378.
[139] See pp. 38 ff, *supra*.

and errors in the Church a large number of men and women have been alienated from the Church and its worship.[140]

One of these preparatory documents was a private circulation in 1916 of *The Report of the Chaplains' Replies to the Lord Bishop of Kensington*[141] which provided the basis of the book *The Army and Religion*[142] eventually published in 1919. In the Report it is said that there was a good deal of evidence that the Prayer Book Services of Matins and Evensong were considered 'difficult and dull' and were 'not understood by ignorant chaps'.[143] The Report asks, 'What is the remedy?' and then provides one:

The persistent reply is—Reform in Church Services. There is a constant request for simpler prayers, greater elasticity, a new lectionary, a selection of psalms, a simpler Prayer Book, clearly printed and paged that all can follow, and a single hymn book for universal use.[144]

The Report goes on to disclose what it describes as 'an altogether surprising demand', that Holy Communion should be 'explicitly treated as the principal service of the Sunday',[145] and in support of this statement it produces quotations from servicemen:

Restore our Lord's own Service to its rightful position as the Service for all baptized to attend. Put the chief Service first. Men do not come to Communion, because they have not learnt what it means.[146]

And then further support is quoted from Chaplains, such as:

The experience of those Chaplains, so far as I know, who have brought it before men by making the Lord's Service the Parade Service, has been that it has produced an extraordinarily deep impression on their minds. There is no need to explain that it is different to any other Service. They know and feel its

[140] *Bulletin of the National Mission of Repentance and Hope (cit. Bulletin)* No. 3, 15 June 1916.

[141] This document is included in a set of bound printed papers catalogued as 'National Mission Papers' at Lambeth Palace Library. They are William Temple's own personal set.

[142] *The Army and Religion. An enquiry and its bearing upon the Religious life of the Nation.* See p. 37, *supra*.

[143] *The National Mission of Repentance and Hope. A Report of the Chaplain's Replies to the Lord Bishop of Kensington.* Private and Confidential, 1916, p. 40.

[144] *Ibid.*

[145] *Ibid.*

[146] *Ibid.*, pp. 40–41.

Divinity, as they would know and feel the Divinity of our Lord, not by explanation, but by instinct. It is reality and not High Church bias that makes men
prefer the Lord's Supper to a Service invented 300 years ago. The meal of the
brotherhood of Jesus is more to them than a Choir Office.[147]

Once again we see the strong pressure, arising from their wartime
experiences, that the Chaplains are bringing to bear on the subject of
the centrality of the Eucharist.

The June 1916 issue of the National Mission's *Bulletin* contained a
very positive statement about the centrality of the Eucharist. In what
is described as an *ad interim* report it is stated quite confidently:

The great alteration which many men, apparently of different types, would
like to see is the Holy Communion made the principal service on the Sunday.
Most seem to desire that this service should be simple, with hymns.[148]

Then in August the same publication printed a description of a
country parish which had 'restored the Eucharist to its rightful
place'.[149] In this parish 8.45 a.m. had been chosen as the most suitable
hour for its simple Sung Eucharist 'at which all who wished to do
could make their communion'.[150] The justification for the parish decid-
ing on such a service was said to be:

Our desire has been that the chief feature of our Sunday morning worship
should be the gathering together of the Christian family in one place, to
present to God the Father the memorial of our Saviour's Death, and partake
in the holy fellowship of the Body and Blood of Christ. Thus by having this
one parish communion only on Sundays we have tried to avoid as far as possible the separation of communion and worship.[151]

This service, described as both parish communion and parish
Eucharist in the article, was followed by a feature which became
increasingly important in many Parish Communion parishes in later
years, the Parish Breakfast. The parish in the article (nowhere identified apart from being called 'a country parish') told the *Bulletin*
readers about the development of the breakfast:

We had been accustomed from time to time to have breakfast in the parish
room after Communion: and it was felt that in view of this parish Eucharist
becoming a regular thing every Sunday, and in view, too, of the distance
which most of the communicants have to come, the establishment of a

---

[147] *Ibid.*, p. 41.
[148] *Bulletin*, No. 4, 20 June 1916, pp. 13–14.
[149] *Bulletin*, No. 9, 15 August 1916, pp. 7–8.
[150] *Ibid.*, p. 7.
[151] *Ibid.*, p. 8.

Sunday breakfast would be necessary for the success of our venture. Accordingly we decided to provide one every Sunday in the parish room. A committee of men was formed, and the whole thing is run by the people themselves. Tea, bread and butter and jam are provided: a box is handed round into which our folk put what they can afford.[152]

The writer says that he feels sure that a Sunday Eucharist of this kind would enable the rising generation to appreciate and become familiar with sacramental worship in a way that no teaching in Church or Sunday School could achieve. He says:

It is very beautiful and encouraging to see parents with their children, and even grandchildren, worshipping side by side at our Lord's Service: and mothers with their infants at the altar rails, and then afterwards sitting down to a common meal in the fellowship of the Christian Family.[153]

This eloquent advocacy is presented in the National Mission's official *Bulletin* as a pattern for others to follow.

The considerable influence in the Church of England which the Christian Social Union had exercised over many years was eventually channelled into the formation of the Industrial Christian Fellowship after the end of the War. The later influence of this organization on the development of the Parish Communion will be considered in its chronological place. In the same way that in its heyday the Christian Social Union had attracted the patronage of some of the episcopate, the Industrial Christian Fellowship had the support of socially-concerned bishops, including Gore, who were keen to support the work. The Archbishops of Canterbury, York, and Wales were Presidents, with the Bishop of Lichfield, the Vice-President, as the public *persona*.[154]

John Augustine Kempthorne, after six years as Rector of Liverpool,[155] became Bishop of Hull in 1904 and was translated to Lichfield in 1913.[156] Just about the time that he was becoming increasingly involved with the Industrial Christian Fellowship, Bishop Kempthorne published his thoughts on the work of the Church at a parochial level, in a book entitled *Pastoral Life and Work*

[152] *Ibid.* Could this be Temple Balsall? See p. 208, *infra.*

[153] *Ibid.*

[154] Studdert-Kennedy, *Dog-Collar Democracy*, pp. 15 and 40.

[155] *The Story of the Church of Our Lady and St. Nicholas, Liverpool*, n.d. (between 1926–1935), p. 27.

[156] Searches in the Dean Savage Library, Lichfield and the Lichfield Cathedral Library have not brought to light any memoir of Bishop Kempthorne. Percy Hartill said that Kempthorne was 'a disciple of Westcott who ordained him', *Industrial Christian Fellowship Journal*, vol. iii, No. 2, February 1935, p. 18.

Today. 'The conditions of acceptable worship are best fulfilled in the Holy Eucharist', wrote Kempthorne, because, he said, it is our Lord's sacred legacy to His Church and has 'the sanction of his plain command.'[157] The **Bishop** believed that the Church could not rest content until all church people were willing and ready to worship God in the Eucharist. He said:

It is a truism to say that the SERVICE which our Lord ordained must be the chief service of the Lord's Day. Whenever or wherever it is celebrated it cannot fail to be the chief service of the day.[158]

To achieve this, Kempthorne advised that services must be arranged so that the largest possible number of the faithful may be able to take part in Eucharistic worship. There is no doubt about the ideal re-arrangement, stated the Bishop: it should be planned in such a way so that the Eucharist is celebrated at an hour not too early for those 'who are weary with the labour of the week' nor too late for 'observance of the Church's ancient principle of fasting communion'.[159] Then **Bishop Kempthorne** uses as the title of the service he is advocating as the cornerstone of his plan, employing capital letters, 'A Parish Communion'. Of this service he wrote:

A Parish Communion at 9 or 9.30 has much to commend it, and we cannot but desire that all communicants should be spiritually ready for weekly communion.[160]

He also commends the encouragement of the presence of children at this service, saying that they would be able to see the Church at worship. Kempthorne also makes reference to the evidence which is available from the experience of the Army Chaplains that the Eucharist is 'conducive to relevant worship',[161] a very late twentieth-century sounding phrase.

All in all, the **Bishop** of Lichfield makes a very strong case for the introduction of the Parish Communion, which is made all the more convincing in that it comes from someone who had already had wide experience of working in the large cities of England and was acutely conscious of the task which was before the Church in the immediate post-war period.

In the late twenties and early thirties, that is, before the publication

[157] J. A. Kempthorne, *Pastoral Life and Work Today*, 1919, p. 30.
[158] *Ibid.*
[159] *Ibid.*, pp. 30–31.
[160] *Ibid.*, p. 31.
[161] *Ibid.*, p. 32.

of A. G. Hebert's seminal book *Liturgy and Society* in 1935, a number of writings advocating the Parish Communion or drawing the attention of English readers to the continental Liturgical Movement had started to appear, so that Hebert's book came as a grand finale to this period.

The monthly journal *Theology*, which described itself as a 'Journal of Historic Christianity', had been founded in 1920 as an organ of liberal catholicism under the editorship of E. G. Selwyn.[162] In an editorial in 1927 Selwyn deplored the continuing 'semi-feudal division of morning and evening church-goers' and stated that he was convinced that the main services of a Sunday 'must be real gatherings ... even if the people are not many they must look many'.[163] Selwyn referred to the Report of the Archbishop's Committee on *The Worship of the Church* already examined,[164] and reminded his readers that it had bidden the church to prepare for drastic change. But he was not over-optimistic about the Church's willingness or ability to cope with change in worship, admitting that the group of articles in that issue of *Theology*, which his editorial was prefacing, were commending a line of development for the main service of a Sunday morning which had been originally advocated by W. H. Frere in 1908.[165] He said that the articles

represent what we believe to be the right line of development ... it has taken long to digest, but that is the common fate of ideas which are soundly based.[166]

The first of the articles is entitled 'The Problem of the Sunday Morning Service'.[167] For evidence that there was indeed a problem, the author, R. H. Sutch, like the Editor, made reference to the report *The Worship of the Church*, and quoted with approval its statement that the whole tradition of the Church is in favour of making the Eucharist 'in some way central'.[168] Sutch wanted to support the idea of conflat-

---

[162] Alec R. Vidler, *Scenes from a Clerical Life: An Autobiography*, 1977, p. 89. Selwyn later edited *Essays Catholic and Critical*, 1926, which claimed an ancestry from *Lux Mundi*, cf. pp. 91 ff, *supra*.

[163] *Theology: a monthly Journal of Historic Christianity* (cit. *Theology*) vol. xiv no. 69, January 1927, p. 4.

[164] See pp. 38 ff, *supra*.

[165] Frere, *Principles*.

[166] *Theology*, vol. xix, No. 69, January 1927, p. 5.

[167] *Ibid.*, pp. 8–14.

[168] *Ibid.*, p. 8 (quoting *The Worship of the Church*, p. 15).

ing an abbreviated form of Matins and the Eucharist (as suggested by the National Assembly)[169] and making this service the centre-piece of Sunday morning worship. As for the hour for this principal service, Sutch suggested that, whatever time was chosen (his parish preferred 10 o'clock), it should be the same each Sunday. He concluded:

Surely it should be possible for clergy and laity alike to recognize as a principle that the chief service on the Lord's Day should be the highest act of worship known to the Church, offered at such a time as is most convenient to the majority; a service so built up as to call forth our spiritual and mental activities; and so ordered as to be recognized by all as the Church's supreme act of weekly worship.[170]

In the same issue of *Theology* A. R. Browne-Wilkinson discussed 'Sunday Morning and the Children'.[171] He was anxious to introduce children at an early age to the kind of Sunday morning worship which was the most valuable to them. Browne-Wilkinson stated that regular attendance at morning Sunday School, however often the lesson might be about Sunday worship, would not build up a habit of Sunday morning Church-going: 'nothing but the actual Church-going can do that'.[172] He asked that churchmen should tackle the question:

What is the habit with regard to Sunday morning which we want to build up? Supposing our aim to be at any rate, taking a long view, to lead the child to be in the future a weekly Communicant, this habit will not be forced by exacting weekly attendance at any non-communicating service, be that service Morning Prayer or even a Eucharist, at which there are no communicants. Further, supposing our aim is to train in the habit of attandance at either of these last-named services, we shall fail even in this so long as they are performed in such a way as to be interesting and delightful only to adults.[173]

The opinions of two other influential ecclesiastics on the problems and opportunities of the Church of England were published during this period, and both wrote about the place of the Eucharist in parish worship. One had not by then been appointed to the episcopate, while the other was climbing by stages to the highest office in the

[169] *Revised Prayer Book (Permissive Use) Measure, 1923,* NA 84, p. 15.
[170] *Theology,* vol. xiv, No. 69, January 1927, p. 14.
[171] *Ibid.,* pp. 15–24.
[172] *Ibid.,* p. 16.
[173] *Ibid.*

Church of England. They were Leslie Hunter[174] and William Temple.[175]

Hunter called his book *A Parson's Job* and in it he said that it was much to be desired that the Holy Communion should become the principal service of a Sunday.[176] Few could be happy with the excessive individualism of Catholic worship, but Hunter thought that things might be corrected if, instead of there being several celebrations at a Parish Church on a Sunday morning, to which individuals could go according to their personal convenience, an effort was made to 'concentrate on one Parish Eucharist'.[177] Hunter puts his point with strong conviction:

As soon as the belief is discarded that God is better pleased with the offering on Sunday morning in a church of five Masses than with one parochial Communion, the case for a multiplicity of celebrations is greatly weakened. A parochial Communion to which the same group of people, more or less, come Sunday by Sunday to share the hospitality of God, does develop a sense of fellowship between the worshippers at least as strong as in the less worshipful rite of the Free Churches.[178]

And in a footnote Hunter, as a 'son of the Manse', states that he speaks from personal experience of both. This group bound together in a eucharistic fellowship would discover itself as 'a fellowship in action, united by a common standard of life and a common action in social service'.[179] So Hunter advocated 'a parochial Communion at nine or ten o'clock' but admitted that, in order to plan this, the question of fasting communion needed honestly to be faced.[180]

Not only is regular fasting communion beyond the reach of many members in a working class home and many other people also, so is early morning com-

[174] Gordon Hewitt, ed., *Strategist for the Spirit—Leslie Hunter, Bishop of Sheffield 1939–1962*, 1985, *passim*.

[175] F. A. Iremonger, *William Temple Archbishop of Canterbury: His Life and Letters*, 1948, *passim*.

[176] Leslie Stannard Hunter, *A Parson's Job: Aspects of Work in the English Church* (cit. Hunter, *Parsons Job*), 1931, p. 47.

[177] *Ibid.*, p. 48.

[178] *Ibid.*

[179] *Ibid.*

[180] *Ibid.*, p. 49. Hewitt, *op. cit.*, makes no mention of Hunter's advocacy of the Parish Communion but it is mentioned briefly in Ronald Preston, 'A Bishop Ahead of His Church; Leslie Hunter: Bishop of Sheffield 1939–62', *Crucible, The Journal of the General Synod Board for Social Responsibility*, April–June 1984, p. 75.

munion as a regular practice ... The truth is that where the rule of fasting is pressed the Church is in fact excommunicating a large number who need the sacraments and is giving others a feeling that they have done something wrong when they communicate after having a cup of tea. It is time that the subject was cleared of cant and humbug.[181]

One person who was trying to clear the church of such 'cant and humbug' was Percy Dearmer.

In 1928 he produced *The Truth about Fasting*, in which, as has been seen, he revealed what he declared to be 'the falsities enveloping the subject'.[182] Dearmer stated that in the wake of the Tractarian revival much confusion had been caused by the introduction of the principle of fasting communion in many parishes.

By this time Dearmer had abandoned the idea of an early morning Sung Eucharist[183] and had reverted to promoting mid-morning Matins followed by a Sung Eucharist, with the omissions proposed in the 1928 Prayer Book (which he calls 'the New Book'):

Once, then, we cease to be trammelled by ideas about fasting, the difficulties which so continually baffle the clergy and offend the laity about the Sunday morning services completely disappear. Matins is at the usual hour of eleven: it is followed by the Holy Communion, and before the Holy Communion the Litany (made optional in the New Book) may be said or sung. The New Book also renders all three services more practicable by avoiding repetitions and allowing convenient adjustments.[184]

Archbishop William Temple gave his views on the subject of the best Sunday timetable in the Charge given at his Primary Visitation to the diocese of York in 1931.[185] It was published as *Thoughts on Some Problems of the Day*, and right at the beginning, in the preface, Temple says that there must be adjustments in the matter of hours of service and suggests that a fair trial might be given to

Matins to Benedictus (said) 8.45
Holy Communion (sung by congregation) 9.00
Sermon (30 minutes at least) with hymns and short prayers 11.00[186]

In a later chapter the Archbishop gave more details of his suggestions:

[181] Hunter, *Parson's Job*, p. 51.
[182] Dearmer, *Fasting*, p. vi.
[183] Cf. p. 132, *supra*.
[184] Dearmer, *op. cit.*, p. 5.
[185] Iremonger, *op. cit.*, p. 369.
[186] William (Temple), Archbishop of York, *Thoughts on Some Problems of the Day. A Charge delivered at his Primary Visitation*, 1931, p. vii.

In many places admirable results have followed the custom of holding a parochial Communion at 9.00, 9.15 or 9.30. No doubt if people have learnt to
value their Communions worthily, they will come at any hour. But to maintain avoidable difficulties in the way of coming is contrary to the method of
our Lord. The inherent difficulties of Christian discipleship are very great,
but they do not lie in this region. I can see no reason why people should be
called upon to cut short their sleep on the morning of their day of rest.
Further, I cannot believe that there are very many people for whom it is
profitable to make their Communion at 8.00 a.m. and then attend the same
service as a Eucharist at 10.30 or 11.00 a.m. That may be good occasionally,
but hardly as a normal practice. I suggest, for some churches at least, a parochial Communion at 9.15 a.m. followed by instruction (a sermon of 30 or 40
minutes with short prayers) at 11.00 a.m. Matins might then be said at 8.45
a.m.[187]

On the subject of fasting the Archbishop gave this advice:

Our aim must be, not to obey some particular regulation, but to come as fully
prepared as possible to receive the divine gift. For many this will involve fasting; for many also it will involve the taking of a little nourishment.[188]

He then summed up his conviction on the matter by saying:

But this is exactly the kind of question which is rightly determined only when
the determination is 'according to every man's conscience in the sight of
God'.[189]

This clearly stated opinion of the Primate must have had a wide-
spread influence on parish priests not only in the Northern Province,
when they came to consider their parochial policies regarding the
planning of their Sunday morning services. The time was still to come
when the people of a parish would be rightly given an opportunity to
express their preferences in respect of the pattern of worship in their
parishes. It was still the prerogative of the Parish Priest to set the pattern and for the congregation to accept what was decided by him—or
vote with their feet.

3   The Liturgical Movement in the Continental Roman Catholic Church

In 1929 *Theology* noted for the first time the influence of the Liturgical
Movement on continental Roman Catholicism in an article by

---

[187] *Ibid.*, pp. 160–161.
[188] *Ibid.*, pp. 162–163.
[189] *Ibid.*, p. 163.

F. Gavin on 'Contemporary Religion in Germany',[190] in which he revealed to English readers that

the Liturgical Movement aims to bring back the old Catholic ideal, and to bind up every worshipper through the service with the action of the Mass and the thought of the Offices. To this end there has been a double aim on the part of the leaders of the movement: addressed to the thinking and scholarly world, a series of solid and scientific essays have attempted to lay sound theological foundations; similarly, a popular series of handbooks and manuals— largely a practical working out of the theories expounded in the larger works—make specific application of the principles for the use of the worshipper in church. Where the Movement has had freedom to develop its own technique, congregational worship has practically become vernacular.[191]

Until the publication of *Liturgy and Society* in 1935, the only other references to the Liturgical Movement on the Continent are contained in two articles by J. Perret in *Christendom*,[192] the journal edited by Maurice Reckitt and already noted as the organ of the Christendom Group.[193] Thus may be seen again the continuing sensitivity of those who were heirs of 'the Maurice Tradition' to an expression of the liturgical life of the Church which manifests its role as being the Body of Christ in the world and its consequent social vocation. Perret underlines these issues in his first article, which is a review of Guardini's *The Spirit of the Liturgy*, by saying that he believed that the teaching of the Liturgical Movement could

help towards the solution of the problem raised more than once by the writers of *Christendom* as regards the intimate relationship of Worship and social action.[194]

Twelve months later in the same journal Perret wrote a fuller article on 'The Significance of the Liturgical Movement',[195] in which he said:

some of the ideas of the Liturgical School may be of some interest and help towards the removal of the great scandal which confronts the Christian

---

[190] *Theology*, vol. xix, No. 113, November 1929.

[191] *Ibid.*, p. 280.

[192] *Christendom*, vol. ii, No. 8, December 1932, pp. 294–298 and vol. iii, No. 12, December 1933, pp. 285–291.

[193] See p. 136, *supra*.

[194] *Christendom*, vol. ii, No. 8, December 1932, p. 296.

[195] *Christendom*, vol. iii, No. 12, December 1933, pp. 285–291.

Sociologists, namely the conscientious indifference of millions of sincere worshippers towards the social problems of the day.[196]

He made it clear that the Liturgical Movement was a reaction
against the religious individualism, subjectivism, and sentimentalism
inherited by the Roman Catholic Church from the eighteenth century. Whereas, in the Liturgy seen properly, there is a tremendous
social power which can transform congregations into 'a strong and
powerful body acting as God's arm interfering in human affairs,
becoming, as it were, an apocalyptic power which alters the course of
history.'[197]

He noted that one of the perversions of the Holy Eucharist which
the Liturgical Movement denounced as obscuring its corporate
nature is the High Mass without communicants at 11 a.m. and goes
on:

It is a poor justification to say that Communion takes place at a 'Low Mass'
in the early morning, and Adoration and Oblation—some add intercessions,
unless they put them with Communion!—take place at 'High Mass' at 11
a.m. If we want to transform our congregations of individuals into a
Church—i.e., an organic body—we will have to make again the solemn
celebration of the Holy Eucharist the great Communion Service of the week,
and teach again and again all that it means.[198]

The socially-aware sacramentalists of the Church of England
obviously recognized in the continental liturgical reformers a shared
concern. Who were these European radicals?

During the same period that the Church of England was involved
in the liturgical debates and upheaval that have been examined,
there were a number of places within the Roman Catholic Church on
the continent of Europe where liturgical matters were very much to
the forefront. Before making an assessment of the possibility that there
might have been some cross-fertilization, the history of this continental Liturgical Movement must briefly be examined, so that its salient
features may be discerned.

It cannot be denied that the twentieth century has seen a most
remarkable renewal by the Roman Catholic Church of its worship
and of the Church's understanding of that worship. This is what is
understood as the Liturgical Movement, a movement which has its
origins in France during the nineteenth century. However, for the

[196] *Ibid.*, p. 285.
[197] *Ibid.*
[198] *Ibid.*, p. 291.

background from which it emerged, it is necessary to look further into the past.

The imposition of the Roman Breviary in 1568 and the Roman Missal in 1570 was the Roman Church's response to the events of the Reformation. This had the effect of inaugurating a period in which the main concern of the Church was to see that these precise liturgical forms were strictly observed. There was great concern that there should be complete uniformity in the Church, and this was ensured by the decrees of a special Roman congregation, the Sacred Congregation of Rites. This period of preoccupation with the exact observance of rites, a strict interpretation of rubrics and decrees, has been called 'the Age of Rubricism'.[199]

For some time these principles were not challenged, but the movements of Jansenism, Gallicanism, and the Englightenment, although disapproved of by the Church and in general condemned as being deviant, just like the Reformation in the sixteenth century, showed up some of the fundamental weaknesses in liturgical practice and were concerned to eliminate them. The motives of these movements were diverse, but they were generally agreed that the liturgy should be simplified and its main ideas should be better worked out.[200]

However, it was the next stage in the intellectual history of Europe which was to prove to have the most influence on the principles of rigid unification and rubricism. The Romantic Revival, with its love of the past, both medieval and classical, did not have as its main motive a desire for the betterment of the people, but it did awaken a sense of history, and led many clergy and laymen to inquire into the origin and meaning of the liturgical gestures, vestments, vessels, rites, and feasts.

It is often maintained that the first stage in the Liturgical Movement began in France with the life and work of a Benedictine monk, Dom Prosper Guéranger. His aim was to reform the spiritual apathy of the Church in France and to restore the ancient (Roman) liturgical traditions. Guéranger went about this by refounding the Benedictine priory at Solesmes in 1833, which he organized on the basis of a mediaeval religious community. In 1841 the first volume of his massive work *L'Année Liturgique* was published. This made clear that Guéranger's aim was that

[199] Joseph Jungmann S. J. (trans. J. B. O'Connell) *Liturgical Renewal in Retrospect and Prospect*, 1965, p. 11.

[200] Theodor Klauser (trans. John Halliburton) *A Short History of the Western Liturgy, An Account and Some Reflection*, 1969, p. 121.

the Roman Liturgy should be the framework of ritual variation because through the Christian centuries the Roman Church was the centre of liturgy, as it was of faith.[201]

However, Ernest Koenker disputes the claim that Guéranger should be seen as the founding-father of the true Liturgical Movement. Koenker states that Guéranger's work never became anything more than a scholarly, academic thing, remaining at the theoretical level. He admitted that Guéranger's work gave impetus to the study and use of Gregorian music.

But the modern Roman Catholic Liturgical Movement is much more than a concern for the proper rendition of the chant.[202]

But Koenker's main point is that he is unable to accept Guéranger as the founder of the Liturgical Movement because his work did not involve bringing liturgy to the masses:

It did not aim at general participation or recognize as its ideal the ancient Christian Church, nor did it embrace the all-pervading social concern of the modern apostolate.[203]

Botte,[204] Bouyer,[205] and Jungmann[206] are agreed that the *Congrès National des Oeuvres Catholiques* at Malines in Belgium was the scene for the birth of the Liturgical Movement. Jungmann says:

The Liturgical Movement broke out all at once, apparently quite suddenly. We can even specify place and time: we can point to the decisive moment when this important phenomenon of our century was made manifest: it was at the meeting of the Catholic organisations of Belgium in Malines in 1909.[207]

Whereas, Koenker believes that the true birth-place was in Germany:

[201] R. W. Franklin, 'Guéranger and Variety in Unity', *Worship*, vol. 5, No. 5, 1977, p. 399.

[202] Ernest Benjamin Koenker, *The Liturgical Renaissance in the Roman Catholic Church*, 1954, p. 10.

[203] *Ibid.*, p. 11.

[204] Bernard Botte OSB, *Le Mouvement liturgique: Témoignage et souvenirs*, 1973, p. 18. Cf. Martin B. Hellriegel at the first National Liturgical Day at St John's Abbey, College-ville, Minn., 15 July 1929: 'Belgium is the oldest daughter of the liturgical movement'. *The Liturgical Movement*, Popular Liturgical Library, Series IV, no. 3, 1930, p. 26.

[205] Louis Bouyer, *Life and Liturgy*, 1956, p. 58.

[206] Jungmann, *op. cit.*, p. 15.

[207] *Ibid.*, pp. 15–16.

The Liturgical Movement as we know it today may ... be traced to the first Liturgical week held for laymen at Maria Laach in Holy Week of 1914.[208]

Even so, it would be mistaken to believe that in any particular year the Liturgical Movement came into being, full-grown. At Maria Laach also it remained largely a scholarly effort. Yet the research promoted there by Ildefons Herwegen, who was Abbot from 1913 until 1946, resulted in scholarly publications for the clergy and cultivated laymen which rapidly revolutionized the understanding of the liturgy among intellectuals, if not ordinary parish priests.

Botte, Bouyer, and Jungmann are perhaps to be followed because it would seem that the Belgian manifestation of the movement was the first to gain a popular following. Once again it was a Benedictine who was the leader, Dom Lambert Beauduin. Beauduin emphasized that the liturgy is not something which we are meant to see and hear alone but rather something in which we all take part. He wrote:

Hence, from the first centuries to our own day, the Church has ever given to all her prayer a character profoundly and essentially collective. By means of living the liturgy wholeheartedly, Christians become more and more conscious of their supernatural fraternity, of their union in the mystic body of Christ. And this is the most powerful antidote against the individualism to which our natural egoism surrenders itself so readily.[209]

Meanwhile in Austria it was an Augustinian monk of Klosterneuburg, Pius Parsch, who introduced the practical applications of what was being studied and taught at Maria Laach. He took over the tiny church of St Gertrude in 1919 and turned it into an experimental parish. Here, in his Bible Hours with laymen, they worked out the relevance of the Bible to liturgy.

Dr Pius Parsch through his Bible publications, devotional literature, periodicals, has made Klosterneuburg and his *Volksliturgisches Apostolat* great names in the Liturgical Movement. He has brought the liturgical research of Maria Laach and other monastic centres to fruitful practical application.[210]

Parsch has written about the doctrine of the Mystical Body:

This great doctrine is that it enables us to see our religion as a whole—as a unity. Some forty years ago many people looked at Christianity only bit by

[208] Koenker, *op. cit.*, p. 12; Margaret Senft-Howie and Radbert Kohlhaas, *Maria Laach Abbey*, 13th ed., 1985, p. 11.

[209] Lambert Beauduin OSB (trans. Virgil Michel OSB) *Liturgy the Life of the Church*, Popular Liturgical Library, Series 1, no. 1 1926, p. 13.

[210] Koenker, *op. cit.*, p. 15; *Liturgy and the Liturgical Movement, A Study Club Outline on the Liturgy in General*, revised ed., 1937, p. 4.

bit—and often the bits they saw most clearly were not the most important bits. But here we are brought right into the centre of our faith, and everything of prime importance is made to stand out clearly and in its context: Christ, the Church, the Holy Ghost, grace, the Eucharist, the sacraments, the entire liturgy, and also sin. All these can be clearly seen as a unity with their due proportions and interconnections when explained in terms of the Mystical Body doctrine.[211]

France, despite Solesmes, appeared to be a liturgical desert for many years. Although there had been a good deal of scholarly liturgical work done there (e.g. Duchesne, Batiffol, Cabrol, and the monumental *Dictionnaire d'archéologie chrétienne et de liturgie*), the practical application of this learning was lacking. This eventually emerged in the 1920s through contact with the German and Austrian movement, although the full pastoral expression of the movement in France had to wait until the Second World War. In 1943 the *Centre National de Pastorale Liturgique* was founded and the periodical *La Maison-Dieu* commenced publication.[211]

Germany also came to greater life during the 1939–45 war. A model liturgical parish was built up in Leipzig during the war,[213] and Klauser's *Short History of the Western Liturgy*, which represented an attempt to introduce to a wide circle of readers both the facts and the problems in the history of worship in the Western Church, started out as a correspondence course for German prisoners-of-war.[214] The centre for the study of the liturgy was founded at Trier in 1947 under Johannes Wagner.

It has been seen that in its very earliest days the Continental Liturgical Movement in the Roman Catholic Church could easily have been dismissed as a mere hankering after the liturgical purities of the past, but as it evolved, it broadened and deepened. It recognized the opportunities and the challenges of the present and was willing to admit that the insights of a new generation were capable of enriching and enlivening the Church's contemporary use of its received liturgical tradition. At the end of a definitive book, *Histoire du Mouvement Liturgique*, Dom Olivier Rousseau says:

The Church is alive, the past is living in it—and it sometimes happens that this generation forgets it—but the present is living there too. Furthermore the

[211] Pius Parsch (trans. Clifford Howell) *We are Christ's Body*, Liturgical Library 17, 1962, p. 14.

[212] Koenker, *op. cit.*, p. 16.

[213] *Ibid.*, p. 15.

[214] *Ibid.*, p. vii.

past cannot exist without the present, nor the present without the past. Let us acknowledge the indisputable supremacy of the first centuries in the Church, a supremacy which will last for ever and about which we shall never be able to change a thing. But let us tell ourselves that if it is to misunderstand the Church to make it begin at some later period in its history it is also a misunderstanding to make it end at some particular moment.[215]

All this activity in the Roman Catholic Church on the Continent had no particular influence on the development of the Parish Communion in the Church of England.[216] As has been seen, scant attention was given to it by Anglican theological journals and, as will be noted later, those responsible for the popularization of the idea, such as Gabriel Hebert, had no contact in any particular way with the continental developments. It is interesting to note further that the English Roman Catholic clergy were reluctant as a whole to take account of what was happening in Europe until the work of Vatican II began to have its effect.[217] To this extent the Anglican pioneers were well ahead of their English Roman Catholic contemporaries.

4   The Writings of A. G. Hebert

(a) Introduction

The various examples which have already been examined in this study have made it abundantly clear that the idea of the Parish Communion service did not spring new-born from the work of A. G. Hebert. However, his writings did bring to the attention of many, who had not previously given it any consideration, that this was a possible way of tackling the problem of Sunday morning worship. Hebert's books must be acknowledged as having ushered in the first period in which there was a rapid spread of the Parish Communion in the Church of England. The second stage came in the post-war period after the formation of the Parish and People organization.

Arthur Hebert was born on 28 May 1886 in the Vicarage at Silloth in Cumberland. After Harrow, he went up to New College, Oxford,

---

[215] Dom Olivier Rousseau, *Histoire du Mouvement Liturgique*, Lex Orandi 3, 1945, pp. 231–232 (own translation).

[216] There is evidence of 'liturgical stirrings' among Continental Protestants in this same period, but they had no influence either on the Church of England. Details of these stirrings have been gathered together in Michael J. Taylor, SJ, *The Protestant Liturgical Renewal: A Catholic Viewpoint*, 1963, *passim*.

[217] J. D. Crichton, H. E. Winston, J. R. Ainslie, eds, *English Catholic Worship: Liturgical Renewal in England since 1900*, 1979, p. 71 and pp. 79–80.

where he had a distinguished academic career. He spent a year at Oxford House before going to Cuddesdon. While in Oxford he met Fr David Jacks SSM, with the result that after two years in a curacy at St Peter's, Horbury, under H. A. Kennedy, he went to Kelham to work as a tutor before joining the noviciate in 1915.[218] From 1917 to 1918 Hebert worked with the YMCA in France and was eventually professed at Michaelmas 1921. At Kelham he came under the influence of the founder, H. H. Kelly, who had resigned as Director in 1910,[219] and almost decided to accompany Fr Kelly, who was considering going out to Japan to inaugurate theological training in that country.[220] In the event Hebert went out to St Augustine's Priory, Modderpoort, in the Orange Free State. But Kelly had already by that time planted a number of important ideas in the mind of his *protégé*, not least a regard for the writings of the man who was the inspiration of his own life, F. D. Maurice.

For Kelly the writings of Maurice were of supreme importance. When he first came across Maurice's work, Kelly said,

I not only read him, I absorbed him, thought him, built my whole mind on him. Maurice has always been the bottom stratum, the true foundation of all that I have tried to do.[221]

Maurice had 'the secret' as far as Kelly was concerned. 'Perhaps it is not true', he wrote,

that we have everything to learn from him but I am convinced we shall learn nothing at all till we have learnt his secret, and I hardly know from whom else we can learn it.[222]

In a study of Kelly's theological contribution to the life of the

[218] A MS *curriculum vitae* in Fr Hebert's own handwriting amongst the *Hebert Papers* (AGH Personal) in the Archives of the Society of the Sacred Mission of Willen Priory, Milton Keynes has been used to correct some of the biographical details in George Every, 'Arthur Gabriel Hebert', *SSM: The Magazine of the Society of the Sacred Mission* (cit. *SSMM*) vol. 64, No. 204, September 1963.

[219] Herbert Kelly, SSM (ed. George Every, SSM) *No Pious Person, Autobiographical Recollections* 1960, p. 98.

[220] MS letter in *Hebert Papers* (AGH Letters Received). SSM Archives.

[221] H. H. Kelly, 'Frederick Denison Maurice', *SSM Quarterly* (cit. *SSMQ*) vol. 60, No. 196, 33, September 1959 (reprinting a personal appreciation written by Fr Kelly in 1910). See also envelope 'Maurice (key to English theological mind)' in *H.K. Papers* 1929, SSM Archives.

[222] *Ibid.*, p. 36.

Church of England Alan Jones said that it had been Kelly and Kelham that had kept Maurice's theology alive during a time when the latter's influence was on the wane.[223] And Michael Ramsey said of Kelham:

An institution which learnt its theology from F. D. Maurice and had its first plans made by the prophet (H. H. Kelly) is not going to be the home of traditionalism or immobility.[224]

Kelly's coming into contact during his undergraduate days with another important figure whose work has already been considered, Henry Scott Holland, further confirmed him in his conviction about the importance of Maurice's teaching. Jones records that

Kelly's four years at Oxford were to shatter his simplistic world view. The change came, when he discovered the works of Charles Kingsley and F. D. Maurice and sat at the feet of Henry Scott Holland.[225]

Scott Holland remained an influence on Kelly after his ordination. George Every has said that Scott Holland was the only person who took any notice of Kelly's developing ideas and also had sympathy for 'this ungainly curate with ill-expressed Maurician ideas'.[226] Scott Holland's sympathetic interest continued for many years.[227]

It is interesting to consider F. R. Barry's assessment of Kelly's role in the work of the Church (and not merely the Church of England). Barry's view was that, while after the First World War two student generations were vouchsafed the religious leadership of giants such as John Mott, J. H. Oldham, Neville Talbot, and William Temple, there was always in the background the *éminence grise*—Fr Herbert Kelly. And he adds, 'Like his acknowledged master he was far more prophet than system maker.'[228]

(b) The development of Hebert's thoughts on the Parish Communion

Hebert did not come suddenly to the conclusions about the Parish

[223] Alan William Jones, *Herbert Hamilton Kelly SSM 1860–1950: A Study in Failure (a contribution to the search for a credible Catholicism)*, University of Nottingham unpublished Ph.D. Thesis (*cit.* Jones, *Kelly*) 1971, p. 370.

[224] A. M. Ramsey, 'Theology and the Priest', *SSMQ*, vol. 51, No. 174, March 1950.

[225] Jones, *Kelly*, p. 27.

[226] Herbert Kelly, *The Gospel of God* (with memoir by Brother George Every, SSM) 1959, p. 21.

[227] HHK letter to AGH, 25 June 1912: 'I have heard from Scott Holland, also from Talbot about training native clergy in India.' *Hebert Papers* (AGH Personal), SSM Archives. (AGH = Fr Hebert)

[228] Kelly, *The Gospel of God*, p. 7.

Communion which he expressed in *Liturgy and Society*.[229] We can see them developing in articles which he contributed to the *SSM Quarterly*.

At Easter 1929 he wrote that

It is one of the failures in the wonderful Anglican revival of recent years that it has not succeeded in restoring the communion of the people as an integral part of the chief Mass on a Sunday.[230]

He further advocated that

if we could aim at having in every Church on a Sunday a Parish Eucharist which was also a communion, such a service would be a great corporate act of adoration of God's glory and thanksgiving for our redemption, the commemoration of God's mighty acts, the setting forth of the One Sacrifice—all this illuminated by the changing lights of the liturgical year; it would be the laying of our corporate life before God at the altar, with all our supplications for one another and for ourselves, and its acceptance and incorporation into Christ through our communion. The Christ in us making our corporate life and our individual lives an offering of his glory. Such a service would supply what the offering of High Mass without communicants can never give.[231]

Hebert called a non-communicating High Mass 'a mutilated rite' and was equally dismissive of the practice of taking communion early in the day and then returning for High Mass. This he condemned because it encouraged the idea that communion means primarily the individual reception of grace by the individual soul.[232] For Hebert the day could not come quickly enough when the Parish Mass again became the Parish Communion.[233] It does not seem to have been until three years later that Hebert made his first visit to the continent to see the Liturgical Movement there in action. At Christmas 1932 he wrote a description of 'The Liturgical Movement in the Church of Rome' in which he said:

We Anglicans are apt to form our ideas of the Roman Church from what we see of it in England: and when we imitate the Roman Church we often imitate its worst and not its best.[234]

He then goes on to describe what he saw in the churches affected by

---

[229] Hebert, *Liturgy and Society*, pp. 207–214.

[230] A. G. Hebert, Review of Yngve Brilioth, *Nattvarden i evangeliskt godstjänstliv*, 1926, in *SSMQ*, vol. 19, No. 106, Easter 1929, p. 46.

[231] *Ibid.*, p. 47.

[232] *Ibid.*

[233] *Ibid.*, p. 48.

[234] A. G. Hebert, 'The Liturgical Movement in The Church of Rome', *SSMQ*, vol. 33, No. 121, Christmas 1932, p. 100.

the Liturgical Movement. Hebert thinks he can discern in the Roman Church a deep inward change 'which amounts to a veritable transformation and holds promise of great things'.[235]

It must be emphasized that this visit came after Hebert had already strongly expressed his views about the importance of the introduction of the Parish Communion in the Church of England. He was advocating building on what he knew already existed in a number of places in England. He was keen to encourage all such efforts and wrote a further series of articles in the year before the publication of *Liturgy and Society*.[236]

In the *Martin Correspondence* there is a revealing letter from Fr Hebert which settles beyond any doubt that there was no continental influence. Hebert himself said:

The Parish Communion certainly was *not* copied from Roman Catholic usage on the Continent. It is very common now in France and Germany, but I am sure we were first in the field here.[237]

In the same letter he writes about the 9 a.m. service every Sunday at St Mary's, Horbury Junction ('I was curate in the next parish 1911–1913'), and the early examples of the service at Temple Balsall and St Saviour's, Poplar, an authoritative statement regarding the fundamentally Anglican provenance of the Parish Communion.

(c) Liturgy and Society

The fact that Gabriel Hebert had come under the self-same influence as his mentor Fr Kelly, albeit at a remove, was recognized from the outset when his book *Liturgy and Society* was published in 1935. The anonymous reviewer in *The Times Literary Supplement* brought out the fact that

Maurice was accustomed to call himself a digger. He believed he was laying foundations. And so he was. His own plans for the structure that was to be raised on the foundations were often not very intelligible. Their scale was too large, and his own interpretation of the world so prophetic that few could understand it. Elucidations, together with fresh light, came with the *Lux Mundi* school. Gore, Holland and their friends joined to the Maurician outlook other visions inherited from Newman and from T. H. Green and John Ruskin. They were far from destitute of prophetic power, but they were far

---

[235] *Ibid.*, p. 101.

[236] A. G. Hebert 'Liturgy and the Parish', *SSMQ*, vol. 35, No. 126, Easter 1934, pp. 18–22 is subtitled 'The Parish Eucharist'.

[237] AGH, letter to R. H. Martin, 5 February (1958) (underlining as in original MS) *Martin Correspondence*.

more practical than Maurice ... Hence Mirfield, and the Christian Social Union and the improved though not yet secure social conscience of English Christianity today.[238]

The reviewer is completely accurate in his confident assessment that, 'Fr Hebert is of that succession'. He goes on to spell out that conviction:

He is a Maurician. He rejects with some indignation the good-natured tolerance which many people are willing to extend to the Church, as a harmless and even praiseworthy provider of a form of spiritual entertainment which those who like that kind of thing are welcome to enjoy.[239]

In this most discerning review it is emphasized that Hebert sees liturgy as supplying the worshipping Church with a perpetual point of contact with the eternal world, yet at the same time the bearing of the liturgy on society is made equally clear.

In the book itself Hebert writes of Maurice as 'that seer and prophet of the future whose importance has never yet been fully recognized',[240] and asserts that it will be Maurice's teaching that will form the basis of the constructive theology of the future.[241]

Liturgy and Society is far more than just a book written to advocate the Parish Communion, however much it became 'the bible' of that movement. It was inevitable that the spread of the Parish Communion should be the liturgical conclusion to which those who were influenced by the book should come. The book clearly made that point itself, but such a conclusion could only be come to as a result of accepting the book's general thesis.

For Hebert the value of the liturgy was that it leads to worship, not to the realm of speculation, but to the heart of the saving work of Christ, and that worship is not individualistic but within the fellowship of the Body of Christ in the Holy Eucharist.

This is the first of the 'three chief aims'[242] he sets himself: to give expression to the view of the Church as the mystical body of Christ, which is not an organization for bringing together a number of religious individuals but a society with an organic life of its own. Hebert

[238] *Times Literary Supplement*, Thursday 13 June 1935.
[239] *Ibid.*
[240] A. G. Hebert, *Liturgy and Society: The Function of the Church in the Modern World*, 1935, p. 108.
[241] *Ibid.*
[242] Hebert, *Liturgy and Society*, p. 12.

believed that this could best be apprehended when the Eucharist was restored to its true place in the life of the Church.

The form that such a service would take would not be a devotional service for the inner circle of the faithful in the early morning.[243]

nor would it be

a mid-morning act of devotion with no communicants but the priest.[244]

It would, in fact, be

the Parish Eucharist with the communion of the people the central act of worship on every Sunday.

By participation in such a serivce, Hebert thought, the meaning of the Fellowship of the Body would be taught more effectively than by 'all our books of theology'.[245]

The second 'chief aim' that Hebert set himself in the book was to show that, over against the opinions of the Liberal theologians, dogma is more than just personal opinion or belief, and that the Creeds, rather than bringing about a bondage of the intellect, do provide a charter of freedom. He writes:

There is no freedom except in allegiance to the truth—to God, whose service is perfect freedom. This is the paradox of Christianity. There is no freedom for man except in acknowledging authority, the authority which ultimately is that of God, not of man, even though it is mediated through men. In being thus under authority man is freed from the domination of other men's opinions and of his own; he is free to obey his conscience and free also from the tyranny of his own conscience, in so far as he has learnt to obey the truth. And thus the Creed, which is man's act of allegiance to God and his acknowledgement of the authority of God's revelation in Christ, is our charter of freedom.[246]

To his aid Hebert once again calls on Maurice, who he denies was a Broad Churchman. There has never been a theologian more radically opposed to the spirit of Liberal theology than Maurice, he alleges, and describes him as a 'thorough dogmatist'.[247]

The final aim of *Liturgy and Society*, Hebert states, is to spell out the mission of the Church to the modern world. In this he hoped that not only church services would speak of the church's mission but also all

[243] *Ibid.*, p. 13.
[244] *Ibid.*
[245] *Ibid.*
[246] *Ibid.*, pp. 110–111.
[247] *Ibid.*, p. 108.

forms of art. Together with all this must go, he quotes from Maurice 'a bond of mutual fellowship among members of a suffering race'.[248] In order to express the bond of mutual fellowship, the Church is compelled

> to criticize the present order far more radically than do those whose minds are fixed upon material well-being. Poverty, bad housing, the wrong distribution of wealth, are material evils; and, because they are evils, they must be fought against. But it is the function of the Church to keep the mind of the community alive to the spiritual side; to such evils as the lack of social life in our land, the harm which is done to the rich by the sin of luxury and the class-distinction which separates them from their fellow-men, and the evil effects of unemployment, not merely in material poverty but in the degradation of mind and soul.[249]

Yet despite Hebert's anxiety to place his advocacy of the Parish Communion in the fullest possible setting, reviewers, and one must presume, the ordinary reader, fastened on to that part of the book which was about the introduction of a particular form of service called 'The Parish Communion'. It was as if they were waiting for some theologian to give his seal of theological approval to what they already knew was a pastoral need. It must be noted that none of those who wrote about the book appeared to think that it was a completely novel idea that Hebert was advocating; they all assumed that their readers knew what was meant by 'The Parish Communion'. It was the backing of a theological rationale for such a service which many were waiting for, it seemed, and they seized on it with enthusiasm.

The Guardian says of 'this remarkable book' that it had been fertilized by many streams, by F. D. Maurice, the Roman Catholic Liturgical Movement, and the theology of modern Sweden, and was of the opinion that Hebert's plea for a Parish Eucharist would have a wide appeal.[250] W. R. Matthews, the Dean of St Paul's[251] commenting that the Anglo-Catholic party in the Church of England had not recovered from the loss of Charles Gore, who had given it 'a philosophy and a voice which was listened to by the country at large', thought that Fr Hebert might fill that gap. Matthews continues:

---

[248] Frederick Denison Maurice, *The Kingdom of Christ or Hints to a Quaker respecting the Principles, Constitution and Ordinances of the Catholic Church* (a new edition based on 2nd ed. of 1842 ed. A. R. Vidler) 1958, vol. ii,p. 28.

[249] Hebert, *Liturgy and Society*, p. 202.

[250] *The Guardian*, 7 June 1935.

[251] W. R. Matthews, *Memories and Meanings*, 1969, pp. 183 ff.

Fr Hebert is critical of modern developments of Eucharistic worship and would advocate a revival of the earlier practice in which the communion of the people took place at the principal service.[252]

R. Ellis Roberts' broadcast review was reprinted in *The Listener*. Roberts said that in what he called a 'prophetic book' Hebert stood for

that vital strain in Anglicanism which we find in the Christian Socialists and belongs to the tradition which gave us Westcott and Stewart Headlam.[253]

He was not as blinded by the liturgical suggestions as others, but, as has been observed, he was unusual in that.

The Modern Churchman, in an editorial, speaks of Hebert's longing

for the time when on every Sunday morning the central service of the Parish Church will be the Eucharist offered by the whole congregation as in primitive Christian times.[254]

Likewise, *John o' London's Weekly* focusses on an

approach which is away from personal beliefs to the corporate faith of the Church as it may be approached through its external liturgy and service.

Artifex[255] in *The Manchester Guardian* agreed with Hebert that

people are drawn in by the active life of the whole body of the faithful as constantly set forth in worship rather than by discussions on doctrine.[256]

The journal *Theology* was anxious to whet the appetite of its readers to study a book of which the author, although staunchly Anglican, had an horizon which 'is not filled and his mind obsessed with the sole merits of our own "incomparable liturgy"'. The editorial is also convinced that

staunchly Catholic as he is, (Hebert) knows that Liturgy must be judged by its power to inspire, illuminate and interpret life.[257]

Amongst the letters that Fr Hebert kept there are two of particular

[252] *The Spectator*, 12 July 1935.
[253] *The Listener*, 17 July 1935.
[254] *The Modern Churchman*, vol. xxv, No. 9, December 1935, p. 489.
[255] Canon Peter Green of Salford: see Lloyd, *op. cit.*, p. 55; Sheen *op. cit.*, p. 43.
[256] *The Manchester Guardian*, 18 May 1935.
[257] *Theology*, vol. xxl, No. 181, July 1935. Further reviews appeared in *Oxford Magazine*, 10 June 1935; *Church of Ireland Gazette*, 21 June 1935; *New Statesman*, 13 June 1935; *Month*, July 1935; *Sydney Morning Herald*, 19 October 1935; *Record*, 16 August 1935; *Church of England Newspaper*, 31 May 1935; *Living Church*, 30 May 1936; *CR*, Michaelmass, 1935; *Blackfriars*, April 1936; *The Outlook*, 18 October 1937. The cuttings are preserved in *Hebert Papers* (Reviews), SSM Archives.

interest. One of them is from W. K. Lowther Clarke the Editorial Secretary of the SPCK,[258] in which he says,

your book is fully up to expectations, what you say *ought* to be commonplace to the clergy. Unfortunately it is not and if widely read, it should do a lot of good. I seem to trace something of the Kelham spirit and the creavity of the founder.[259]

The other letter is from the distinguished theologian O. C. Quick, at that time Professor of Divinity and Ecclesiastical History at Durham University.[260] In his letter to Hebert he says he must send him 'a line of deep and personal gratitude' for the book.

I do hope it will have a deep and wide influence. The great trouble to people like myself is that we can really only be religious in a worshipping fellowship through sacramental acts and yet we are told by the modern masters of the spiritual life to cultivate private mystical powers which we do not feel anxious to possess. And so we need to seek for a genuinely *corporate* and *incorporating* religion, the more isolated and individualistic we are made to feel. I'm sure you will understand what I'm trying to say. I don't say it to other people because I don't think they would.[261]

(d) *The Publication of* The Parish Communion

As has been already seen and noted, the particular suggestions about the Parish Communion service in *Liturgy and Society* were eagerly seized upon by readers. They were perhaps not unaware of that type of service but they were glad to have the advocacy that Hebert's book had provided. In the wake of that book they now wanted further information. They wished to know how it could best be introduced in either town or country parishes, and whether there was a supply of accumulated wisdom available from those parishes which had already had some years of experience of the Service. It was to fulfil this need that it was suggested to Hebert by Brother Edward that he should edit a book of essays to which was given the straightforward title: *The Parish Communion*.

This book of essays . . . owes its orgin to a suggestion made by Brother Edward to Father Hebert in 1935. The idea came to him during one sleepless night

---

[258] Hebert's book was published by Faber and Faber.

[259] W. K. Lowther Clarke, letter to AGH, 19 May 1935, *Hebert Papers* (AGH letters received), SSM Archives.

[260] *DNB 1941–1950*, 1959, p. 702.

[261] O. C. Quick, letter to AGH, 13 March 1936 (underlining as in original MS), *Hebert Papers* (AGH Letters received), SSM Archives.

while he was in Chelmsford Hospital after his serious operation, but (he says) 'It was like an ostrich's egg, too large for me to hatch'. At Michaelmas of the following year, Father Hebert writes, 'It is exactly a year ago since you spent a sleepless night, and the idea came to you that there ought to be a book on the Parish Eucharist ... and you told me I must do it—you remember about the ostrich egg? Well, I tried to get out of it and I couldn't, and the idea grew, till now a book of essays is nearly ready to be sent to the publishers. It follows the line laid down in your letter'.[262]

The book was produced just two years after the publication of *Liturgy and Society*, and 2500 copies were sold in the first nine months, proof positive, if it was needed, of an unfulfilled appetite.[263]

Although it was a practical book, Hebert was anxious that it should not get bogged down with the minute details of the best arrangements for the Sunday service; for him 'the real question is ... deepened understanding of the meaning of the Sacrament and the Church'.[264] He was equally anxious that the movement for the establishment of the Parish Communion should not be side-tracked by being made into some sort of new ritualistic movement.[265] In fact, he prophesied that, if in the following twenty years the Parish Communion became the normal practice in English Parish Churches, it could do much to heal party divisions.[266] There is a good deal of enthusiasm in the book. Hebert himself admitted that he had, of the Parish Communion service,

a great and glorious hope that it may be the appointed means by which the Church of England may come to a true understanding of herself and her calling.[267]

To this end the book contained background theological essays, which included contributions by Hebert, J. O. Cobham, Charles Smyth, and Austin Farrer, while Gregory Dix wrote on 'The idea of "The Church" in the Primitive Liturgies'.[268] Then there were the more practical essays which included W. S. Baker on the way in which the service was introduced at St John's Newcastle in 1927[269] and Henry de Candole on instruction in worship and particularly Liturgical

[262] Packard, *Brother Edward*, p. 140 footnote.
[263] A.G.H., *Starting the Parish Communion. A Letter to a Congregation by a Priest of the Church of England*, n.d., p. 3. Initials in original.
[264] Hebert, *The Parish Communion*, p. v.
[265] *Ibid.*, p. 7.
[266] *Ibid.*, p. 6.
[267] *Ibid.*, p. 7.
[268] *Ibid.*, pp. 95–143.
[269] *Ibid.*, pp. 271–287.

Missions.[270] Some of these authors, who were not well-known in 1937, have since made major contributions to the revival and renewal of the worshipping life of the Church of England.

One of these writers was Henry de Candole, of whom his biographer could claim that

The History of the Liturgical Movement within the Church of England is in many ways inseparably interwoven with the life and work of Henry de Candole.[271]

It is true that what Temple Balsall had been for the previous generation, St John's, Newcastle became for the next. A Parish Communion at 9.15 a.m. was established at St John's in December 1927 while de Candole was senior curate to Noel Hudson.[272] It became the basis of parish policy and mission.[273] Henry de Candole set out his convictions about the Parish Communion in a book which appeared in the same year as Hebert's *Liturgy and Society*. In this book *The Sacraments and the Church*, recommending a Eucharist between nine and ten, he said:

Some such arrangement of a Parish Eucharist as the regular and expected meeting-place of the whole Christian family in a given parish for worship and Communion will do very much to revive, as well as to express, the sense of corporate membership in the Church ... It will in fact be the practical embodiment, which is needed to put into concrete, intelligible, teaching form the ideas which otherwise easily remain mere theory.[274]

He was later asked to write a pamphlet based upon his experience at St John's, which had a wide circulation. In it de Candole stated,

This corporate act of worship—offering and communion—is meant to be a living picture of the Church. The Church is the Body of Christ, that is the instrument he uses to continue down the ages his work of redeeming man to God and reuniting man with man. That is the purpose for which the Church exists.[275]

De Candole was wont to speak of the Eucharist as 'a whole society

[270] *Ibid.*, pp. 249–251.

[271] Jagger, *de Candole* p. 13.

[272] *Ibid.*, p. 72; see also W. S. F. Pickering, ed., *A Social History of the Diocese of Newcastle 1882–1982*, 1981 (*sic*) pp. 59–61.

[273] Jagger, *de Candole*, p. 74.

[274] Henry de Candole, *The Sacraments and the Church: A Study in the corporate nature of Christianity*, 1935, p. 141.

[275] Henry de Candole, 'The Parish Eucharist', pamphlet issued in 1936, in Peter J. Jagger, *Being the Church Today: A Collection of Sermons and Addresses by Bishop Henry de Candole*, 1974, p. 79.

doing something together before God'[276] and it was on this kind of teaching that he concentrated when he conducted his first Liturgical Mission early in 1936,[277] and continued throughout the time that he was Liturgical Missioner in the Diocese of Chichester (1937–1939), with the result that the diocese became a stronghold of the Parish Communion movement.[278]

At the same time as de Candole was doing his work as Liturgical Missioner in Chichester, a rather different style of approach but with the same end in view, was being adopted by Brother Edward, an itinerant priest and evangelist.

5 The Pioneering Work of Brother Edward

Edward Gordon Bulstrode, known to thousands in various parishes up and down the length of England as 'Brother Edward', was a striking figure. Kenneth Packard, his biographer, tells this intriguing story about him:

He was a Man of God, and the remark most often heard on the lips of folk when they had just met him for the first time was that he seemed to have stepped straight out of the pages of the Bible. His very appearance was Christ-like, as people of very different types and divergent views have testified. On one of his missions a child, opening the door to his knock, ran excitedly into the kitchen saying, 'Mummy, Jesus is on the doorstep and wants to come in'.[279]

After Keble, Oxford, in 1904–1908[280] and training at Ely Theo-

---

[276] Henry de Candole, *The Church's Offering, A brief study of Eucharistic Worship*, 1935, p. 20.

[277] Jagger, *de Candole*, p. 102.

[278] *Ibid.*, pp. 106–123; Jasper, *Bell*, pp. 177–178. Henry de Candole worked under the guidance of a diocesan Liturgical committee under the chairmanship of J. C. H. How (*ibid.* p. 177). How had recently arrived in the diocese after having been Rector of Liverpool from 1926–1935. How was the leader of Liberal Catholicism in Cambridge in the early years of this century and a founder of the Oratory of the Good Shepherd, of which Eric Milner-White was also a member, thus providing another link with 'sub-Tractarians'. George Tibbatts OGS, *John How, Cambridge Don, Parish Priest, Scottish Primus*, 1983, *passim*.

[279] Packard, *Bro. Edward*, pp. 11–12.

[280] *Ibid.*, p. 20. His greatest friend there was David Railton, Rector of Liverpool 1935–1942. Railton was an outstanding First World War Chaplain and the originator of the idea of the Unknown Warrior Tomb in Westminster Abbey. Moynihan, *op. cit.*, pp. 77 ff.

THE EMERGENCE OF THE PARISH COMMUNION

logical College in 1908–1909[281] Bulstrode served his title at St Columba's, Wanstead Slip in the diocese of St Albans, being ordained Deacon on Trinity Sunday 1909.[282] After just over three years as a curate in the parish[283] he left to go and live with the Society of St John the Evangelist (the Cowley Fathers) in Oxford, but he remained there for less than twelve months.[284] He then moved restlessly from one place to another, without seeming to have any settled pattern of living or any definite plans for the future, but then an event occurred which was to have great significance for his future work. He discovered Temple Balsall, and for many years it was his regular resting place amidst his wandering apostolate.[285]

So, during the years of the first World-War and the decade that followed, Brother Edward made Temple Balsall his home, from which he went out as calls came or as the need arose, refreshed and sustained by the life he loved ... Temple Balsall was one of the first parishes in England to establish a Parish Communion and Breakfast, an arrangement which came to mean a great deal to Brother Edward in later years.[286]

At Temple Balsall Brother Edward came in contact with Fr E. Seyzinger CR, who with Fr Fairbairn (The Master of Temple Balsall) had inaugurated the Parish Communion and Breakfast there in 1913.[287] This experience of the Parish Communion obviously had a great impression on him, so that when in 1923 he conducted his first parochial mission in St Silas, Pentonville, he decided that the outcome of the Mission would be to 'plant the Parish Communion and Breakfast in which he had firm faith'.[288] This became the pattern in all Brother Edward's Missions, and he always hoped that the establishment of the Parish Communion would be a 'memorial of the Mission'.[289] His enthusiasm for the Parish Communion had a wide effect on the adoption of the service. It has already been seen how he was instrumental in persuading Fr Hebert to gather together the authors of *The Parish Communion*. In the correspondence between

[281] Packard, *Bro. Edward*, p. 30.
[282] *Ibid.*, p. 36.
[283] *Ibid.*, p. 47.
[284] *Ibid.*, p. 55.
[285] *Ibid.*, p. 57.
[286] *Ibid.*, pp. 83–84.
[287] *Ibid.*, p. 84; *Sunday Morning*, p. vii; *The Leap*, no. 7, August 1945, p. 10.
[288] Packard, *Bro. Edward*, p. 89.
[289] *Ibid.*, pp. 139–140.

Hebert and Brother Edward they spoke of that book as an 'ostrich egg' and of another book as a 'sparrow's egg'. This book, the 'sparrow's egg', was edited by Brother Edward himself and was an even more basically practical book than *The Parish Communion*. It was called *Sunday Morning: The New Way* and appeared in 1938. Brother Edward did not care for the title the book was given, strongly maintaining that the Parish Communion was not 'a new way', least of all some novelty for attracting people to church, but a recovery of the 'old way' and the practice of the Early Church.[290] Brother Edward was insistent:

We must never think of this thing as a 'stunt', or a bright idea for 'getting people to church'. If it is anything, it is a mighty movement of the Holy Spirit. It is the principle that matters: the fashioning of our worship, and of our lives, according to the Mind of Christ. Numbers are of little account with God; our Lord said, not 'When two or three thousand', nor 'When two or three hundred,' but 'When two or three are gathered together in My Name, there am I in the midst of them'.[291]

Sunday Morning: The New Way contained descriptions of the introduction of the Parish Communion in widely differing types of parishes in England and also included a section containing examples from other provinces of the Anglican Communion.[292] It also contained Fr Hebert's *A Letter to a Congregation*[293] and a description and plan of the John Keble Church at Mill Hill, which was one of the first churches built with the Parish Communion in mind.[294]

Throughout his minstry there was always a number of men and women who wished to associate themselves actively with Brother Edward's work. In the 1920s the Servants and Handmaids of Jesus of Nazareth (SHJN) were formed, who became in 1937 the Disciples of Jesus of Nazareth (DJN).[295] They were bound together by a simple Rule of Life and they supported him on his travels, so that in the case of poor parishes he had no need to ask for help for any expenses for himself or for his helpers. They themselves were most often these

[290] *Ibid.*, p. 140.
[291] *Sunday Morning*, p. vii.
[292] *Ibid.*, pp. 44–61.
[293] In *Sunday Morning* Fr Hebert's name is not given.
[294] *Ibid.*, pp. 144–146. See also Rex Walford, *John Keble Church, Mill Hill 1932–1964. The early years of a modern parish church*, 1964, *passim*; Peter Hammond, *Liturgy and Architecture*, 1960, pp. 72–73.
[295] Packard, *Bro. Edward*, p. 87.

helpers, giving a week or fortnight a year to work with him on the missions he conducted up and down the country.[296] In 1947 they started to use the title Village Evangelists,[297] and it was through this group that Brother Edward continued to conduct his Missions in which the spread of the idea of the Parish Communion was so important. Writing about the aims of the Village Evangelists he wrote:

We cannot leave people unconvinced that Worship, Fellowship, and Witness are the Will of God. All this is the background and the follow-up of pure Evangelism.

I myself belief that the Parish Communion, uniting Offering, Communion and Fellowship has been restored to us by God at this time to meet this need.[298]

It is on this evidence that Kenneth Packard,[299] who was instrumental in bringing together the group which became Parish and People,[300] could confidently declare:

Twelve years after the publication of *Sunday Morning*, there was born the movement called Parish and People, which seeks to co-ordinate and develop the whole *nexus* of principle and practice which lies behind the Parish Communion. This movement, which is now having considerable and growing influence in the Church of England and beyond, is the Anglican expression of a trend which is making itself more and more evident in many parts of Christendom, in the Iona Fellowship, for instance, and in the Liturgical Movement in French and German Catholicism. Brother Edward may undoubtedly be reckoned as a progenitor of Parish and People.[301]

6   The Influence of the Industrial Christian Fellowship

That the Industrial Christian Fellowship (ICF) was the result of an

---

[296] *Ibid.*, p. 135.

[297] *Ibid.*, p. 148.

[298] Brother Edward Priest-Evangelist, V.E., *Village Evangelism*, 1947, p. 17.

[299] Kenneth Packard was himself the author of a popular leaflet published by the SPCK: Kenneth Packard, *The Parish Communion: A Simple Explanation*, 1941. It was reprinted in 1956 and again in 1961.

[300] Jagger, *History*, pp. 20–24.

[301] Packard, *Bro. Edward*, p. 145.

amalgamation of the Christian Social Union and the Navvy Mission Society has already been noted.[302] Now that organization's contribution to the development of community-conscious worship has to be analysed to see what influence it brought to bear on the growth of the Parish Communion in the Church of England.

The ICF formed a Worship Committee[303] which planned a Conference, mainly for clergy, which was held at Swanwick in January 1939. In preparation for this conference a syllabus for study was prepared, and in that syllabus the corporate nature of the Eucharist is emphasized.

By all together, as a corporate act, the production of bread and wine in the Offertory, the breaking and uplifting in Consecration, are performed. It is Christ in and through His Body, the Church, Who says, 'This is My Body'.

The climax of Christian worship is reached when, having seen the vision of God fulfilling His Purpose in the redemption of the world, we unite ourselves to Him and to one another in Communion, and He fills us with His Life, that we may work with Him for the cause of His Kingdom, and suffer with Him, if need be, to the breaking of our bodies and the shedding of our blood.[304]

It is no cause for surprise that such Christian Socialists as J. V. Wilson and Jack Bucknall were enthusiastic about this conference. Writing in *Church Militant*, Wilson said:

There was more agreement on the fact of there being a social significance in the Christian religion than I remember at previous conferences and there was a welcome desire for information and understanding.[305]

Bucknall also spoke of it as 'a very important Conference'.[306] Wilson said that when the Conference discussions were published they would provide 'a new approach to the whole subject of worship and to liturgical reform'.[307] These documents were duly published later that year with a foreword by P. T. R. Kirk, who had acted as Chairman of the Conference.

In a powerful address to this Swanwick Conference the Archdeacon of Aston (the Ven. H. McGowan) said,

---

[302] See p. 93, *supra*.
[303] The Minutes of the Worship Committee are not in the ICF Archives at Sion College (List B: Minutes and Other Records Navvy Mission, ICF, CSU).
[304] *The Social Significance of Worship (A Syllabus for Study with Questions for Discussion)*, 1939, p. 14.
[305] *Church Militant*, No. 28, February 1939, p. 5.
[306] *Ibid.*
[307] *Ibid.*

What I want to feel when I come to the Eucharist is that I can join whole-heartedly, not only with angels and archangels and all the company of Heaven, but with the city council and the motor works and the teaching profession and the staff of the hospitals, and so can laud and magnify His holy name. Until we do that, we shall never offer worship as it ought to be.[308]

The Conference asked itself the question, 'Are our present forms of worship adequate?' and a number of speakers stated that they were not. Canon J. S. Bezzant of Liverpool Cathedral blamed insistence on fasting communion for weakening the social significance of the sacrament. He said that he was unable to conceal his opinion that

insistence upon fasting communion has in fact had results which are as unfortunate as they were unintended, and that it now tends to a confusion of values. I can speak disinterestedly, as I always observe the rule myself, though it is a discipline too trivial to be useful or even to deserve the name. But it has had the effect of forcing the act of communion to an hour at which we have grievously failed to persuade the mass of church-people to make it a great corporate act of worship, in which the great majority of the full members of a local church participate. From the point of view before us, it is a real loss that the reception of Holy Communion has become in popular esteem the mark of the specially devout.[309]

In the main speeches at the conference no specific mention of the Parish Communion was made, although Archdeacon McGowan spoke of the 'strong current flowing' in the Liturgical Movement.[310]

Arising out of the Conference, the ICF produced a series of publications which were intended to lead church people to a fuller understanding of the meaning of worship 'and to a desire for a fuller expression of its meaning in the services of the Church'.[311] In one of these a 'note on the presentation of the Eucharist' said:

The service is one in which the whole Church in the parish should normally take part. It should be at an hour when most people can make their commu-

---

[308] *Worship: Its Social Significance*, 1939, p. 125. There is also a description of the Conference in *ICF Review*, vol. vii, no. 2, February 1939, pp. 32–35 which reports that a parish priest made this appeal to the Conference: 'If your faith in the Eucharist's primary place in Christian Worship is sure, then cannot you get down to the real matter of showing Dick, Tom and Harry that Worship is for him the way to his spiritual satisfaction, and trust that, as he expands in Christian understanding, he will be led to the sacrament of the Altar'. *Ibid.* p. 33.

[309] *Worship: Its Social Significance*, pp. 146–147.

[310] *Ibid.*, p. 121.

[311] J. V. Wilson, R. T. Howard, H. McGowan, *The Social Significance of the Liturgy*, Popular Series No. 4, new and revised ed., 1941, p. 2.

nion together as a body. (Some time between 8.30 and 10 a.m. has been found to be suitable in many parishes.)[312]

In 1941, in the middle of the Second World War, the ICF was associated with the Christendom Group in setting up the Malvern Conference under the chairmanship of William Temple.

Temple, who had strong contemporary links with Scott Holland and Gore,[313] gathered together a conference of 240 bishops, clergy, and laity in order that they might find the

'middle axioms'—maxims for conduct which mediate between fundamental principles and the tangle of particular problems.[314]

The Malvern Conference was critical of much of the worship of the Church of England finding that it was not 'so directed and conducted that its relevance to life and man's actual needs'[315] was evident. Regarding the Eucharist the Conference was of a mind that

the Eucharist is to be appreciated as the offering of ourselves and all we are—for the bread and wine are the produce of man's labour expended upon the gifts of God—in order that Christ may present us with Himself in His perfect self-offering, and that we may receive again from Him the very gifts which we have offered, now charged with the divine power, to be shared by us in perfect fellowship; so in our worship we express the ideal of our common life and receive strength to make it more real.[316]

In this way this important conference, which could be seen directly as part of the main stream of the social thought and concern in the Church of England stretching back to the days of Kingsley, Maurice, and Ludlow, made its own significant contribution to preparing the way for that upsurge of liturgical, pastoral, and parochial enthusiasm which resulted in the Eucharist, in the form of the Parish Communion, becoming increasingly the principal mode of worship in a very large proportion of the parish churches of England in the ten years (1945–1955) immediately after the Second World War,[317] so that the

[312] *Ibid.*, p. 25.

[313] Robert Craig, *Social Concern in the Thought of William Temple*, 1963, p. 14.

[314] *Malvern, 1941: The Life of the Church and the Order of Society being the Proceedings of the Archbishop of York's Conference*, 1941, p. vii.

[315] *The Malvern Conference, Edition for Study*, 1941, iii(8), p. 5.

[316] *Ibid.*, iii(9), p. 5 and *Christ the Lord of All Life*, ICF, 9th ed., 1960, p. 160.

[317] No statistics for the introduction of the Parish Communion are available on an annual basis, so that it is not possible to detect statistically the precise period when it was being most rapidly adopted in English parishes. However in a sample of 470 parishes questioned by Vere Ducker between April and June 1961 (Paton, *The Parish Communion Today*, pp. 138–140) 310 parishes stated that it was in the ten years 1951–61 that they had adopted the service, compared with 123 parishes which had started in the fifteen years between 1935 and 1950.

point could be reached where Arthur Couratin could speak to an assembly of the leaders of the Church of the necessity that any revision of the Eucharist should be based on the pattern of the Parish Communion.[318] The Parish Communion had arrived.

[318] See pp. 3–4, *supra*; Welsby, *op. cit.*, pp. 68–71.

PART FOUR

CONCLUSION

Little surprise is expressed these days at the latest example of so-called 'contemporary' worship when it is featured in the pages of the church press. Readers have become inured to accounts of services held on horseback, Pets' Services, services in which all dress up as clowns, services containing mime or dance, toy services, puppets in the pulpit, Flower Festivals, Christingles, and so on and so on. Many of these, in the final analysis, appear to be nothing more than somewhat pathetic pew-filling enterprises using the latest 'gimmick' (a crude word which has almost become the property of the Church), but there are those who would justify them theologically.[1]

In the light of such recent phenomena it would be easy to look back on the evolution of the Parish Communion as a similar attempt by an earlier generation to devise their own form of experimental worship, designed for their times, which would make the liturgy relevant and contemporaneous to their age and its experience. That this is a completely facile and fundamentally inaccurate assessment can be seen from the evidence assembled in this book. The emergence of the Parish Communion was based upon much more solid foundations, which were theological as well as pastoral.

The debate on how far the Oxford Tractarians saw a relationship between their teaching and social action has continued for many years and the contrasting views, for instance, of W. G. Peck and A. M. Allchin have been noted previously in this work.[2] In a recent article R. W. Franklin, commemorating the one hundred and fiftieth anniversary of Keble's Assize Sermon on 14 July 1833, came down decisively in favour of discerning in the work of Edward Pusey an attempt to present an interpretation of the gospel for Victorian society in which the good news is that faith in Jesus Christ establishes a living organic relationship with others and that the Eucharist is the body of this fellowship. That is, as long as the English recovered a Catholic belief in the Real Presence. Franklin wrote that he believed that it was possible to see the beginnings of such a fusion between an

[1] Some of these approaches are advocated in such works as J. G. Davies, *New Perspectives on Worship Today*, 1978; Harvey Cox, *The Feast of Fools: A Theological Essay in Festivity and Fantasy*, 1969; John Killinger, *Leave it to the Spirit, Commitment and Freedom in the New Liturgy*, 1st British ed., 1971.

[2] See p. 109, *supra*. On Pusey's political liberalism, see Peter Nockles, 'Pusey and the Question of Church and State' in Perry Butler, ed., *Pusey Rediscovered*, 1983, pp. 265–268. Keble's 'radicalism' is defended in John R. Griffin, 'The Social Implications of the Oxford Movement', *Historical Magazine of the Protestant Episcopal Church*, vol. 44, No. 2, 1975, pp. 155–165.

appreciation of the Doctrine of the Real Presence with a communal understanding of the Church in W. E. Gladstone's hymn 'O lead my blindness by the hand'.[3] In the last verse of the hymn Gladstone wrote:

> We, who with one blest Food are fed,
>   Into one body may we grow,
> And one pure life from thee, the Head,
>   Informing all the members flow;
> One pulse be felt in every vein,
> One law of pleasure and of pain.[4]

From an examination of the work of many of the pioneers of Anglo-Catholic worship such as Charles Lowder[5] and A. H. Mackonochie,[6] Franklin comes to the conclusion that 'liturgical change was in some way linked to the recovery of the communal dimension and social mission of the church.'[7] It is the fact that this underlying association between liturgical development and social witness has existed in one vigorous and lively part of the Catholic party in the Church of England over the past one hundred and fifty years which gives the thesis of this book its momentum.

It has been shown that, from the time of Headlam and Scott Holland and through the life of the various Christian Socialist societies, there has always been the strongest possible teaching by them about the inter-connection which they believed to exist between the Eucharist and the Church's calling to serve sacrificially in the world. This is why at each stage they can be accurately described as 'Sacramental Socialists'. But it cannot be emphasized too often that it was from the Catholic wing of the church that they came. They were those who wished to emphasize the proposition that the Church is the extension of the Incarnation, and they are also one in acknowledging F. D. Maurice as their prophet and inspirer. If they are to be given another label it would be 'Liberal Catholic', a thread which would serve to join Maurice, through Headlam and Scott Holland and Gore, to Temple and Ramsey. They stand out in contrast with the imitative 'Romanizing' tendencies of other parts of the Anglo-Catholic Move-

---

[3] For a discussion on the extent to which Gladstone might be described as a Tractarian, see Perry Butler, *Gladstone: Church, State and Tractarianism, A Study of his religious ideas and attitudes, 1809–1859*, Oxford Historical Monographs, 1982, pp. 157–171.

[4] *The English Hymnal*, 1933, Hymn no. 322.

[5] Ellsworth, *op. cit.*

[6] Reynolds, *op. cit.*; Bentley, *op. cit.*

[7] R. W. Franklin, 'Pusey and Worship in Industrial Society', *Worship*, vol. 57, September 1983, pp. 396–402.

ment; but slowly, not least through the influence of Widdrington's Anglo-Catholic Summer Schools of Sociology,[8] the Liberal Catholics were able to fill the vacuum of theological leadership in the party. Robert Woodifield described the theological position of the Liberal Catholics with enthusiasm:

A Catholic is one who lives in the stream of that common Catholic life and experience and developing thought—that living tradition—which, having its ultimate source in the revealing activity of God in the whole life of all humanity and its immediate origin in his supreme and most objective self-revelation in Jesus, fertilises the life of the whole body of humanity through which it flows, and also absorbs into itself tributaries from the life and experience and thought of that same body of humanity.[9]

For Woodifield, to be a Catholic is not a static state, but rather it is to be one who 'seizes upon the values of the past and is alive to the present and a master builder for the future'.[10] Within such a vision the Eucharist further 'extends' the Incarnation. The bread and wine of the Eucharist represents all the material products of God's earth and human labour, and they are declared to be the Body and Blood of God the Son, and are shared by the Christian Community representing the whole body of mankind in his spirit of fellowship and equality in a Common Meal. In the fellowship of that meal, in which the universal presence of the Eternal Son through symbols of the human material world is manifested and also focussed, that Christian Community unites itself (and the whole human race that it represents) with Jesus in the response, or sacrifice, which he eternally offers to the Father within the life of the Holy Trinity.

The First World War chaplains had pleaded for a rebirth of fellowship within the Church; perhaps it would not be unfair to suggest that such a developed theology of fellowship around the Eucharistic meal as has just been described was more than they were spelling out at the time. Nevertheless, they and the servicemen they represented, had an instinctive (and admittedly accurate) feeling that something was very lacking in a church where there were institutionalized divisions in worship, with the divide being either between the rich and the poor or between the devout and the more casual. Unfortunately the abolition of such divisions was an ambition which few of the bishops of the

---

[8] See pp. 135 ff, *supra*.

[9] Robert Woodifield, *Catholicism: Humanist and Democratic*, Theology for Modern Man iv, 1954, p. 22.

[10] *Ibid.*, p. 22.

Church of England were willing to support, the notable exceptions being those who had been influenced at some stage in their lives by the Christian Social Union.

In consequence, when the War was over, a great opportunity for liturgical renewal was missed. The Church had before it the task of liturgical revision. As a result of the findings of the Royal Commission of 1904 this was not something they could avoid, yet the 'official' church proved to be consistently deaf to the promptings of the war-time experiences of many dedicated and committed priests and lay-men who were convinced that out of the red-hot furnace of war some of the more precious elements should be preserved. Among the most valuable, they believed, was the discovery, in reality a rediscovery, of that dimension in worship which is the joy and inspiration to be gained by the open recognition of one's fellow-worshippers around the Table of the Lord rather than the anonymity which obtains when each disappears into the pew. Officer and soldier alike discovered in the grim surroundings of battlefield worship that each was 'the brother for whom Christ died'. They discovered this fact as together they prepared for the very real possibility of their own impending death by receiving together the symbols of Life under the signs of His death: the broken Body and the poured-out Blood. Here was a deep corporate experience crying out to be built upon and developed for the good of the whole nation; but the Bishops and Convocations in their blinkered anxiety to produce their 'Answer to the Royal Letters of Business' were in no mood to be deflected by such matters. Even such erstwhile Christian Socialists as Walter Frere were too pre-occupied with liturgical minutiae and the consequent church politics to find time to listen to those who wished to persuade them to design a form of worship which would have linked the unique fellowship of a simple Eucharist in a Flanders field with the Sunday morning wor-ship of urban England, despite the evidence being available from the work of the National Mission that such a service was widely sought after.[11] The opportunity was lost and it might be thought that God's judgement was passed on such an unadventurous church when the parliamentary fiascos of the 1927 and 1928 Prayer Book debates occurred.

With the benefit of hindsight we can feel relieved that the Church was not saddled with the 1928 Prayer Book because it is very possible that it would have prevented the Church of England from giving its mind to that later process of revision which resulted in *The Alternative*

---

[11] See pp. 181–2, *supra.*

Service Book with its tacit recognition of the Parish Communion as the 'type' of Anglican worship for the contemporary Church.[12] However, that does not grant a reprieve to those who were unwilling to accept the challenge of change in the nineteen-twenties.

The unwillingness to change at that time was not confined to any particular church party. We have identified throughout this book the continuing concern of the Liberal Catholic/Christian Socialist group to witness to the Eucharist as being pre-eminently the service which gathers up and at the same time expresses all that the Church of the Incarnation ought to be. It became increasingly apparent to this group that this principle could only be worked out practically and parochially in terms of a service of the type which became known as the 'Parish Communion'. But its advocates had to maintain that principle and over against the 'no-change' policies of both the High and Low church parties. They received some support from those who were associated with the 'Grey Book',[13] but there was no enthusiasm whatsoever for their ideas from the more traditional wings of the Catholic and Evangelical parties.

Fr Hebert was conscious that he was not representative of the extreme Anglo-Catholics who were 'ruling the whole business',[14] and was caught up in the internal battles within his own community over extra-liturgical Devotions of the Blessed Sacrament.[15] Hebert described himself as 'an old-fashioned Anglo-Catholic' in an address given to Manchester University in which he spoke of a 'vivid sense of the meaning of "common prayer"' in which the pronouns are 'us' and 'ours',[16] but this was not the approach of the more conservative High Churchmen. The individuality of the worshipper was still paramount, whether it was on his or her visits to the Blessed Sacrament outside Mass[17] or for guidance about personal piety within it. Books of devotion suggested prayers like this to be said at the end of the Canon:

My Jesus, I believe that thou art truly and really present in the Sacrament of the Altar. I adore thee; I love thee; come into my heart. May the Body of our Lord Jesus Christ preserve my soul to everlasting life.[18]

[12] See pp. 3–4, *supra*.

[13] See p. 55, *supra*.

[14] AGH, letter to his father, 11 August (1922) from St Augustine's Priory, Modderpoort, OFS. AGH (Personal), SSM Archives.

[15] Jones, *Kelly*, pp. 238–260.

[16] *SSMQ*, vol. 52, no. 178, March 1951.

[17] 'A Quarter of An Hour before the Blessed Sacrament', *Let Us Pray: A Simple Book for Lay Folks* (*cit. Let Us Pray*) Catholic Literature Association n.d., p. 61.

[18] *Ibid.*, 'Prayers during Mass', p. 31.

It was this same individuality that was further emphasized through insistence on the personal preparation of fasting before Communion. It has already been seen how this discipline caused much heart-searching amongst the Catholics of the Church of England. For those Anglicans who sought disciplinary guidance from the Roman Catholic Church there was no room for discussions or arguments; the Papal directions were clear. But for the 'Prayer Book Catholics' there was the desperate need to justify the practice from writings and teachings of the Anglican Divines, and also, if possible, to persuade the Convocations to speak out uncompromisingly on the subject. As has been seen, the Convocations eventually only spoke with an unclear voice to the dissatisfaction of the Anglo-Catholics.[19] However, the compilers of books of Catholic devotion went on undeterred. For example, in one such book in a list of over fifty possible 'sins' the order commenced:

Did you keep back any sin in your last confession?
Did you say your penance?
Did you go to Holy Communion without preparing yourself, or after having broken your fast?[20]

Stealing, violence, lies, jealousy, and deeds 'against purity or modesty' came much lower in the published list. Even Fr Hebert felt he had to sum up his 'Note on the Fast before Communion' in *The Parish Communion* with:

The fact that the Prayer Book neither enjoins nor abrogates the Fast before Communion implies that it assumes the universal rule as a matter of course. To call it a 'laudable custom' or an 'ideal' is thoroughly unsatisfactory; we must uphold it as a rule.[21]

All this had an effect on the Sunday morning arrangements in parishes. In many places, although the principle of a corporate parochial celebration was accepted, it was still thought necessary that the service should be held at an hour at which there could be a reasonable assurance that the communicants would arrive fasting, some consideration having also been given to the need for additional rest in an industrial society. For the important point began to be taken that there ought not to be any division between the 'offering' and 'communion', and that there should be general communion at every celebration.

[19] See pp. 20 ff, *supra*.
[20] *Let Us Pray*, pp. 42–43.
[21] Hebert, *Parish Communion*, p. 29.

The strait-jacket into which regard for this fasting principle forced both parishes and parishioners had one positive result in that in a number of places it gave the notion of following the Parish Communion with a Parish Breakfast a practical, as well as a theological, justification.[22]

Meanwhile, amongst Evangelicals there can be seen to be an equal preoccupation with the individual and consequently little interest in the need for the Church to work out its gospel in terms of the society into which it is set. This was an attitude of Evangelicals in the Church of England which had lingered on for many years and needed, as was seen earlier, powerful and influential voices like that of Max Warren, then General Secretary of the Church Missionary Society,[23] to make the criticism. Warren wrote in 1946 about what he called the decay amongst his fellow Evangelicals of the confident proclamation of the Gospel by both Word and by Sacrament.

This failure, in turn, led on to the other failure to see when a fuller understanding of the corporate emphasis of the Sacrament could, without any sacrifice of Evangelical principle, have provided the Evangelicals with the prophetic message which a society disillusioned by individualism was looking for, and failing to find from Evangelicals.[24]

There is a further issue which has been examined and that is the extent to which the introduction of the Parish Communion in the Church of England can be said to be as a result of the influence of the Liturgical Movement of the Roman Catholic Church on the continent.

One of the eventual outcomes of that Roman Catholic Liturgical Movement was the use of the vernacular in the liturgy.[25] Of course, this step had been taken by the Church of England in its public worship in the sixteenth century,[26] so this development could not be said to demonstrate a point of contact between the Churches. Instead it might be suggested that the Church of England's first 'Liturgical Movement' dated back to that particular period in her history when the Church consciously tried to revise its worship on the twin bases of

[22] *Sunday Morning, op. cit.*, pp. 8–9, pp. 67–68, pp. 110–114.
[23] F. W. Dillistone, *Into All the World: A Biography of Max Warren*, 1980, p. 67 ff; Max Warren, *Crowded Canvas: some experiences of a lifetime*, 1974, *passim*. See pp. 146–8 above.
[24] Warren, *Strange Victory*, p. 116.
[23] *Constitution on the Liturgy, Sacrosanctum Concilium*, 4 December 1963: AAS 56 (1964) 97–138, Const. Dect. DEC1, 3–69, Chapter 1, ii, C 36.
[26] Cuming, *History*, pp. 31 ff.

scripture and the then prevailing knowledge of the practice of the Early Church. Equally it could perhaps be claimed that a second Anglican 'Liturgical Movement' was co-terminous with the Oxford Movement, having in mind the recall, in its early stages, to the principles of the Prayer Book,[27] and then the continuing and determined efforts in the Movement's later stages to restore the Eucharist to the centre of the worshipping life of the Church.

We have noted the awakening of interest among Anglicans in the liturgical activities in France, Germany, Austria and Belgium and also the fact that Fr Hebert studied them,[28] but this interest came long after those first stirrings within the Church of England which were to result in the eventual wide-spread introduction of the Parish Communion. There was a considerable 'head of steam' already built up long before there was any awareness in England that there were corresponding liturgical activities in Europe. It can be stated with confidence that the idea of the Parish Communion is a home-grown Church of England plant, the seed of which had been well sown and had become a hardy plant in many parishes long before any study of the Roman Catholic work had taken place.[29] Subsequent knowledge and study of the writings of the leaders of the Liturgical Movement admittedly strengthened and inspired those who were working to establish a Parish Communion, but it was not the original stimulus in the Church of England.

It is the submission of this book that this 'plant' grew out of the concern of those who are to be described as 'Sacramental Socialists'. They saw the Church as God's instrument in the world, commissioned to tackle its injustices and inequalities, and were strengthened by the assurance that the Church was sustained and fed by the Holy Food of the Eucharist for this task. As has been seen they were deeply convinced that the Church was the *Corpus Christi*, and it was fed by the *Corpus Christi* in order that it might *be* the *Corpus Christi* in the world. The Sacramental Socialists took very much to heart the words of St Teresa of Avila:

> Christ has no body now on earth but yours,
>   no hands but yours,
>   no feet but yours.

[27] Gray, *op. cit.*, pp. 1–3; Horton Davies, *Worship and Theology in England*, 5, 38.
[28] See pp. 198–9, *supra*.
[29] 'None of this (the Liturgical Movement) had the slightest influence on the Anglican Prayer Book of 1928'. Geoffrey Cuming, 'Liturgical Change in the Church of England and the Roman Catholic Church' in Rupert Davies, ed., *The Testing of the Churches 1932–1982: A Symposium*, 1982, p. 121.

Yours are the eyes through which Christ's compassion is
   to look out onto the world.
Yours are the feet with which He is to go about doing good.
Yours are the hands with which He is to bless men now.

Thus they saw the People of God around the Altar on a Sunday morning as preparing themselves for whatever political or social action they were to be called to in the coming week. They were not receiving the precious gifts of the Body and Blood of Christ for their own spiritual welfare or comfort but for the sake of the World. And therefore they saw no incongruity in the fact that the holiest of gifts was given to them under the signs of bread and wine, because as Christian Socialists they saw all creation as being redeemable by the Incarnation of the Son of God. In fact the Offertory Procession, in which representatives of the People of God placed on the altar the bread and wine, together with their gifts of money, represented for them the totality of their life and the life of the society from which they came and to which they would shortly return.

In more recent years this concept of the inter-relationship of worship and social action has broken out of its seeming captivity in the High Church party within the Church of England. The connection between worship and the life of the community is no longer the sole prerogative of Catholics. It can be said that the Liberal Catholic/ Christian Socialists' supreme contribution to the life of the Church of England in the twentieth century, is the spread of such a realization. Such writers as Kenneth Leech[30] and David Sheppard,[31] whose origins derive from quite different party stables within the Church, have each entered into a heritage which is in direct succession from Maurice, through his disciples in the intervening decades. They are not espousing some new principle when they seek to attempt to work out the practical, and even political, consequences for the Church of its incarnational role.[32]

[30] 'A number of us are very disturbed at the trend in the Catholic movement towards a sickly pietism and a right-wing reactionary stance in social and political issues.' Kenneth Leech and Rowan Williams, eds. *Essays Catholic and Radical, A Jubilee Group Symposium for the 150th Anniversary of the beginning of the Oxford Movement 1833-1983*, 1983, p. 7.

[31] 'In urban working class areas where the corporate sense of belonging is very strong, it is all gain to use forms of worship which encourage as many as possible to participate', David Sheppard, *Bias to the Poor*, 1983, p. 203.

[32] Thus *Faith in the City. A Call for Action by Church and Nation*, The Report of the Archbishop of Canterbury's Commission on Urban Priority Areas (ACUPA), 1985, can be seen to be in this same succession.

This stance has never been an uncontroversial one for Churchmen to take up,[33] and it is certainly not a new one. Writing in *The Modern Churchman* in 1932 H. D. A. Major[34] said that whereas in the past the Church of England had been aptly described as 'the Conservative Party at prayer' now, through the influence of Bishop Gore, at least in the persons of her Anglo-Catholic clergy, it might be more accurate to describe it as 'the Socialist Party at Mass'.[35] In 1981 Canon Alan Wilkinson of Leeds in a letter to *The Times* brought it all up to date when he wrote to the Editor reporting that:

The other day I attended a meeting of bishops and clergy. I discovered that virtually all of us were supporters of the Social Democrats. Should the Church of England now be described as the Social Democratic Party at the parish Eucharist?[36]

Even such a humorous comment as this can serve to remind us that the Parish Communion had its origins in a determination to link the social and political concerns of the church with its eucharistic worship. The pity is that in many places this connection has been lost, if it was ever there, and the Parish Communion has become nothing more than the accepted liturgical fashion. It is time for a recalling to fundamentals.

[33] The most recent criticism can be found in Digby C. Anderson, ed., *The Kindness that Kills: The Churches' Simplistic Response to Complex Social Issues*, 1984, *passim*.

[34] A. M. G. Stephenson, *The Rise and Decline of English Modernism. The Hulsean Lectures 1979–80*, 1984, pp. 78 ff.

[35] *The Modern Churchman*, vol. xxl, No. 11, February 1932, p. 583.

[36] *The Times*, 18 July 1981. By March 1985 some partial confirmation of Canon Wilkinson's impression was available in the Report of the Gallup Survey conducted for ACUPA which asked clergy their voting intentions. Almost half (49%) of Church of England Clergy, it was reported, stated they would vote Liberal/SDP Alliance. *Gallup Survey of Church of England Clergymen prepared for the Archbishop's Commission on Urban Areas*, 1986, 29.0, p. 48.

PART FIVE

BIBLIOGRAPHY

Books

(The place of publication is London unless otherwise stated.)

Abraham, W. H., *The Position of the Eucharist in Sunday Worship*, 1904.
Adderley, J., *Christian Social Reformers*, 1927.
The Alternative Service Book: A Commentary by the Liturgical Commission, 1980.
Anson, P. F., *Fashions in Church Furnishings, 1840–1940*, 1965.
The Army and Religion. An Enquiry and its bearing upon the Religious Life of the Nation, 1919.
B., W., *A Postscript on some points in Mr. Kindon's work on Fasting Communion*, 1876.
Barry, F. R., *Mervyn Haigh*, 1964.
Beauduin, OSB, Lambert, (trans. Virgil Michel, OSB) *Liturgy the Life of the Church*, Popular Liturgical Library, Series 1, no. 1, Collegeville, Minn., 1926.
Beer, Max, *A History of British Socialism*, 1923.
Benoit, J.-D., (trans. Edwin Hudson) *Liturgical Renewal. Studies in Catholic and Protestant Developments on the Continent*. Studies in Ministry and Worship 5, 1958.
Bell, G. K. A., *Randall Davidson, Archbishop of Canterbury*, 3rd edition, 1952.
Bennett, F., *The Life of W. J. E. Bennett*, 1909.
Benson, Arthur Christopher, *The Life of Edward White Benson*, new edition abridged, 1901.
Bentley, James, *Ritualism and Politics in Victorian Britain: The Attempt to Legislate for Belief*, Oxford, 1978.
Bettany, F. G., *Stewart Headlam: A Biography*, 1926.
Billington, Raymond J., *The Liturgical Movement and Methodism*, 1969.
Binyon, G. C., *The Christian Socialist Movement in England—An Introduction to the Study of its History*, 1931.
Blomfield, Alfred, ed., *A Memoir of Charles James Blomfield DD*, 1863.
Botte, OSB, Bernard, *Le Mouvement liturgique: Témoignage et Souvenirs*, Paris, 1973.
Bouyer, Louis, *Life and Liturgy*, 1956.
Brabant, F. H., *Neville Stuart Talbot, 1879–1943—A Memoir*, 1949.
Brightman, F. E., *The English Rite*, 2 vols, 1915.
Brilioth, Yngve, *The Anglican Revival: Studies in the Oxford Movement*, 1925.
Brilioth, Yngve, (trans. A. G. Herbert) *Eucharistic Faith and Practice: Evangelical and Catholic*, 1930.
Brill, Kenneth, ed., *John Groser: East London Priest*, 1971.
Brose, Olive J., *Frederick Denison Maurice, Rebellious Conformist*, Ohio, 1971.
Buchanan, Colin O., *Patterns of Sunday Worship*, Grove Booklet on Ministry and Worship no. 9, Bramcote, 1972.
Buchanan, Colin O., *The End of the Offertory: An Anglican Study*, Grove Liturgical Study no. 14, Bramcote, 1978.

Burson, Malcolm, ed., *Worship Points the Way: A Celebration of the Life and Work of Massey Hamilton Shepherd, Jr.*, New York, 1981.

Butler, Perry, *Gladstone: Church, State and Tractarianism, A Study of his religious ideas and attitudes, 1809–1859*, Oxford, 1982.

Butler, Perry, ed., *Pusey Rediscovered*, 1983.

Buxton, R. F., *Eucharist and Institution Narrative*, ACC 58, Great Wakering, 1976.

Candole, Henry V. de, and Couratin, Arthur, *Re-shaping the Liturgy. Invitation to a Parish Enquiry*, 1964.

Candole, Henry V. de, *The Church's Offering*, 1935.

Candole, Henry V. de, *The Sacraments and the Church*, 1935.

Carlile, Wilson, *Congregational Communion. Music without Choir Lasting thirty minutes apart from the administration*, n.d. (1894?).

Carpenter, James, *Gore: A Study in Liberal Catholic Thought*, 1960.

Carpenter, S. C., *Duncan-Jones of Chichester*, 1956.

The Central Records of the Church of England. A Report and Survey presented to The Pilgrim and Radcliffe Trustees, 1976.

Chadwick, Owen, *The Victorian Church*, vol. i, 1966, vol. ii, 2nd edition, 1972.

Chadwick, Owen, *Hensley Henson: A Study in the friction between Church and State*, Oxford, 1983.

Chesterton, G. K., *Autobiography*, 1937.

Christ the Lord of All Life, ICF, 9th edition, 1950.

Christensen, Torben, *Origin and History of Christian Socialism, 1848–54*, Aarhus, 1962.

Christensen, Torben, *The Divine Order: A Study in F. D. Maurice's Theology*, Aarhus, 1973.

Church of England Liturgical Commission, *Prayer Book Revision in the Church of England*, 1957.

Clayton, Joseph, *Bishop Westcott*, 1906.

Cole, G. D. H., *A Short History of the British Working Class Movement*, 1927.

Colloms, Brenda, *Victorian Visionaries*, 1982.

Coombs, Joyce, *George Anthony Denison: The Firebrand, 1805–1896*, 1984.

Couratin, A. H., and Tripp, D. H., eds., *E. C. Ratcliff: Liturgical Studies*, 1976.

CR 1892–1952, Wakefield, 1952.

Craig, Robert, *Social Concern in the Thought of William Temple*, 1963.

Creighton, Mandell, (ed. Louise Creighton) *The Church and the Nation: Charges and Addresses*, 1902.

Crichton, J. D., Winstone, H. E., Ainslie, J. R., *English Catholic Worship: Liturgical Renewal in England since 1900*, 1979.

Cross, F. L. and Livingstone, E. A., eds., *The Oxford Dictionary of the Christian Church*, 2nd edition (revised), Oxford, 1983.

Cross, F. L., *Darwell Stone*, 1943.

Crosse, Gordon, *Charles Gore. A Biographical Sketch*, 1932.

Cuming, G. J., *A History of Anglican Liturgy*, 2nd edition, 1982.

Cuming, G. J. *The Godly Order: Texts and Studies relating to the Book of Common Prayer*, ACC 65, 1983.

Daniel, Evan, *The Prayer Book; its History, Language and Contents*, 26th edition, 1948.

Dark, Sidney, *Wilson Carlile, the Laughing Cavalier of Christ*, 1944.

Dark, Sidney, ed., *Conrad Noel, An Autobiography*, 1945.

Davidson, R. T., Archbishop of Canterbury, *The Prayer Book: Our Hope and Meaning*, 1928.

Davidson, R. T., and Bentham, W., *Life of Archibald Campbell Tait, Archbishop of Canterbury*, 1891.

Davies, Horton, *Worship and Theology in England. Vol. V, The Ecumenical Century 1900–1965*, Princeton, 1965.

Davies, J. G., *A Dictionary of Liturgy and Worship*, 1972.

Davies, Rupert, ed., *The Testing of the Churches 1932–1982*, 1982.

Dawson, G. P. H., ed., *Edward Keble Talbot. His Community and his friends*, 1954.

Dearmer, Nan, *The Life of Percy Dearmer*, 1940.

Dearmer, Percy, *The Art of Public Worship*, 1919.

Dearmer, Percy, *The Truth about Fasting with special reference to Fasting-Communion*, 1928.

Dearmer, Percy, *The Parson's Handbook*, 12th edition, 1931.

Demant, V. A., *Theology of Society*, 1947.

The Dictionary of National Biography, Twentieth Century (various editors), Oxford, 1912 ff.

Dillistone, F. W., *Into All the World: A Biography of Max Warren*, 1980.

Dix, Dom Gregory, *The Shape of the Liturgy*, 1945.

Donovan, Marcus, *After the Tractarians*, 1933.

Duncan-Jones, A. S., *Why Change the Communion Service?*, Alcuin Club Papers, 1934.

Edward [G. Bulstrode], Brother, (ed.) *Sunday Morning: The New Way. Papers on the Parish Communion*, 1938.

Edward [G. Bulstrode], Brother, *Village Evangelism*, Eastbourne, 1947.

Edwards, David L., *Leaders of the Church of England 1828–1978*, 1978.

Edwards, David L., *Christian England (vol. three) from the Eighteenth Century to the First World War*, 1984.

Ellsworth, L. E., *Charles Lowther and the Ritualist Movement*, 1969.

Evans, Stanley, *Christian Socialism: A Study Outline and Bibliography*, Christian Socialist Movement Pamphlet 2, 1962.

Foakes-Jackson, F. J., ed., *The Faith and the War*, 1915.

Frere, W. H., *The Principles of Religious Ceremonial*, The Oxford Library of Practical Theology, 1906.

Frere, W. H., *Some Principles of Liturgical Reform. A Contribution towards the Revision of the Book of Common Prayer*, 1911.

Frere, W. H., *The Anaphora or Great Eucharistic Prayer*, 1938.

Fullerton, Thomas G., *Father Burn of Middlesbrough*, Bradford, 1927.

Garbett, C. F., ed. *The Work of a Great Parish*, 1915.

Gilbert, A. D., *Religion and Society in Industrial England. Church, Chapel and Social Change 1740–1914*, 1976.

Gore, Charles, ed., *Lux Mundi*, 1889.

Gore, Charles, *The Body of Christ*, 1901.

Green, Peter, *The Town Parson*, 1919.

Groves, Reg., *Conrad Noel and The Thaxted Movement, An Adventure in Christian Socialism*, New York, 1968.

Groves, Reg., *The Catholic Crusade: A reprint of its original Manifesto with an introduction and notes*, 1970.

Hammond, Peter, *Liturgy and Architecture*, 1960.

Hankey, Donald, *A Student in Arms*, 1916.

Harcourt, Melville, *Tubby Clayton: A Personal Saga*, 1953.

Härdelin, Alf, *The Tractarian Understanding of the Eucharist*, Uppsala, 1965.

Harrison, D. E. W., *The Book of Common Prayer: The Anglican Heritage of Public Worship*, 1946.

Harrison, D. E. W. and Sansom, Michael C., *Worship in the Church of England*, 1982.

Headlam, A. C., *The New Prayer Book, being a Charge delivered to the Clergy and Churchwardens of the Diocese of Gloucester on the occasion of his Second Visitation*, 1927.

Headlam, Stewart B., *A Lent in London, A Course of Sermons on Social Subjects*, 1895.

Headlam, Stewart B., *The Meaning of the Mass*, 1905.

Headlam, Stewart B., *Christian Socialism*, Fabian Tract no. 42, 1892, 5th reprint August 1907.

H(ebert), A. G., *Starting a Parish Communium. A Letter to a Congregation by a Priest of the Church of England*, n.d.

Hebert, A. G., *Liturgy and Society: the Function of the Church in the Modern World*, 1935.

Hebert, A. G., (ed), *The Parish Communion. A Book of Essays*, 1937.

Henson, Herbert Hensley, *Retrospect of an Unimportant Life*, 3 vols., 1943.

Hewitt, Gordon, ed., *Strategist for the Faith: Leslie Hunter, Bishop of Sheffield 1939–1962*, 1985.

Higham, Florence, *Frederick Denison Maurice*, 1947.

Holland, Henry Scott, *Personal Studies*, 1905.

Holland, Henry Scott, *Sacramental Values*, n.d. (1917?).

Hollingworth, Tully Kingdon, *Fasting Communion historically investigated from the Canons and the Fathers, and shown to be not binding in England*, 2nd ed., 1875.

Huelin, Gordon, *King's College, London 1828–1978*, 1978.

Hugh SSF, Father, *Nineteenth-Century Pamphlets at Pusey House, An Introduction for the prospective user*, 1981.

Hughes, Dom Anselm, *The Rivers of the Flood, A Personal Account of the Catholic Movement in the Twentieth Century*, 2nd ed., 1963.

Hunter, Leslie Stannard, *A Parson's Job; Aspects of Work in the English Church*, 1931.

Inglis, K. S., *Churches and the Working Classes in Victorian England*, 1963.

Ingram, A. F. Winnington, *Work in Great Cities*, 1895.

International Commission on English in the Liturgy, A Joint Commission of the Catholic Bishops' Conference, *Documents on the Liturgy 1963–1979, Conciliar, Papal, and Curial Texts*, 1982.

Iremonger, F. A., *William Temple, Archbishop of Canterbury, His Life and Letters*, 1948.

Jagger, Peter J., ed., *Being the Church Today. A Collection of Sermons and Addresses by Bishop Henry de Candole*, Leighton Buzzard, 1974.

Jagger, Peter J., *The Alcuin Club and its Publications. An Annotated Bibliography 1897–1974*, 1975.

Jagger, Peter J., *Bishop Henry de Candole. His Life and Times 1895–1971*, Leighton Buzzard, 1975.

Jagger, Peter J., *A History of the Parish and People Movement*, Leighton Buzzard, 1977.

Jasper, R. C. D., *Prayer Book Revision in England 1800–1900*, 1954.

Jasper, R. C. D., ed., *Walter Howard Frere. His Correspondence on Liturgical Revision and Construction* ACC xxxix, 1954.

Jasper, R. C. D., *Arthur Cayley Headlam, Life and Letters of a Bishop*, 1960.

Jasper, R. C. D., *Bishop Bell, Bishop of Chichester*, 1967.

Jasper, R. C. D., ed., *The Renewal of Worship*. Essays by members of the Joint Liturgical Group, 1965.

Jasper, R. C. D., ed., *The Eucharist Today. Studies on Series 3*, 1974.

Jones, Cheslyn; Wainwright, Geoffrey; Yarnold, Edward, eds, *The Study of Liturgy*, 1978.

Jones, Peter d'A., *The Christian Socialist Revival 1877–1914: Religion, Class and Social Conscience in Late-Victorian England*, Princeton, 1968.

Joynson-Hicks, William, *The Prayer Book Crisis*, 1928.

Jungman, J. (trans. Clifford Howell), *Liturgical Renewal in Retrospect and Prospect, with a section on the Liturgical Movement in Great Britain and Ireland* by J. B. O'Connell, 1965.

Kelly, SSM, Herbert, *The Gospel of God* (with memoir by Brother George Every, SSM), 1959.

Kelly, SSM, Herbert (ed. George Every, SSM), *No Pious Person, Autobiographical Recollections*, 1960.

Kempthorne, J. A., *Pastoral Life and Work Today*, 1919.

Kingsley, Charles, *His Letters and Memories of his Life*, 1877.

Klauser, Theodor (trans. F. L. Cross), *The Western Liturgy Today*, 1963.

Klauser, Theodor (trans. John Halliburton), *A Short History of the Western Liturgy, An Account and Some Reflections*, 1969.

Knox, Edmund Arbuthnott, *Reminiscences of an Octogenarian 1847–1934*, 1934.

Knox, W., and Vidler, A., *The Development of Modern Catholicism*, 1923.

Koenker, Ernest Benjamin, *The Liturgical Renaissance in the Roman Catholic Church*, Chicago, 1954.

Lacey, T. A., *Liturgical Interpolations*, Alcuin Club Tract iii, 1898.

Lacey, T. A., *Liturgical Interpolations and the Revision of the Prayer Book*, Alcuin Club Prayer Book Revision Pamphlets i, 1912.

Lang, C. G. *The Opportunity of the Church of England*, 1905.

Leech, Kenneth and Williams, Rowan, *Essays Catholic and Radical*, 1983.

Lewis, John; Polanyi, Karl; Kitchin, Donald K., eds, *Christianity and the Social Revolution*, 1935.

Liddon, H. P., *Evening Communion contrary to the Teaching and Practice of the Church in All Ages*, 1876.

Liddon, H. P., *Life of Edward Bouverie Pusey*, 4 vols, 1893–7.

The Liturgical Conference 1966, Report of Proceedings, 1966.

The Liturgical Movement, Popular Liturgical Library, Series IV, no. 3, Collegeville, Minn., 1930.

Liturgy and the Liturgical Movement. A Study Club Outline on Liturgy in General, Collegeville, Minn., revised ed. 1937.

Lloyd, Roger, *The Church of England 1900–1965*, 1966.

Lockhart, J. G., *Cosmo Gordon Lang*, 1949.

Lowry, Charles W., *William Temple. An Archbishop for all seasons*, Washington, 1982.

Lowther Clarke, W. K., ed., *Liturgy and Worship*, 1932.

Lowther Clarke, W. K., *The Prayer Book of 1928 Reconsidered*, 1943.

Malvern 1941: The Life of the Church and the Order of Society being the Proceedings of the Archbishop of York's Conference, 1941.

The Malvern Conference, Edition for Study, 1941.

Manifesto of the Catholic Crusade, n.d.

Marrin, Albert, *The Last Crusade, the Church of England in the First World War*, North Carolina, 1974.

Martimort, A. G., ed., *The Church at Prayer*, Shannon, Ireland, 1966.

Martin, Hugh, ed., *Christian Social Reformers of the Nineteenth Century*, 1926.

Masterman, C. F. G., *Frederick Denison Maurice*, 1907.

Matthews, W. R., *Memories and Meanings*, 1969.

Maurice, F., ed., *The Life of Frederick Denison Maurice Chiefly told in His Own Letters*, 1884.

Maurice, F. D., *The Kingdom of Christ*, 1838.

Maurice, F. D., *The Kingdom of Christ* (a new edition based on 2 ed. of 1842, ed. A. R. Vidler), 1958.

Maurice, F. D., *Sermons Preached in Lincoln's Inn Chapel*, 1892.

Moynihan, Michael, *God on our Side: the British Padre in World War I*, 1983.

Murray, A. D., ed., *John Ludlow, the Autobiography of a Christian Socialist*, 1981.

Mackenzie, Kenneth, ed., *The Liturgy Papers read at the Priests' Convention, Tewkesbury May, 1938*, 1938.

Mackenzie, Kenneth, *Sunday Morning*, n.d.

Macnutt, F. B., ed., *The Church in the Furnace. Essays by seventeen Temporary Church of England Chaplains on Active Service in France and Flanders*, 1918.

The National Mission of Repentance and Hope. A Report of the Chaplains' Replies to the Lord Bishop of Kensington.

Newbolt, W. C. E., *Consolidation*, Alcuin Club Tract ii, 1897.

Noel, Conrad, *Jesus the Heretic*, 1940.

Noel, Conrad, *The Sacraments*, n.d.

Norman, E. R., *Church and Society in England 1770–1970*, Oxford, 1976.

Ollard, S. L.; Crosse, Gordon; Bond, Maurice F., eds., *A Dictionary of English Church History*, 3rd ed., 1948.

Orens, John R., *The Mass, the Masses and the Music Hall: Stewart Headlam's Radical Anglicanism*, 1979.

Owen, Robert, *The Life of Robert Owen*, 1857–8, repr. 1965.

Oxenham, F. N., *The Duty of Fasting Communion*, 1873.

Packard, Kenneth, *The Parish Communion: A Simple Explanation*, 1941.

Packard, Kenneth, *Brother Edward, Priest and Evangelist*, 1955.

Paget, Stephen, ed., *Henry Scott Holland: Memoirs and Letters*, 1921.

Pare, Philip, and Harris, Donald, *Eric Milner-White*, 1965.

Parsch, Pius (trans. Clifford Howell), *We are Christ's Body*, Liturgical Library 17, Tenbury Wells, 1962.

Paton, David M., ed., *Parish Communion Today*, 1962.

Peck, W. G., *Social Implications of the Oxford Movement*, New York, 1933.

Pickering, W. S. F., ed., *A Social History of the Diocese of Newcastle 1882–1982*, Henley, 1981 (*sic*).

Pike, James A., ed., *Modern Canterbury Pilgrims and Why they Chose the Episcopal Church*, New York, 1956.

A New Prayer Book. Proposals for the Revision of the Book of Common Prayer and for additional Services and Prayers drawn up by a Group of Clergy together with a foreword by William Temple, D. Litt., Bishop of Manchester, 1923.

Prayer Book Revision in the Church of England. A Memorandum of the Church of England Liturgical Commission, LC 1958/2, 1957.

Prayer Book (Alternative and Other Services) Measure, 1965.

Prestige, G. L., *The Life of Charles Gore: A Great Englishman*, 1935.

Principles of Prayer Book Revision. Report to Review the Principles of Prayer Book Revision in the Anglican Communion, LC 1958/3, 1957.

Puller, F. W., *Concerning the Fast before Communion*, 2nd ed., 1895.

Purcell, William, *Woodbine Willie*, 1962.

Putterill, Jack, *Thaxted Quest for Social Justice*, Marlow, Bucks, 1977.

Ramsey, Arthur Michael, *F. D. Maurice and the Conflicts of Modern Theology*, 1951.

Ramsey, A. M. *Durham Essays and Addresses*, 1956.

Ramsey, Arthur Michael, *From Gore to Temple*, 1960.

Raven, C. E., *Christian Socialism 1848–54*, 1920.

Reckitt, Maurice, ed., *The Social Teaching of the Sacraments. Being the Report of the Second Anglo-Catholic Summer School of Sociology held at Keble College Oxford, July 1926*, 1927.

Reckitt, M. B., *Maurice to Temple, A Century of the Social Movement in the Church of England*, 1947.

Reckitt, Maurice B., *P. E. T. Widdrington, A Study in Vocation and Versatility*, 1961.

Reckitt, Maurice B., ed., *For Christ and the People, Studies of four Socialist Priests and Prophets of the Church of England between 1870 and 1930*, 1968.

The Report of the Keele Conference 1967, 1967.

The Report on the Place of the Holy Communion in the Service of the Lord's Day (Diocese of Worcester), 1910.

Reservation. Report of a Conference held at Farnham Castle on October 24–27, 1925, 1926.

Revised Prayer Book (Permissive Use) Measure, 1923.

Richardson, Alan, ed., *A Dictionary of Christian Theology*, 1969.

Robinson, J. A. T., *Liturgy Coming to Life*, 1963.

Rogers, Clement, *Principles of Parish Work*, 1905.

Rogers, Clement, *Pastoral Theology and the Modern World*, 1920.

Rousseau, Olivir, *L'Histoire du Mouvement Liturgique. Esquisse historique depuis le début du XIXe siècle jusqu'au pontificat de Pie X*. Lex Orandi, 3, Paris, 1945.

Rowell, Geoffrey, *The Vision Glorious: Themes and Personalities of the Catholic Revival in Anglicanism*, Oxford, 1983.

Royal Commission on Ecclesiastical Discipline. Minutes of Evidence taken before the Royal Commission on Ecclesiastical Discipline, vol. i (cd 3069), vol. ii (cd 2070), vol. iii (cd 3071), 1906.

Royal Commission on Ecclesiastical Discipline. Record of Commissioners' Attendances, Appendices, Index and Analysis of Evidence, vol. iv (cd 3072), 1906.

Royal Commission on Ecclesiastical Discipline. Report of the Royal Commission on Ecclesiastical Discipline (cd 3040), 1906.

Seasoltz, Kevin R., *New Liturgy, New Laws*, Collegeville, Minn., 1980.

Shands, Alfred R., *The Liturgical Movement and the Local Church*, 1959.

Sheen, Harold E., *Canon Peter Green*, 1965.

Sheils, W. J., ed., *The Church and War*, Studies in Church History, vol. 20, Oxford, 1983.

Shepherd, Massey H., Jnr., *The Reform of Liturgical Worship*, New York, 1961.

Sheppard, David, *Bias to the Poor*, 1983.

Shield, E. O., *At Parish Communion: The Prayer Book Service with a Commentary*, 1958.

Smyth, C. H., *C. F. Garbett*, 1959.

Smythe, John, *In this Sign Conquer: the Story of the Army Chaplains*, 1968.

The Social Significance of Worship (A Syllabus for Study with Questions for Discussion), 1939.

Southcott, E. W., *The Parish Comes Alive*, 1956.

Sparrow Simpson, W. J., *Non-Communicating Attendance*, 1913.

Srawley, J. H., *The Liturgical Movement, its Origin and Growth*, Alcuin Club Tract 27, 1954.

Staples, Peter, *The Liturgical Movement in the Netherlands Reformed Church 1911–1955, with Special Reference to the Anglican Dimension. Interunivsitair Instituut voor Missiologie en Oecumenica*, Research Pamphlet no. 9, Utrecht, 1983.

Stephenson, Alan M. G., *The Rise and Decline of English Modernism*, 1984.

Stephenson, Gwendolen, *Edward Stuart Talbot 1844–1934*, 1956.

Stevens, T. P., *Father Adderley*, 1943.

Stevenson, Kenneth W., *Gregory Dix—Twenty-Five Years On*, Grove Liturgical Study no. 10, Bramcote, 1977.

Stone, Darwell, *The Prayer Book Measure and the Deposited Book—The Present Situation: a plea for an Agreed Book*, 1928.

Studdert Kennedy, G. A., *The Unutterable Beauty*, 17th ed., 1964.

Studdert Kennedy, G. A., *The Hardest Part*, 1918.

Studdert Kennedy, Gerald, *Dog-Collar Democracy: The Industrial Christian Fellowship 1919–1929*, 1982.

A suggested Prayer Book being the text of the English Rite altered and enlarged in accordance with the Prayer Book Revision proposals made by the English Church Union, 1923.

A Survey of the Proposals for the Alternative Prayer Book part i, The Order of Holy Communion, Alcuin Club Prayer Book Revision Pamphlet xii, 1923.

A Survey of the Proposals for the Alternative Prayer Book, part ii Occasional Offices, Alcuin Club Prayer Book Revision Pamphlets xiii, 1924.

A Survey of the Proposals for the Alternative Prayer Book, part iii, the Calendar etc., the Collects, Epistles and Gospels, the Ordination Services, Alcuin Club Prayer Book Revision Pamphlet xiv, 1924.

Talbot, Neville S., *Religion Behind the Front and After the War*, 1918.

Taylor, M. J., *The Protestant Liturgical Renewal: A Catholic Viewpoint*, Westminster, Maryland, 1962.

(Temple), William, Archbishop of York, *Thoughts on Some Problems of the Day. A Charge delivered at his Primary Visitation*, 1931.

Thinking about the Eucharist. Papers by Members of the Church of England Doctrine Commission, 1972.

Tibbatts, OGS, George, *John How, Cambridge Don, Parish Priest, Scottish Primus*, Oxford, 1983.

Towards a Catholic Standard of Life. Being a Short Report of the First Summer School of Sociology under the auspices of the Anglo-Catholic Congress held at. Keble College Oxford in July 1925, 1926.

Tracts for the Times by Members of the University of Oxford, 1833 ff.

Trollope, Constance, *Mark Napier Trollope, Bishop in Korea 1911–1930*, 1936.

Underhill, Francis, ed., *Feed My Sheep. Essays in Pastoral Theology*, 1927.

Underhill, Francis, *The Revival of Worship. A Primary Visitation Charge to the Clergy and Churchwardens of the Diocese of Bath and Wells*, 1938.

Vidler, Alec R., *Witness to the Light. F. D. Maurice's Message for Today*, New York, 1948.

Vidler, Alec R., *F. D. Maurice and Company: Nineteenth Century Studies*, 1966.

Voll, Dieter (trans. Veronica Ruffer), *Catholic Evangelicalism*, 1963.

Wagner, Donald O., *The Church of England and Social Reform since 1854*, New York, 1930.

Wainwright, Geoffrey, *Doxology*, New York, 1980.

Ward, Maisie, *Gilbert Keith Chesterton*, 1944.

Warren, Max, *Strange Victory: A Study of the Holy Communion Service*, 1946.

Warren, Max, *Crowded Canvas: some experiences of a lifetime*, 1974.

Ways of Worship, Report of a Theological Commission of Faith and Order, 1951.

Weil, Louis, *Sacraments and Liturgy: the Outward Signs, A Study in Liturgical Mentality*, Oxford, 1983.

Welsby, Paul A., *A History of the Church of England 1945–1980*, Oxford, 1984.

West, Frank H., *'FRB'—A Portrait of Bishop Russell Barry*, Bramcote, 1980.

Westcott, Arthur, *Life and Letters of Brooke Foss Westcott DD, DCL*, 1903.

Westcott, Brooke Foss, *The Incarnation and Common Life*, 1893.

White, James F., *The Cambridge Movement*, Cambridge, 1979, reissue.

Wickham Legg, J., *English Church Life: from the Restoration to the Tractarian Movement, considered in some of its neglected and forgotten features*, 1914.

Wilberforce, R. I., *The Doctrine of the Holy Eucharist*, 1853.

Wilkinson, Alan, *The Church of England and the First World War*, 1978.

Williams, N. P., and Harris, Charles, eds., *Northern Catholicism*, 1933.

Williamson, Joseph, *Father Joe*, 1963.

Wilson, J. V.; Howard, R. T.; McGowan, H., *The Social Significance of the Liturgy*, Popular Series no. 4, new and revised ed., 1941.

Woodifield, Robert, *Catholicism: Humanist and Democratic*, 1954.

Woodworth, A. W., *Christian Socialism in England*, 1903.

Wordsworth, John, *The Holy Communion, Four Visitation Addresses AD 1891*, 1893.

Wordsworth, John, *The Ministry of Grace*, 1901.

Wordsworth, W. A. (compiler), *Quam Dilecta: A description of All Saints' Church Margaret Street with historical notes of Margaret Chapel and All Saints' Church*, 1891.

The Worship of the Church, being the Report of the Archbishops' Second Committee of Enquiry, 1918.

Worship: Its Social Significance, with a Foreword by P. T. R. Kirk, 1939.

Yates, Nigel, *The Oxford Movement and Anglican Ritualism*, 1983.

Theses

Heaton, Richard L., *The Inter-Relation of Sacramental and Ethical Concerns in the thought of Frederick D. Maurice, Henry S. Holland, Charles Gore and William Temple*, unpublished Ph.D. thesis, University of Edinburgh, 1968.

Jones, Alan William, *Herbert Hamilton Kelly SSM 1860–1950: A Study in Failure (a contribution to the search for a credible Catholicism)*, unpublished Ph.D. thesis, University of Nottingham, 1971.

Martin, Robin H., *The Act of the Brethren, A History of the Parish Communion Movement*, unpublished BD thesis, University of Birmingham, 1961.

Storey, Kenneth, *Wilson Carlile and the Church Army: A Study of his life and teaching*, unpublished Ph.D. thesis, University of Manchester, 1984.

Periodicals and Newspapers Consulted

Alcuin.

Blackfriars.

Bulletin of the National Mission of Repentance and Hope.

CR: Quarterly Review of the Community of the Resurrection.

The Christian Socialist.

Chronicle of Convocation (Canterbury).
Church of England Newspaper.
Church of Ireland Gazette.
The Church Militant.
The Church Reformer.
The Church Socialist Quarterly.
The Church Times.
Commonwealth.
The Guardian.
Historical Magazine of the Protestant Episcopal Church.
ICF Journal.
ICF Review.
The Journal of Ecclesiastical History.
The Journal of the Royal Army Chaplains' Department.
LKG Quarterly: The Organ of the League of the Kingdom of God.
The Leap.
The Leap Leaflets.
The Listener.
Liverpool Parish Magazine.
The Manchester Guardian.
The Modern Churchman.
The New Statesman.
The Optimist.
Oxford Magazine.
Parish and People, incorporating 'The Leap'.
The Quarterly Review.
The Record.
SSM: the Magazine of the Society of the Sacred Mission.
SSM Quarterly.
Salisbury Diocesan Gazette.
Salisbury and Winchester Journal.
Southern History.
The Spectator.
Studia Liturgica.
Theology.
The Times.
The Times Literary Supplement.
Worcester Diocesan Magazine.
Worship (formerly *Orate Fratres*).
York Journal of Convocation.

General Index

Index of Parishes